DISARMAMENT AGREEMENTS AND NEGOTIATIONS: THE ECONOMIC DIMENSION

UNIDIR

United Nations Institute for Disarmament Research

UNIDIR is an autonomous institution within the framework of the United Nations. It was established in 1980 by the General Assembly for the purpose of undertaking independent research on disarmament and related problems, particularly international security issues.

The work of the Institute aims at:

1. Providing the international community with more diversified and complete data on problems relating to international security, the armaments race, and disarmament in all fields, particularly in the nuclear field, so as to facilitate progress, through negotiations, towards greater security for all States and towards the economic and social development of all peoples;

2. Promoting informed participation by all States in disarmament efforts;

3. Assisting ongoing negotiations in disarmament and continuing efforts to ensure greater international security at a progressively lower level of armaments; particularly nuclear armaments, by means of objective and factual studies and analyses;

4. Carrying out more in-depth, forward-looking and long-term research on disarmament, so as to provide a general insight into the problems involved, and stimulating new initiatives for new negotiations.

The contents of UNIDIR publications are the responsibility of the authors and not of UNIDIR. Although UNIDIR takes no position on the view and conclusions expressed by the authors of its research reports, it does assume responsibility for determining whether they merit publication.

UNIDIR

Palais des Nations
CH-1211 Geneva 10
Tel. (022) 734 60 11

Disarmament Agreements and Negotiations: The Economic Dimension

Serge Sur
Editor

UNIDIR
United Nations Institute for Disarmament Research
Dartmouth
Aldershot · Brookfield USA · Hong Kong · Singapore · Sydney

Published by
Dartmouth Publishing Company Limited
Gower House
Croft Road
Aldershot
Hants GU11 3HR
England

Dartmouth Publishing Company Limited
Distributed in the United States by
Ashgate Publishing Company
Old Post Road
Brookfield
Vermont 05036
USA

A CIP catalogue record for this book is available from the British Library and the US Library of Congress

ISBN   1 85521 257 9

Printed in Great Britain at the University Press, Cambridge

Table of Contents

Part IV: Economic Implications of a Chemical Weapons Convention

Preface

The link between disarmament and economics is obvious. The United Nations Charter refers to the Security Council's task "to promote the establishment and maintenance of international peace and security with the least diversion for armaments of the world's human and economic resources" (Article 26).

In an earlier phase the economic dimension of disarmament was confined to the relationship between disarmament and development. The linkage between military expenditure and economic and social development, especially in developing countries was made in the Final Document of the First Special Session of the General Assembly devoted to disarmament (SSOD-I).

The UN study on "The Relationship between Disarmament and Development" requested in the Final Document of SSOD-I together with the 1987 International Conference on the subject were important milestones. They led to an understanding that, while disarmament and development were independent processes, there was a complex relationship between them stemming from their common use of finite resources and their common goal of security.

The acceleration of the pace of disarmament in the aftermath of the improvement in US-USSR relations and the signature of the INF and CFE Treaties has led to a fresh approach to the economic aspects of disarmament. This has involved focusing on the adjustment process in economies following the implementation of disarmament treaties, as well as on the reality of the costs of disarmament in terms of human and material resources. Policy-makers and others have begun to look closely at these economic aspects of disarmament; certainly a need for a pragmatic analysis of the issues exists. In this context, UNIDIR in association with the International Defence Economiscs Association organized a workshop in Leningrad in July 1990 on the subject. We invited a number of specialists in the field, mainly economists, from different regions to consider a number of related questions. The papers presented by them and the discussions in Leningrad form the content of this publication. The research project was co-ordinated and this research report edited by Professor Serge Sur, Deputy Director of UNIDIR. Sophie Daniel has prepared the manuscript for publication.

I would like to thank the International Defence Economics Association for their assistance in organizing the workshop and express my appreciation to the participants for their contributions. The UN Association of the USSR assisted UNIDIR in the practical arrangements of the workshop in Leningrad, which was financed out of the voluntary contributions of the Government of the USSR to UNIDIR.

Jayantha DHANAPALA
Director

Acknowledgements

UNIDIR wishes to express its thanks
to the International Defence Economics Association (IDEA)
for their assistance in the preparation of this work.

Introduction

From the moment they started preparing for this meeting, the organizers of the Leningrad Symposium had the feeling that they were going to be dealing with a range of questions of great complexity. They also felt that the time had come to tackle, them and that UNIDIR had a useful contribution to make.

The time had come because disarmament is no longer just a subject for speeches, schemes and vain regrets; it is now, at least partially, a matter of fact. Hence it is not only possible but also necessary to analyse its economic implications, which are going to become more and more of a practical issue.

More and more practical, but also more and more specific. In other words, the approach to these questions will as far as possible have to be divorced from ideological presuppositions, rhetorical phrases and vast general claims. It will demand a great deal of caution, a great deal of skill and a great deal of modesty.

This comment, moreover, applies generally. The time of ideological breakthroughs, of global objectives - the time of unification and globalization - is in reality a time when we are all still feeling our way, as in the early stages of any venture. It is a time of hope, but also of confusion. As people come closer together in their views, they are faced with more and more varied problems, and it becomes essential to take an approach that is both analytical and positive. Seen from a distance, things are, if not simple, at least integrated into a broader context governed by an intellectual vision. Seen from close up, they may be easier to distinguish, but they become more ambiguous. They present contradictory aspects and a sort of intrinsic opacity.

This process is already well under way for the military aspects which are naturally the core of disarmament. There are separate negotiations, often in different bodies, on questions which are not unconnected but have to be dealt with independently, such as the limitation of nuclear weapons, the reduction of conventional weapons, or the elimination of chemical weapons, for example.

When, on the other hand, new problems arise or, more precisely, when the implications of disarmament come to be viewed in a broader context, what is needed first and foremost is a general approach, so as to identify and conceptualize the problems and determine the general issues involved. That applies to the non-military aspects of disarmament; as well as to the exploration of the various security aspects, which are tending to attract more and more attention of research workers nowadays. Obviously one day, these problems will need to be given individual treatment in the light of the differences between them, once they have each been classified and analysed on the basis of their specific features, but at the initial stage they need to be grasped in their totality, as a necessary preliminary to any more individual approach.

The problems connected with the economic aspects of disarmament might be said to be in an intermediate situation. They can no longer be dealt with in a purely theoretical and abstract fashion. But they have not yet been grasped clearly enough to be duly distinguished from each other, identified and assessed. The weight they carry in current negotiations is also difficult to gauge, even if it seems obvious that they are already taken into consideration and constitute a significant element in national positions on the subject.

It is interesting to note in this connection the change that has taken place over the past 15 years or so. The final document adopted by the General Assembly at its tenth special session on disarmament in 1978, which lays down the United Nations' general philosophy and sets forth the international community's objectives in this area, only alludes briefly to the economic sphere. If the subject has attracted attention and research, it has done so as a parallel development. At the same time it has diversified. Long concentrated on the topic of "disarmament-development", it has now extended to the problems of conversion. These remain the two main ideas one thinks of when referring to the economic aspects of disarmament. But now we ought, perhaps, to go further.

- I -

Going further means changing our approach in various ways.

We should begin by abandoning, at least to start with, any normative approach aiming at a general statement of what is good and what is bad or seeking to set global objectives for the international community - e.g. in terms of cuts in military budgets, reallocation of resources, etc. Not only would there probably be no consensus on these objectives, but in any case they need to be dealt with first from a national or possibly a regional standpoint.

In the same way, we should not be too eager to start making recommendations about the policies that States might follow or the negotiations they might enter into. An attempt should first be made to arrive at an objective and independent analysis, as precise and well-informed as possible, in order to provide a solid basis for any future action.

From this viewpoint, the most logical immediate approach would be to base one's analysis on the agreements recently concluded and the negotiations under way. There are no negotiations regarding the economic aspects of disarmament on the international community's agenda at present. But we can ask ourselves about the economic consequences of the elimination of certain categories of weapons, whether agreed or still under negotiation, and about the impact of certain kinds of arms reductions. We need to assess the consequences not just for the parties to the agreements in question, but for all States and more particularly for the developing countries. This approach has quite logically guided the way UNIDIR has organized its research and presented its results.

UNIDIR is surely an appropriate body for this type of analysis. It is a research institute whose work is based on the criteria of academic independence and objectivity. It is also a multilateral institute, which can bring together people from different cultures with different attitudes. It is, finally, a United Nations institute, sharing the Organization's philosophy and guided in its work by the concern for balance and respect for the legitimate views of all parties which characterizes the Organization as a whole.

Thus for the purposes of this research UNIDIR assembled a number of personalities who together form a group with various characteristics. It includes well-known economists with established international reputations in the field of defence and disarmament questions. In this work UNIDIR has benefited from the very helpful assistance of IDEA, to which the main specialists in this area belong.

The group also includes diplomats participating in the various negotiations under way, who are thus in a position to share their experiences and to raise the questions which emerge from those negotiations or to which their success could lead in the near future. Finally, it includes research workers and experts on security and disarmament, who are able to establish the general relationship between the economic approach, the strategic approach and the prospects for disarmament, or at least to identify the questions thus raised.

It is the results of these talks, these communications and these exchanges that are reproduced here. There is no point in concealing the fact that any initial research is preliminary and no doubt incomplete in nature (as it is bound to be if the research is done properly). Not only is the subject not exhausted, but it has probably not yet been fully mapped out. That is only to be expected at the transitional stage through which the research is now passing, from the general and normative to the analytical and concrete.

It must also be stressed that the transition in question is not just an intellectual process. It is also occurring in practice. The speed of the changes that have occurred in the world in recent years and the new course taken by international relations cannot fail to modify in depth the traditionally accepted basic data, including the economic data. The consequences of these changes remain in doubt, particularly since they are far from finished, while the speed, direction and significance of the process is far from being fixed once and for all, or even temporarily. The whole of the research is thus proceeding in a context which is in many ways uncertain.

In these circumstances it would be pretentious and premature to try to arrive at final conclusions. One can only speak of immediate and no doubt subjective impressions. They are at all events more a reflection of questions being asked than answers being arrived at. Some of these questions raise doubts about expressions and policies which, rather like sacred cows, are normally treated with reverence on principle in international forums rather than subjected to any critical examination.

Others are more directly concerned with the role and capacity of economics in the field of disarmament.

- II -

The first series of questions involves the traditional formula of the "disarmament-development" relation, with the corollary of "peace dividends", together with the infinitely complex question of conversion. None of these issues has been tackled head on in the contributions that follow, but they largely constituted the background, implicit or explicit, to the discussions.

The link between disarmament and development, which has reasonably aroused great hopes and continues to do so, was very much called in question by most participants and rarely defended. It is true that efforts to realize these hopes have so far had very limited results. But it was the actual idea behind them - the use of public and private savings from disarmament to further harmonious development which could benefit the disadvantaged countries first and foremost - that was strongly contested. At the same time, the very idea that disarmament would yield automatic returns - the famous peace dividends - was called in question. On the contrary it was argued that, at least during an initial phase of indeterminate duration, disarmament was likely to be expensive. It would entail destruction and verification operations together with the reorganization of military systems, the cost of which, while difficult to evaluate, could be high. At the same time, conversion also has its cost - but we will come back to that in a moment.

At all events, the peace dividends are likely to be some time coming. Does this mean that the disarmament-development formula should be abandoned as a piece of misleading rhetoric? Perhaps we may confine ourselves to observing that it is not an economic concept, but a political one, intended to guide behaviour by fixing objectives. Its economic aspects, the conditions for it, the speed and manner in which it might be implemented, no doubt call for further analysis. That analysis should be concerned with the domestic level as much as the international level, inasmuch as disarmament by a particular country will have consequences first of all for its own development, before affecting other countries more indirectly. In this respect it is similar to conversion.

As far as conversion is concerned, it is probably more easily dealt with at this stage by economic analysis. Firstly because there are a number of precedents; after the major international conflicts, for example, the problems of moving from a wartime to a peacetime economy had to be identified and resolved. Though, less spectacular and more limited, a process of even relative demilitarization of our economies would not fail to raise related problems. This process, moreover, has in certain respects already begun, for instance, as a result of the shrinking of the international arms market.

That does not mean, however, that it can be taken for granted; caution is called for here as in all matters connected with disarmament and security. The word "conversion" suggests something instantaneous, complete and final. The term "transition" would probably be more in keeping with the gradual, slow and uncertain process involved. We should think in terms of a process, a movement, rather than of fixing on an arbitrary point of departure and point of arrival. Such a transition requires case studies and analyses, not general dissertations.

- III -

Secondly, any attempt to deal with these matters inevitably confronts economics with other questions that are more fundamental. It is legitimate to formulate them naively, as they may appear to non-specialists who expect to be given as clear a picture as possible - even if it is illusory to hope for simple and definitive solutions to problems that are complex and constantly changing. We may mention three of them here.

The first is the easiest to state, but that does not make it easy to solve. It is also very familiar. It is the problem of basic data, of information on military expenditure, on the knowledge, identification, comparison and development of such expenditure. It is on the one hand a question of the facts and on the other a question of agreeing on definitions. In some respects the military element permeates the whole of economic activity. It is nonetheless essential to isolate and identify a certain type, or several categories, of expenditure which one can regard as relating to the defence of the State and to assess their impact on the overall economy.

An additional difficulty results from the nature of the relationship between such expenditure and the overall economy, depending on the economic system in question. In other words, can one use the same type of reasoning when dealing with liberal economies and socialist economies? What is the influence of levels of development on the impact of military expenditure? What would be the consequences of a reduction in such expenditure from this standpoint? What happens when a market economy is being established in place of a planned, State-run economy? It can be seen what complex issues these are, demanding transparency, a good knowledge of the quantitative data and a proper understanding of the qualitative elements in the economy.

A second problem can now be raised. Can one regard economics as a single science, is it sufficiently well established and uniform to speak with one voice on these questions? Is there just one economics, or more than one? The possibility of there being more than one can be explained by differences in ideological systems. The disagreements in this area are well known, and almost as old as economics itself. It is true that the triumph, at least for time being, of the market economy and the collapse of Marxist doctrines have left the field completely free for liberal analyses and doctrines.

However, even if we stay within the liberal camp, there are several schools of thought and they sometimes differ. By definition, liberal thinking tends towards diversity. Even if people could agree on the scientific axioms, that would not eliminate the differences in the way they feel and the way they approach things.

Furthermore, the economics of disarmament is still in its infancy, and there is no point in expecting it to come forward as a discipline with recognized status and conclusions confirmed by practical experience, which is largely non-existent. Economics has to be both factual and, if not experimental, at least operational. The general uncertainty that pervades its teachings and precepts applies with particular force here. Any pedantry or dogmatism therefore has to be avoided.

This leads to a third problem. In the last few decades, since the Second World War, economics has taken the lead among the social and political sciences. Rapid growth in some periods and crisis in others, vigorous development in some countries or regions while others lag behind or decline, all these factors have contributed to the rise of economics. Economists are asked to diagnose, to forecast, to provide remedies. The logic of business management is tending to take over all institutions, both public and private.

This situation raises two questions, one of factual nature, the other normative. First of all, there is the question whether economics is capable of meeting all the challenges confronting it - yesterday the challenge of prosperity, today and tomorrow the challenge of peace. One may then ask whether such an approach can be expected to tell us what objectives to achieve, what goals to pursue. In other words, if it could be shown - or seem to be shown, at least partially and provisionally - that disarmament was expensive and perhaps economically unproductive for certain economies, would that be a reason or an acceptable argument for abandoning the idea? Should not narrowly economic considerations be subordinate to political goals, to questions of peace and security - in a word, to the principles of the United Nations, which are the charter of the international community?

In formulating the objective of respect for human rights and fundamental freedoms for all, in stating that there should be "the least diversion for armaments of the world's human and economic resources", the Charter of the United Nations is setting political and not economic goals. Economics is being called upon to contribute to the analyses which will throw light on the conditions for disarmament and the obstacles to it. It can help to smooth the path and ensure that disarmament proceeds in the best possible way. It cannot set its objectives and priorities.

Reference was made during the proceedings to the way security questions constantly interfered with disarmament. Security can scarcely be reduced to a matter of economics, and the expenditure it involves is only partially governed by economic logic. In the same way, domestic systems of social protection can seem too expensive and in some ways anti-economic. Quite reasonably, they respond to other imperatives. We have not yet reached the stage where the administration of things can take the place of the government of men.

The important thing for a scientific approach is to formulate the right questions, those which imply a rational way of setting about things, which do not stray beyond their proper sphere and which throw new light on observable phenomena. It is to that vast but modest undertaking that the texts that follow are intended to contribute. They end with a question mark about the present state and future tasks of economic research into disarmament.

- IV -

By Resolution 45/62 G, adopted without a vote on the tenth anniversary of UNIDIR, the General Assembly asked the Institute to prepare, with the assistance of independent experts, a research report on the economic aspects of disarmament and to report to the General Assembly, through the Secretary-General, at its forty-seventh session. This request highlights both the interest of the subjects dealt with here and the preliminary nature of the research. For this new task, the present report provides a sound basis. Like disarmament, research is a process which never reaches its final stage, but in which no stage fails to serve its purpose.

Serge SUR[*]

---

[*] Professor Serge Sur is Deputy Director of UNIDIR. The views expressed are those of the author.

Part 1

Economic Aspects of the INF Treaty and the START Negotiations

Chapter 1

The INF Treaty: An Appraisal and Long-Term Prospects

Gennady Khromov

Implementation of the Treaty between the United States of America and the Union of Soviet Socialist Republics on the Elimination of their Intermediate-Range and Shorter-Range Missiles (the INF Treaty), signed at the end of 1987 and ratified in June 1988, is proceeding successfully.

The elimination of Soviet and American shorter-range missiles was completed in 1989. As at the beginning of the month of July 1990, the situation with regard to the elimination of intermediate-range weapons was as follows:

- The Soviet Union had eliminated 715 out of 889 missiles (80.4 per cent) and 425 out of 587 missile launchers (72.4 per cent);
- The United States of America had eliminated 372 out of 677 missiles (54.9 per cent) and 132 out of 288 missile launchers (45.8 per cent).

The difference in the percentage of missiles and missile launchers eliminated by the Parties is chiefly due to the fact that, under the terms of the Treaty, by the time the missiles have been eliminated (less than a year from July 1990) the Parties should have approximately equivalent military capabilities with their remaining missile forces. (It should be remembered that one Soviet RSD-10 missile - or SS-20 as it is known in NATO - carries three nuclear warheads, while all American missiles carry only one; on the other hand, one American GLCM launcher carries four missiles, while each of the remaining Soviet launchers carries only one).

Soviet and American missile bases and support facilities are continuing to be dismantled and the corresponding military units disbanded.

The Parties have no doubts of a successful outcome to the implementation of the Treaty.

Despite the fact that only three to four per cent of the nuclear potential of these two great countries is covered by the INF Treaty, it is of considerable significance militarily, politically and even economically. It is particularly important in that it is the first specific agreement on the practical elimination of weapons in modern times.

The Treaty has given the green light to a whole range of highly practical military undertakings, extending not only to the elimination of intermediate-and shorter-range missiles and the ending of their production, but also to the reduction of the corresponding military units in both strategic missile and land-based forces.

The United States obviously has and is making use of similar opportunities. Thus, to take one example, by decommissioning its GLCM and Pershing II missile forces the United States has been able to save over $1 billion in operating costs alone, as against a total cost of over $6 billion to create such a force. In fact, maintaining any particular missile force involves not only operating costs, but also the design and manufacture of more and more missiles to replace those which have become obsolete.

People often ask whether the cost of implementing the Treaty (control, inspection, the elimination itself, etc) is not higher than the costs which would have been incurred if intermediate- and shorter-range missiles had continued in use. The answer to that question is an unequivocal no.

Information published to date on expenditure by the American On-Site Inspection Agency, which handles all activities under the Treaty, shows a figure of about $50 million a year. The Soviet Union is spending roughly the same as the United States although it carries out only about a third as many inspections; on the other hand, the amount of equipment it has to dispose of is far greater. Total expenditure arising from the implementation of the INF Treaty has turned out to be lower than many experts had supposed.

In addition, it is worth remembering that some of the materials from the missiles eliminated (including precious materials from missile guidance systems power-supply and communications equipment, vehicle chassis, etc) are either transferred to the domestic economy (at reduced prices, in view of wear and tear) or remain available to the Ministry of Defence, thereby enabling expenditure on new military equipment to be reduced. It can be argued that these recycled resources alone entirely offset the expenditure involved in implementing the INF Treaty.

There are other economic factors, too, which to some extent "vindicate" earlier expenditure on the deployment of intermediate- and shorter-range missile forces. For example, the billions' worth of infrastructure developed for these missiles - roads, bridges (specially reinforced to carry heavy missile launchers), telecommunications and power lines, residential towns - has added to the wealth of the whole country. This wealth remains, virtually in its entirety, available both for military use (for example, the SS-25s now based partly in regions where the now banned SS-20s were formerly deployed, or the missile bases built by the Americans in Europe now used for aircraft installations) and for use within the domestic economy.

The INF Treaty is also an important step forward politically. It has acted as a stimulus to all the current negotiations on arms limitation and reductions. This includes the talks on the reduction of conventional weapons and on the elimination of chemical weapons, and the negotiations over the ratification of the agreements limiting nuclear testing which have already been signed. The talks on a 50 per cent reduction in strategic offensive arms are particularly significant here. When the new round of Soviet-American talks (on nuclear and space weapons) started in March 1985, the problems of intermediate- and shorter-range missiles and of reducing strategic arms generally were treated as a single issue. Joint methods and approaches to the reduction of both kinds of arms and common approaches to verification were worked out, building confidence on both sides. The successful implementation of the INF Treaty has undoubtedly done an enormous amount to advance the negotiations on the reduction of strategic offensive arms, and will have a favourable effect on the talks on increasing stability which are due to start immediately after the signing of the agreement on a 50 per cent reduction in strategic offensive arms.

The INF Treaty has also been conducive to changing the political climate in Europe. The countries of Europe where Euro-missiles aimed at other European nations were sited have now changed from an oppositional, confrontational policy to the building of a "common home". Merely by looking at the chronology of events in Europe, it can be seen that the signing (in December 1987) and ratification (in June 1988) of the INF Treaty coincided with the first real manifestations of those political processes which have so completely changed the face of Europe. The Treaty can thus clearly be regarded as one of the foundation stones of the new Europe.

At the present time the USSR and the United States are not only more actively engaged in talks on arms reduction of various kinds, not only cutting their military budgets from previous levels and planning to cut them still further, but they are also taking unilateral action on arms reductions.

It was announced in June 1990 that the Soviet Union was unilaterally making additional cuts in its tactical nuclear weapons in Europe. By the end of the year, 60 tactical missile launchers, 250 artillery pieces capable of firing nuclear ammunition and 1,500 nuclear warheads will be withdrawn from Central Europe, while 140 tactical missile launchers and 3,200 artillery pieces capable of firing nuclear ammunition will be removed from Europe as a whole, including the territory of the USSR, in 1990.

Almost as if it were competing with the Soviet Union, the United States Administration has recently decided to discontinue work on replacing the Lance tactical missile (the FOTL programme) and halt the modernization of nuclear artillery shells; it is also putting forward for examination by a meeting of NATO a proposal to withdraw around 1,500 rounds of nuclear ammunition from Europe.

The INF Treaty has sparked off completely new processes which previously had not even been thought of. Under the Treaty, a significant number of missiles are being cut, and consequently the nuclear warheads for them are also becoming "redundant". At a rough estimate, the number of such "redundant" warheads in both countries combined will exceed 2,000 (over 1,600 on the Soviet side and more than 400 on the American). More nuclear warheads will become redundant after the signing of the agreement on a 50 per cent reduction in strategic offensive arms. According to the most modest estimates, by the end of the seven-year reduction period we can expect there to be not less than 7,000 to 8,000 redundant warheads in both countries. The two great Powers are therefore presented with an opportunity to agree to halt the (highly dangerous) production of fissionable materials for nuclear weapons and close the factories producing them. Quite enough material would be "freed" to maintain the nuclear arsenals of both sides ready for action at a lower level, and indeed to modernize them if necessary.

One result of the processes set in train by the INF Treaty which may be seen as typical is the "Missile Technology Control Regime" (MTCR) proposed by seven of the most developed Western countries. This, in its aims, resembles the IAEA safeguards, being intended to limit the spread of such a dangerous form of weaponry as missiles on our planet. While the adoption of this regime should be seen as a positive move, it must be said that it is not effective enough at present and does not deal evenhandedly with all possible participants; for this reason the Soviet Union cannot associate itself with the regime *de jure*.

Unfortunately, the positive aspects of the arms limitation and reduction process, including those resulting from the INF Treaty, are attended by some thoroughly negative ones. Among these are attempts to "compensate" for the arms cuts and the eliminated weapons by designing and deploying various new weapons which do not come under the treaty limitations. The most striking example of such "compensation", which reflects no credit on its originators, is the attempt to replace the eliminated intermediate- and shorter-range nuclear missiles with air-launched tactical nuclear cruise missiles based around Europe.

The undesirable consequences of the current elimination of intermediate- and shorter-range missiles also include the harmful effects - which many people have so far considered unimportant - of the elimination process itself on the environment. In drawing up the INF Treaty the two great Powers, with their vast scientific and manufacturing potential, could find no better way of destroying their missiles than to burn their solid-fuel motors or blow up the missiles completely. Either way (and from the environmental point of view they are practically identical), a significant quantity of nitrous oxides, carbon, hydrochloric acid and other harmful substances are released into the atmosphere. While it may be possible, given the relatively small number of missiles to be destroyed, to continue dealing with the intermediate- and shorter-range missiles in this way, it will be necessary to find new, more acceptable methods when far greater numbers of missiles become due for elimination under future agreements. The best course would be for several countries to combine their efforts in the search for ecologically sound methods of elimination. The elimination of missiles is already a problem not only for the Soviet Union and the United States but also for other countries. It would appear that it is now confronting Germany (Federal Republic of) in particular, which, according to statements by the country's leaders, is due to destroy its Pershing IA missiles and 72 launchers for them.

The elimination of intermediate- and shorter-range missiles, and consequently their discontinued production, should give rise to further thought about the question of conversion. Although these missiles did not, in either the Soviet Union or the United States, amount to a significant burden on the munitions industry, and the proportion of military expenditure devoted to them was by no means crucial, the experience gained deserves some attention.

The INF Treaty was the first step (we are talking here of the last 10 to 15 years) towards reducing military production in the USSR and the United States and shifting industry towards civilian production. The question of conversion in the light of the INF Treaty has already been discussed in print, and papers on this topic were presented by Soviet and American representatives at a seminar organized by the International Labour Organisation in Geneva in May 1989.

It might be thought that the process of conversion, having already been approved by the world community several times this century and being of great importance to many countries, would be clear-cut and easy to understand, and that recommendations on how to go about it would be straightforward. At the moment, however, things are not working out like that at all.

Information in print on the problems of conversion is highly contradictory. There is no consensus on what conversion actually is, the directions given are contradictory, there are no indications of priorities for dealing with the problem and no clear division of responsibility between the Government and business. The result is that those actually doing the job - specific enterprises or groups of enterprises - have to work by trial and error, advancing towards their goal along a path which is anything but straight.

Things have progressed to the point where it is simplistically assumed that the mere presence of a good manager ought to guarantee that a factory will prosper, even when it moves from military to civilian production overnight. Still, the plain fact is that wherever military production, is discontinued and there is a move to civilian production the initial outcome is a (chiefly) financial loss on the part of the worker, the enterprise and the Government. The main reason for this is that the value of military products in relation to labour costs is generally higher than the corresponding value of civilian products.

There is only one option here: to cut down on military expenses as conversion proceeds. The INF Treaty has done a good deal to improve matters by enabling us to come to grips with this task, albeit on a small scale.

Our experience with converting the factories which used to produce intermediate- and shorter-range missiles is helping considerably in the conversion of the entire munitions industry in the Soviet Union. A notable feature of the conversion of these factories was the significant help received from the State which, in order to cover the expense involved in stopping missile production and increasing civilian output, allocated funds for the period 1988 to 1990 to compensate for the fall in that part of the profits from which deductions for the social development funds are made. State resources allowed special measures to be taken to protect the average wage of workers, technicians and engineers over this period. A relatively small number of enterprises were affected by these measures.

It is common knowledge that the Soviet Union has drawn up a long-term conversion plan affecting the whole range of military production. In this case, whether the State can provide assistance on the same scale as to the enterprises previously producing intermediate- and shorter-range missiles will be much harder to decide: it simply may not have the resources to ensure that conversion is carried out under optimum conditions on a short time-scale.

Each country's experience of conversion merits individual consideration. There are some problems, however, which it would be sensible to tackle on an intergovernmental basis. There has already been talk of co-ordinating conversion plans. Such plans should mesh with arms reduction "schedules". The expense of conversion for each country individually could be cut through international distribution of labour and sensible co-operation among the "ex-munitions" factories in various countries.

Chapter 2

Arms Control, Disarmament and Budgetary Implications of START

Edward A. Kolodziej

Introduction

The US-Soviet treaty to eliminate long- and shorter-range nuclear weapons in Europe and Asia marked a major breakthrough in the Super Power nuclear arms and disarmament process. For the first time in the postwar era, an entire class of nuclear weapons, with ranges between 500 and 5,000 kilometres, was to be dismantled. Once completed, approximately five per cent of current US-Soviet nuclear arsenals will have been destroyed. The economic and strategic implications of the INF Treaty promise to be greater than the actual number of missile delivery systems and the amount of nuclear explosive power that will be dismantled. The treaty signalled a strong desire on the part of the United States and the Soviet Union to slow and reverse the strategic nuclear arms race, to decrease the size of their nuclear arsenals, and to regulate the process of research, development and testing in modernizing these weapons.

The importance of the treaty also lies in the elaborate verification regime that it has established. The creation and training of bilingual inspection teams and their experience in overseeing the destruction of the US and Soviet missiles covered by the treaty are important for the institutionalization of the arms control and disarmament process between the Super Powers on a permanent basis. The lessons learned by these teams and the willingness of Moscow and Washington to tolerate deep, intrusive on-site inspections are directly relevant to follow-on nuclear and conventional arms reduction accords. It is difficult to underestimate the significance of constructing credible and reliable verification regimes. This latter dimension of the INF Treaty is perhaps its most important and lasting feature since mutual Super Power confidence in verifying their arms cuts and redeployments is a *sine qua non* for the long-run success of the process.

The success of the INF Treaty prompts a preliminary examination of the arms control, disarmament and budgetary implications of the emerging START Treaty between the United States and the Soviet Union. Part one outlines the current strategic force structures of the Super Powers and the principal understandings reached by Washington and Moscow in defining their strategic forces under the proposed treaty at the close of 1990. The essential features of the treaty were reportedly completed at that time, but the signature was postponed, partly due to the Persian Gulf war and partly by on-going negotiations to resolve several unresolved issues.

Part two examines the strategic nuclear modernization programmes of the Super Powers and their implications for the US-Soviet balance in a post-START environment. Even a cursory review of US and Soviet improvements in their nuclear forces reveals that the START Treaty places few restraints on either side in completing their present modernization plans. This outcome of the treaty is in line with the results of previous Super Power arms control accords, including the Partial Test Ban Treaty of the 1960s and the SALT-II Treaty a decade later. Neither of these accords significantly limited Washington or Moscow in developing its nuclear arsenal; indeed, both accords as well as the START Treaty may be viewed as rationalizations of Super Power nuclear modernization programmes and as mechanisms of restraining domestic political pressures, for ever deeper cuts in Super Power long-range nuclear capabilities. Moreover, whatever its final form, START will not affect the military exploitation by either side of space technologies for defence against offensive nuclear forces.

The final section identifies some of the budgetary and security problems that START raises, but does not address. This section also presents an alternative proposal for strategic nuclear modernization to that proposed by the Washington and the cost and security implications of each. The paper concludes that, for reasons to be discussed below, alternative force structures which would reduce US and presumably Soviet capabilities are not likely to be adopted in their present, or in some revised, form in the near future. Of course a significant downturn in US and Soviet economic prospects or a major political convulsion within the Soviet Union, leading to new limits being placed on socio-economic reforms and on a cut of defence expenditures, could have a fundamental impact on the strategic nuclear structures of the United States and the Soviet Union in the post-START era. Barring such structural economic or political changes, START promises to be only a modest start on reducing the nuclear arsenals of the Super Powers, on enhancing the stability of the nuclear balance and on restraining defence expenditures. The counting rules of START actually favour increased spending for new systems, most notably for penetrating bombers and mobile ICBM systems, like US Midgetman and Soviet SS-25 missiles.

If START cannot be viewed as a decisive break from previous Super Power assumptions about what each considers to be an acceptable nuclear posture at tolerable cost and risk, there is reason to believe that a START treaty will be an instalment in the development and strengthening of a long-term US-Soviet strategic relationship that could move more towards co-operation and progressively reinforce the trend of the late 1980s away from conflict. This cautiously optimistic appraisal of the treaty's results is occasioned by the success of the INF Treaty and growing US-Soviet co-operation across a wide spectrum of political and economic issues. These are highlighted by recent and unprecedented levels of US-Soviet agreement in the United Nations Security Council. These signs of enlarging Super Power co-operation have been furthered, arguably, by successful US-Soviet mediation efforts in Southern Africa, Cambodia and, more recently, in their close working relations in addressing the Persian Gulf crisis. Until now, US-Soviet differences over the final form of the START

Treaty, over implementation of the conventional arms reduction accords signed in Paris in November 1990, or over Western concerns about the pace and scope of the political and socio-economic reforms within the Soviet Union and Eastern Europe have not offset these gains in US-Soviet understanding. However modest the emerging START Treaty may be, it should be viewed, in the final analysis, as a significant part of a larger political and strategic process of co-operation that promises to lead to ever wider and deeper accords on arms reductions.

The START Accord and its Implications for Current Nuclear Force Structures and Capabilities

START Rules

President Reagan and General Secretary Gorbachev agreed at Reykjavik in October 1986 on limits of 6,000 nuclear warheads (including bombs) and of 1,600 deployed land-based intercontinental ballistic missiles (ICBMs), submarine-launched ballistic missiles (SLBMs) and heavy bombers. The Washington Summit of December 1987, which also led to the signing of the treaty banning all theatre nuclear weapons in the range between 500 and 5,000 km, also resulted in an agreement on a sublimit of 4,900 on the aggregate number of ICBM and SLBM warheads. A further sublimit of 1,100 has been established for mobile ICBM warheads and 1,540 for 154 heavy Soviet ICBMs. Moscow has also agreed to a cut of 50 per cent in the aggregate throw-weight of its ICBMs and SLBMs. In contrast to SALT, the number of warheads on each ICBM or SLBM will be specified by its actual load, and not by the upper limit of what tests were conducted on the missile. An acceptable monitoring and inspection regime to verify warhead totals is expected to build on the INF experience.[1]

STARTalso defines bomber warhead/bomb totals in a new way. Penetrating bombers, including the US B-1 and B-2 and the Soviet Union's Blackjack, are counted as one warhead per bomber when equipped with gravity bombs or Short-Range Attack Missiles (SRAMs). Heavy bombers, loaded with Air-Launched Cruise Missiles (ALCMs), are discounted under START limits: each of the first 150 US heavy bombers carrying ALCMs will be counted as ten; the corresponding reckoning for the Soviet Union is eight for the first 210 bombers. In contrast, both the B-1 and the B-2 are capable of carrying at least 16 gravity bombs and short-range attack missiles (SRAMs). The B-1 is reportedly capable of actually transporting up to 24 weapons.[2]

---

[1]   An early summary of US-Soviet progress on START may be found in US, Arms Control and Disarmament Agency, *Nuclear and Space Talks: US and Soviet Proposals*, 22 January 1990. For an updated version see Arms Control Association, *Fact Sheet, US and Soviet Positions at the Nuclear and Space Talks*, Washington, D.C, November 1990.

[2]   See Michele A. Flournoy, "START Cutting Soviet Strategic Force", *Arms Control Today*, June/July, 1989, p.20, and Arms Control Association, *Background Paper*, Washington, D.C., June 1990.

Fully loaded, US B-52s are capable of carrying 20-24 weapons, depending on the mix of SRAMs, ALCMs and bombs.

START has also made some progress on limiting ALCMs and Sea-Launched Cruise Missiles (SLCMs). ALCMs with ranges over 600 kilometres are counted against START warhead limits. Both sides are also expected to limit their SLCMs to 880.

The Super Powers also have different views about nuclear defence and space issues. The US is actively pursuing defensive nuclear capabilities and is pressing for treaty assurance for these programmes. The Bush administration has affirmed the Reagan administration's commitment to the development of these systems and the possible "co-operative transition" to a mix of offensive and defensive forces in the future. Moscow is wary of this development. Both sides sharply disagree on the permissible limits for research, development, and testing of defensive systems and on the number of satellites in orbit to "test" a defensive system. Both agree, however, to sign START without the need for a new Defence and Space treaty to regulate ABM development.

Implications of START for Current Super Power Force Structures

United States Capabilities

Figure 2.1 summarizes current and potential post-START strategic force levels. US total launchers are composed of 1,872 ICBMs, SLBMs and bombers. Total US strategic warheads and bombs are estimated at 12,304, including approximately 350 SLCMs. ICBM warheads are divided between 450 single-warhead Minuteman IIs, 500 three-warhead Minuteman IIIs, and 50 ten-warhead MXs. SLBMs are presently carried by 11 Poseidon submarines, each carrying 16 C-3 missiles with 10 warheads per missile; 12 Poseidon submarines carrying 16 C-4 missiles each with eight warheads per missile; eight Trident submarines carrying 24 C-4 missiles each with eight warheads per missile; and one Trident submarine carrying 24 D-5 missiles, each with eight warheads per missile.[3]

The US Air Force presently has approximately 1,600 ALCMs and some 1,100 SRAMs. Bomber levels include 191 B-52s stand-off systems and 97 B-1s. Excluded from these totals are 58 FB-111 aircraft under the control of the Strategic Air Command (SAC) and an additional 300 B-52s in storage, on display or converted to conventional roles. About a third of these strategic bomber forces are kept on 24-hour alert. This contrasts with 55 per cent for SLBMs and 90 per cent for ICBMs. Overall, approximately 20 per cent of the pre-START US strategic arsenal is assigned to ICBMs; 43 per cent to SLBMs or SLCMs; and 37 per cent to bombers.

---

[3]   Current strategic levels are drawn from Arms Control Association, *Fact Sheet*, no. 1.

Figure 2.1
Potential Strategic Forces Under START

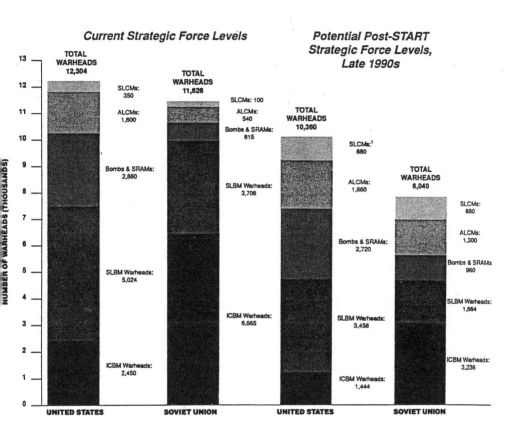

Source: Arms Control Association, *Fact Sheet, US and Soviet Positions at the Nuclear and Space Talks* (Washington, D.C., November 1990. This chapter went to press before slight changes in US and Soviet warhead totals under the proposed START treaty could be incorporated into the final text. The US total is scheduled to increase by 35 warheads to 10,395, reflecting small increases in ALCMs and Bombs & SRAMs and deductions in ICBMs; the Soviet total will remain at 8,040, but an increase of 8 SLMBs will be offset by a decrease of 8 ICBMs.

[1] Permitted ceiling on long-range SLCMs is 880; current US plan calls for 758 or fewer.

Soviet Capabilities

The Soviet Union concentrates most of its warheads on land-based systems. These include SS-11, -13, -17, -18 and -19 ICBMs. Except for the older SS-11 and SS-13s, all carry multiple independently-targeted vehicles (MIRVs). US negotiators consider the Soviet Union's 308 SS-18s as the most threatening of these systems because of their accuracy, throw-weight (10 warheads per missile), rapid and reliable response rate, and hard-target capability. These are designed to destroy US land-based ICBM and bomber bases. To these totals have been added 40 silo-based and 27 rail-based SS-24 missiles, each with 10 warheads. Approximately 200 single-warhead road-mobile SS-25s have also been added to the Soviet arsenal, replacing SS-11s, in conformity with the SALT II limits informally observed by the Soviet Union.

The Soviet Union also has about 60 nuclear-carrying missile submarines.[4] These cover Yankee (I and II), Delta (I-IV), Hotel III, and the newer Typhoon class of submarines. These platforms carry a range of eight different kinds of missiles. Of these, the most important are SS-N-18s, each with seven warheads on 14 Delta IIIs (1,568); SS-N-20s on six Typhoon submarines, each with 10 warheads (1,200); and SS-N-23s on six Delta IVs, each with four warheads (384).

The bomber force includes older Bear A, B, and C heavy bombers introduced in the late 1950s and early 1960s. The Bear A is reported to carry two bombs and its upgraded version about twice this number. The Bear G, deployed in 1984 for the first time, carries four bombs or two air-to-surface missiles. The newer Bear H is estimated to be able to transport up to 10 AS-15 ALCMs. Ten Blackjack bombers are the newest addition to the Soviet arsenal. Although counted only as one warhead per bomber under START, the Blackjack can carry 24 SRAMs or 12 ALCMs. Relative to the United States, Soviet bomber, ICBM and SLBM forces are usually kept on low alert status. Overall, 57 per cent of the pre-START Soviet strike force is carried by ICBMs; 33 per cent by SLBMs; and the remaining 10 per cent by bombers.

START and the Modernization of US and Soviet Nuclear Forces

United States Nuclear Modernization

START limits impose little or no impediment to the modernization of US and Soviet nuclear forces, nor to the development of defensive capabilities. While the precise mix of a modernized US triad is still to be decided, the programmes now underway or proposed by the United States provide some idea, subject to Congressional cuts or administration revisions, of how the US arsenal will look at the turn of the century. Most of the 4,900 long-range ballistic missiles permitted for the United States would

---

[4]   Compare Arms Control *Background Paper* with Flournoy's analysis, p.17 which, list 61 and 63 submarines respectively.

be placed on 18 Trident submarines by the end of the 1990s. The Bush administration has requested full funding for the eighteenth Trident submarine; budgetary agreements with Congress will limit the Navy to this number. Each Trident is scheduled eventually to carry 24 D-5 missiles, each armed with eight warheads. Once deployed, the D-5 will approach, if not match, the MX in accuracy and hard-kill capability thanks partly to improvements in satellite navigation and missile accuracy. However, retrofitting the eight Trident submarines carrying C-4 missiles with the D-5 has been deferred until beyond Fiscal Year (FY) 1997.

Initial negotiations over START would have excluded up to three submarines from START totals for overhaul, conversion or modernization. That would conceivably exclude 72 SLBMs, carrying up to 576 warheads from the 6,000/4,900 limits under START. This issue has now apparently been resolved by including all SLBM-launching submarines under START limits whatever their status. If 18 Trident submarines are assumed as the counting base, the US would concentrate approximately 3,456 warheads in its sea-based force (excluding SLCMs) or about 70 per cent of the 4,900 sublimit permitted by START. Older Poseidon submarines, along with C-3 and C-4 missiles, would be retired from service as the Trident D-5 force became operational.

For land-based ICBMs, planned upgrades in the US arsenal include 50 silo-based MXs and the development of the Midgetman missile to be road-mobile and armed with one warhead (although proposals of up to three have been voiced). These systems would be complemented by a smaller number of silo-based Minuteman III missiles than those currently deployed. These ground-based forces are expected to comprise the difference between the 4,900 limit on such systems and the 3,456 assigned to SLBMs. These ground forces would represent about 944 warheads on Minuteman III missiles and 500 on MX for a total of 1,444 warheads or 20 per cent of the ICBM-SLBM sublimit. Minuteman II missiles are scheduled to be withdrawn, beginning in FY 1992. The shift from ICBMs to SLBMs is justified by the greater invulnerability of sea-based systems; their capacity to be withheld longer from use than land-based systems; and the longer range and accuracy of Trident D-5 missiles which will replace less advanced systems. SLBMs still fall short of the degree of precision and hard-kill capacity of the MX and are less responsive to rapid use or to long-range control, shortcomings arising partially from the impediments to speedy and direct communication between command centres and submarines on patrol.

The most striking difference between SALT-I and START, however, concerns the counting rules for bombers. Since each penetrating bomber is counted as only one warhead, a large disparity immediately arises between accountable warheads under START and the actual number likely to be carried in each Super Power arsenal. The reported 50 per cent cut in warheads, first announced at Reykjavik, is likely to be more in the order of 20 per cent, largely because of the bomber discounts and SLCM exclusion rules.[5] Although the B-1 can carry up to 24 weapons, the force as a whole will be reckoned at only 97 weapons, a potential difference of 2,231 warheads/bombs (2,328 minus 97 B-1s).

Similarly, the B-2 can be armed with up to 16 weapons making a difference between accounted and potential arsenal totals of 1,125 (1,200 minus 75 B-2s). The disparity between accountable and actual bomb/warhead totals for B-52s, as noted earlier, can be roughly estimated by a factor of two. In the extreme, actual bomber force totals, combining B-1, B-2 and B-52 bombers, could exceed accountable START totals by over 3,000 warheads. Anticipated budgetary constraints, which are discussed below, are likely to narrow the potential disparity between START counting rules and the actual number of ballistic missile and bomber warheads that will be deployed.

Moreover, the Bush administration is pushing ahead with plans to develop an advanced Air-Launched Cruise Missile to enhance the stand-off capabilities of the United States. These qualitative improvements, combined with the discounting of bomber forces under SALT, promise actually to strengthen, in the short run, overall US nuclear capabilities. START will essentially leave the US nuclear arsenal in an overall stronger position as a strike force than the comparable arsenal available to the United States when the Carter-Reagan modernization programmes got underway in the late 1970s. Also excluded from START totals, as noted earlier, will be an estimated 880 SLCMs which the US prefers to address in a follow-on treaty, if at all.

If the estimates of Figure 2.1 are accepted for illustrative purposes, the post-START US force will have almost 11,000 warheads. Of this total, 43 per cent will be launched from the sea (including D-5s and SLCMs), 43 per cent from bombers (including ALCMs, SRAMs, and gravity bombs); and 14 per cent from land-based ICBMs.

Soviet Nuclear Modernization

Soviet nuclear strategic forces are also expected to undergo significant changes in the number and composition of missile platforms and warhead delivery systems. The most dramatic change is in the number of SS-18s. This force of 308 missiles will be cut in half to 154 and the remaining missiles upgraded in performance. Since the Soviet Union has indicated that it intends to deploy no more than 3,300 ICBM warheads under START, it also means that Moscow will cut its overall ICBM inventory from 6,665 to half that number. A modernized ten-warhead SS-18 fleet will account for 1,540 warheads, with the remainder to be deployed primarily on SS-24s (in a railcar mode) and SS-25s, and (during the transition to this posture), older SS-19s.[6] Only the SS-18 is believed to have hard-target capability.

---

[5]   According to the Arms Control Association, the reduction in warheads for the United States, is likely to be approximately 16 per cent; for the Soviet Union, about 22 per cent. See Figure 2.1.

[6]   The Arms Control Association, *Fact Sheet*, estimates that the Soviet Union will deploy about 36 SS-24s and 736 SS-25s.

Also sharply cut will be the number of submarines carrying SLBMs. The current level of slightly over 60 submarines is likely to be cut at least in half and to stabilize somewhere between 15-30 vessels. SLBMs will be concentrated on Delta IV and Typhoon submarines. If 880 SLCMs were added to *accountable* SLBM totals under START, the Soviet Union could conceivably have approximately 2,544 sea-launched warheads in its inventory.

Like the United States, the Soviet Union may take advantage of bomber counting rules. The 10 Blackjacks in the Soviet arsenal may be increased to upwards of 60 or more aircraft and the fleet of Bear Hs could theoretically be increased to 100, although the likelihood of so large an increase does not appear high. While START would account for most of the ALCMs on Bear H bombers, it would not count up to 1,400 SRAM warheads and bombs that an expanded fleet of 60 Blackjack bombers would be able to carry.

The overall make-up of the Soviet triad would, like its American counterpart, become less vulnerable to a first-strike attack. About 40 per cent of the actual Soviet arsenal, reckoned in warheads and bombs, would be carried on ICBMs; another 32 per cent on SLCMs and SLBMs; and the remaining 28 per cent or so on Bear and Blackjack bombers.

START rules, as they currently stand, assign priority to bombers and sea-launched systems over silo-based and immobile ICBM forces. The discount rate for penetrating bombers and the anticipated discount of ALCMs, especially favourable for US heavy bombers, puts major pressure on the defence priorities of the two Super Powers to favour bombers and sea-based systems. The discount rate for submarines reinforces these incentives. The result will likely be a more stable Super Power nuclear balance than was the case at the start of the 1980s, but also one that carries significant cost implications for both sides.

The Cost of Strategic Nuclear Force Modernization

The Bush Plan and Alternatives

Table 2.1 summarizes the 25-year life cycle costs of the principal strategic programmes of the Reagan-Bush modernization plan for US strategic forces as of April 1990. The total cost for the five systems, including acquisition and support, is approximately half a trillion dollars. This expenditure is estimated to be sufficient to produce a force of 120 B-2 bombers, 20 Trident submarines (armed with D-5 missiles), and 500 Midgetman single-warhead missiles. The B-1, whose operational shortcomings continue to be a problem, would be upgraded and retained as a penetrating bomber.

The most costly new programmes under this plan are the B-2 and the Midgetman. They appeal to different constituencies within the Washington security community. The Air Force is committed to the B-2 as a penetrating bomber. Meanwhile the Bush administration has initially scaled down its request of 132 B-2s to 75, but has kept open the option of requesting more, pending the outcome of START and the follow-on in START-II. Midgetman, which has always enjoyed Congressional support, is also favoured by General Brent Scowcroft, President Bush's National Security Advisor. In 1983, Scowcroft chaired a special presidential commission, established by President Reagan, that recommended development of the Midgetman and the deployment of the MX. Since both systems have strong support and partisans of one or the other resist any compromise that would eliminate their preferred choice, there is a presumption in favour of both systems being adopted at some level. The past record of compromises on these two weapons systems suggests that some mix will eventually be accepted and deployed.[7] While a rail-based MX system was dropped indefinitely from the Bush administration's revised defence budget for FY 1992-93, spending for Midgetman would increase from $202 million in FY 1991 to $715 million in FY 1993.

Of these systems, among the most vulnerable to strategic and budgetary constraints is the B-2. Depending on the number that might be produced, a single B-2 is expected to cost somewhere between $700-800 million dollars in acquisition costs and an equal amount in operations and support per aircraft over the lifetime of the programme. A price tag of one and a half to two billion dollars for each B-2 is difficult to justify on cost-benefit grounds. Several arguments are advanced by B-2 advocates in support of the B-2:

1. Capacity to hunt mobile targets;
2. Flexibility of mission assignment;
3. Target-kill reliability;
4. Air-defence penetrability and increased burden on enemy defences;
5. Conventional role; and
6. START rules favouring penetrating bombers.

Objections have been raised to all these purported assets.[8] Hunting mobile Soviet missiles is likely to be difficult in a post-attack environment with large-scale devastation where broken communications are likely to be the rule and not the exception. Once the radar of a B-2 is functioning, presumably in pursuit of Soviet mobile missiles, it would itself be a target to alerted defences. Moreover, relatively inexpensive countermeasures - such as decoys - can frustrate its mission from the outset. Doubts also arise regarding the ability of the B-2 to assess damage and identify new targets or to be recalled in the wake of a Super Power nuclear exchange. In an environment of high radiation, smoke and dust, it will be very difficult, if not impossible, to make accurate damage assessments and to be in contact with command

---

[7]   See Strobe Talbott's informed discussion of US strategic nuclear acquisitions decision-making in *Deadly Gambits*, New York, Vintage, 1985.

[8]   A useful, succinct critique of the B-2 on budgetary and strategic grounds is found in *A Report of the Union of Concerned Scientists: The B-2 Bomber: Impossible Cost, Dubious Mission*, Washington, D.C., April 1990.

authorities. Those hard targets that can be destroyed by gravity bombs will most likely be empty, having been used in the initial attack.

Table 2.1
25-Year Life Cycle Costs for Major Nuclear Strategic Systems

	Acquisition Cost in US $ (billion)	O&S Cost in US $ (billion)	Total Cost in US $ (billion)
B-2[a]	77.9	77.1	155.0
B-1B[b]	36.8	53.1	89.9
B-52 (ACM)[c]	26.2	28.8	55.0
MX Rail Garrison[d]	13.4	6.0	19.4
Midgetman[d]	23.8	25.0	48.8
Trident II/D5[d]	71.0	50.0	121.0

Notes
[a.] The B-2 acquisition cost includes $64.9 billion for the baseline programme plus 20 per cent for anticipated non-baseline items, based on experience with the B-1B programme. O&S costs are for 120 B-2s and 240 KC-135 tankers.
[b.] The B-1B acquisition cost includes $31.4 billion for the baseline programme (FY 1990 dollars) plus $5.4 billion for non-baseline items. See GAO, *Estimated Costs to Deploy the B-1B*, GAO/NSIAD-88-12 (Washington, D.C., GAO, 1987), p.1, and GAO, *B-1B Cost and Performance Remain Uncertain*, GAO/NSIAD-89-55 (Washington, D.C., GAO, 1989), p.24. O&S costs are for 90 B-1Bs and 270 tankers.
[c.] The B-52 acquisition cost assumes 96 bombers at $200 million each, plus $7 billion for the advanced cruise missile. O&S costs are for 84 active-duty bombers and 90 tankers.
[d.] Acquisition and O&S data for the MX Rail Garrison, Midgetman and Trident II/D5 systems are adapted from Michael E. Brown, "B-2 and Beyond: What Future the US Bomber Force?" *International Security*, Fall 1989, p.34. The acquisition cost of the Rail Garrison MX includes the purchase of 85 missiles, 50 of which would be deployed on MX trains. The Midgetman system would consist of 500 single-warhead missiles on hard mobile launchers. The Trident II/D5 system would consist of 20 submarines equipped with 480 D5 missiles. Brown's 20-year O&S costs are converted to 25-year O&S costs by multiplying by 1.25. N.B.: The Bush administration has dropped indefinitely the MX Rail Garrison, and plans to retrofit the first eight Trident submarines with new Trident II missiles have been deferred beyond FY 1997. The Trident submarine fleet would be held to 18. Spending for R&D for MX Rail Garrison will, however, continue.

Source: A Report of the Union of Concerned Scientists: The B-2 Bomber: Impossible Cost, Dubious Mission, Washington, D.C., April 1990, p.16.

B-2s might complicate Soviet air defences, but bombers or air platforms carrying cruise missiles (ALCMs) would pose even more troublesome problems for Soviet defences since these systems would be deployed over a larger space than the B-2. Area defence is always more difficult than point defence. Using the Stealth bomber for conventional missions would not only be highly costly but its purpose could be accomplished much less expensively by using other systems, such 25 B-52s, B-1s, F-111s, F-117A stealth attack aircraft, and F-15 and F-16 fighters. Finally, there is a self-serving circularity to Air Force claims that START favours bombers. To gain JCS and Air Force support for START, US negotiators have had to be sensitive to the interests of these parties in large discount rules for manned bombers. Now START counting rules can be relied upon to justify a weapon system which, within a stressed US and Pentagon budget, might have difficulty proving itself on its own military and strategic merits on a cost-target kill basis.[9]

The Midgetman is attractive to arms control advocates and also to strategists who place more value on stability over striking power. The cost of the system, however, is not negligible at approximately $50 billion over its life. It offers no more in the way of invulnerability than Trident or Poseidon submarines, nor more accuracy than the D-5. The cost of maintaining these systems on constant alert makes it likely that they will be garrisoned, like the MX, a deployment mode that will dilute Midgetman's invulnerability and attractiveness as a ground-based strategic weapon. Conversely, the Midgetman might well be used, as critics suggest, as a bargaining chip in a follow-on to START to cut Soviet land-based forces further and to lower the number of nuclear weapons in Super Power arsenals to around 3,000 on both sides. If mutual concessions cannot be achieved, then the decision to develop and deploy Midgetman or the Garrison MX could be taken at that time.

The favourable atmosphere for Super Power arms control accords, created by fundamental changes in Soviet domestic society and politics as well as by the budgetary and economic pressures confronted by the American government, has prompted a great deal of thinking, particularly outside the Pentagon and the official US defence establishment, about ways to cut strategic forces and new defence programmes on both sides without endangering peace. Besides a lower external threat and severe resource constraints on both sides, the evolving strategic environment itself argues for additional cuts. As the nuclear forces of the US and the Soviet Union increase in their invulnerability, there is less reason to build offensive systems capable of destroying these targets in a first-strike or in a pre-emptive attack to limit damage to one's own forces as well as to valued human and material resources.

Moreover, as newer Soviet and US nuclear forces are increasingly invulnerable to a disarming surprise attack, there will be less urgency in political and military command centres to commit these assets before efforts to end an armed conflict and

---

[9]   If the Bush administration's original plan to purchase 132 B-2s were stretched out, the total cost of the programme would of course be even higher than the estimates of the Union of Concerned Scientists. On the other hand, the Congressional Budget Office estimates that the cost per plane for a buy of 132 vs. 120 planes would be somewhat lower than the Union of Concerned Scientists' estimates, but the acquisition costs would still be over $600 million per copy, easily the most expensive bomber ever purchased by any country. See Congressional Budget Office, *Alternative Procurement Programs for the B-2 Bomber: Effects on Capability and Costs*, Washington, D.C., April 1990.

check escalation have been tried. Under these conditions, smaller, invulnerable forces would be sufficient to deter an aggressor. Parity in the number and throw-weight of nuclear weapons would also not be necessary from a strategic point of view. Many may well continue to argue that the ostensible political and psychological leverage afforded by these weapons should not be discounted, despite the increasing difficulty of locating and destroying an adversary's strategic nuclear systems. Those pressing this nuclear war-fighting strategy for deterrence will also insist that deterrence is strengthened, at least in psychological terms, if an opponent's strategic reserve could still be held at risk. These considerations lose much of their force as the Super Powers rely increasingly on invulnerable systems, like sea-based ALCMs and SLBMs.

As vulnerable strategic targets decrease, the maintenance of high levels of nuclear striking power cannot easily be justified on strictly military grounds. William Kaufmann estimates, for example, that there will be less than 400 aim points available to US forces to destroy vulnerable Soviet hard and soft strategic nuclear targets by the end of the century.[10] A US arsenal of more than 10,000 warheads, which would be consistent with START rules, would be redundant on its face. Kaufmann estimates that there will be approximately 1,380 urban-industrial targets available.[11] His estimates permit a considerable margin for error if it is remembered that approximately 100 Soviet metropolitan cities, with a population of 250,000 or more, contain roughly half of the Soviet population.[12] Half the number of soft targets cited by Kaufmann would be sufficient to destroy the Soviet Union as a viable society. The Soviet Union is faced with a similar dilemma of retaining more strategic warheads than there are lucrative targets to destroy.

If these new strategic conditions are recognized by Moscow and Washington, then a basis is created for cutting strategic forces further. Savings would then be substantial, especially for the United States, which is investing heavily in advanced systems. The joint proposal of a panel of defence experts, many of whom have served in high posts in the Pentagon, illustrates the possibility of substantial savings if current US modernization plans are revised in light of these new strategic and budgetary realities and constraints.[13]

Table 2.2 summarizes the recommendations of the Committee for National Security and the Defence Budget Project. If all land-based systems are either cancelled or held at R&D levels pending arms control negotiations, upwards of $37 billion could be saved on the Rail-Garrison MX, MX testing and the Midgetman missile. Another $43 billion (and likely more) would be saved by keeping the B-2 at a level of 15 buys.

---

10 William W. Kaufmann, *Glasnost, Perestroika, and U.S. Defense Spending*, (Washington, D.C., Brookings Institution, 1990), Table 8.

11 *Ibid.*

12 See *The Great Soviet Encyclopedia*, (New York, Macmillan, 1975, Third ed.), pp.30-33.

13 *Restructuring the U.S. Military: Defense Needs in the 21st Century*, A Report by the Defense Budget Task Force of the Committee for National Security and the Defense Budget Project (Washington, D.C., March 1990), especially pp.1-17.

Table 2.2
Recommendations for Potential Savings from Major Strategic Weapons
(current billions)

	Bush Administration	Task Force	Task Force Savings
Rail-Garrison Basing for the MX Missile	Deploy	Cancel	$5
MX Missile (production for test programme)	Continue	Cancel	$7
Midgetman Missile	Deploy	Low-level R&D	Potentially $20-25
Trident Submarine*	Build 21 to 24	Build 17	$6
Small Strategic Submarine	Begin R&D	Begin R&D	$0
D-5 Missile	Deploy on all Tridents	Deploy on 9 Tridents	$6
C-4 Missile	Retire	Keep on 8 Tridents	$0
B-2 Bomber	Build and Deploy 132	Build 15 for Test Programme	At least $43
B-1B Bomber	Upgrade as Penetrating Bomber	Turn into Cruise Missile Carrier	Potentially $6
Advanced Cruise Missile	Deploy	Hold Pending START	Potentially $3-4
Short-Range Attack Missile (SRAM II)	Deploy	Cancel	$2
SDI	Deploy	R&D Only	?

* Savings estimate based on assumption that the Navy would have built 21 Tridents. (N.B.: Since this number will be held to 18, additional savings than those estimated by the Task Force are possible).

Estimates are based on savings from weapons acquisition costs only. Additional savings would accrue in operations and support, particularly from cancelling the B-2 bomber and from achieving a follow-on START agreement limiting strategic warheads to 3,000.

Source: Restructuring the US Military: Defence Needs in the 21st Century, A Report by the Defence Budget Task Force of the Committee for National Security and the Defence Budget Project (Washington, D.C., March 1990), p.17.

Remaining savings could be secured by deploying a mix of Poseidon and Trident submarines to carry, respectively, C-4 and D-5 missiles. The Minuteman and MX systems would remain in their silos and the B-52 and B-1 would become ALCM launchers. This force would still be twice larger than the number of warheads that would be necessary to strike a receding number of Soviet strategic targets and an essentially fixed number of urban and industrial centres. Total savings in adopting a reduced modernization programme could be over a $100 billion.

Other proposals come to much the same conclusion although they differ with respect to the nuclear programmes that they would retain or revise.[14] They essentially concur in their general critique of the current Bush-Reagan budget on strategic and budgetary grounds, viz., too many weapons searching for an insufficient number of targets within an international environment marked by the end of the Cold War, the dissolution of the Warsaw pact, rising socio-economic, ethnic, national and political problems within the Soviet Union, and an increasingly embattled United States, facing mounting budgetary deficits at home and balance of payment difficulties abroad.

Prospects for Additional Cuts

But will US and Soviet nuclear modernization programmes soon be adapted to the new conditions of international life? In the long run, it will be difficult to sustain the tension between the strategic and socio-economic needs of both countries with the massive nuclear arsenals that each will retain under START. In the short run, however, one should not count on rapid change and a sharp decrease in spending on strategic systems. If the experience with SALT-I and II is a guide, the Bush administration's ability to get START through the Senate will depend in some measure on its commitment to modernization and the insurance policy that modernization purportedly offers against an uncertain future. Despite START's evident shortcomings, it is only reasonable to expect that negotiators responsible for its provisions will portray the treaty as a breakthrough in US-Soviet nuclear relations and that this argument, when viewed against the backdrop of the Cold War, promises to have some political force.[15]

---

[14] See Kaufmann, *Glasnost, Perestroika, and U.S. Defense Spending* as well as his *A Reasonable Defense*, (Washington, D.C., Brookings Institution, 1986). Useful, too, is his evaluation of the 1990 defense budget with Lawrence J. Korb: *The 1990 Defense Budget*, (Washington, D.C., Brookings Institution, 1990). Alternate plans for cutting spending on strategic forces while preserving the U.S.-Soviet nuclear balance are found in Lawrence J. Korb and Stephen Daggett, "The Defense Budget and Strategic Planning", *American Defense Annual*, Joseph Kruzel ed. (Lexington, Lexington Books, 1988), pp.43-66; Cindy Williams, "Strategic Spending Choices", *International Security*, XIII, No.4 (Spring 1989), pp.25-35; Stephen Alexis Cain, *Strategic Forces Funding in the 1990s: A Renewed Build-up?*, (Washington, D.C., Defense Budget Project, April 1989); and Congressional Budget Office, *Budgetary and Military Effects of the Strategic Arms Reduction Talks (START) Treaty*, (Washington, D.C., February 1990).

[15] See, for example, the interview with Ambassador Richard Burt, chief US negotiator at START until January 1991, in *Arms Control Today*, February 1990, pp.3-8.

Even those advocating substantial cuts in deployed systems advise spending on R&D and continuing modernization measures.[16] There is also the heavy hand of the past. US defence budgets favour procurement over personnel, support and logistics. This bias is also reinforced by large amounts of funds already authorized and appropriated by Congress for strategic systems. Finally, the bureaucratization of nuclear weapons into the military structures of the United States and the Soviet Union is a formidable impediment to quick across-the-board cuts. The modest result of the START treaty and the discount rules that have been agreed upon as a consequence of internal bureaucratic pressures on both sides suggests the difficulty of overcoming the past and the powerful interests supporting large and expensive strategic nuclear programmes.

Finally, the Persian Gulf war and the stand-off between Iraqi Scud missiles and US-produced Patriot anti-missile missiles have stirred renewed interest in the United States in ABM systems and in the SDI programme. President Bush's revised FY 1992-93 defence budget proposes to increase spending for the Strategic Defence Initiative from $2.87 billion in FY 1991 to $4.93 billion in FY 1993. US Defence Department priorities also favour preparation for a phase one space-based strategic defence system. Increased spending for the development of such systems will not in principle preclude the signing of START. However, expanded anti-ABM programmes, reinforced by the factors just noted, will likely have the effect of discouraging further cuts in offensive nuclear arsenals and impeding progress on a new Defence and Space treaty. START certainly represents a discernible step forward in bringing Super Power arsenals under control. Further progress in this direction and in slowing the modernization of US and Soviet defensive and offensive nuclear systems promises to be difficult and by no means certain.

---

[16]   See Kaufmann, *Glasnost, Perestroika, and U.S. Defense Spending.*

Chapter 3

Responses

First Response

Andrej Cima

The question of economic consequences, or results, of disarmament seems to be a highly topical theme to address. There is no doubt about the positive political and, in the long run, also economic consequences of arms control and disarmament measures. However, a number of complex problems will have to be addressed during the transitional period, conversion being high on the list.

In connection with the scaling down of military programmes in Czechoslovakia, namely the reduction of tank and armoured personal carrier production, a number of economic consequences need to be tackled. It does not seem to be an easy task to convert a facility specialized in production of heavy military equipment to civilian production. There were attempts to find items that could be manufactured instead of tanks or other military vehicles. For instance, the idea of producing vibrating cylinders was suggested and considered. The conclusion was negative, though it is not entirely clear whether the representatives of the relevant production facilities were indeed interested in the suggestion. Thus, for the time being money is being used to pay partially for the lost salaries and for products which will not be used. It might be interesting to study, in specific cases, the question of how long the cessation of military production will have to be financed and when the conversion to civilian production becomes economically sound.

Hopefully, researchers in Czechoslovakia, who must very soon address these hot issues, will pay due attention to the experience of real-life conversion and will share their experience internationally.

For the time being there is no reduction of military expenditure resulting directly from disarmament measures. However, the political changes in Central and Eastern Europe and, hopefully, the approaching first agreement on the reduction of conventional armaments in Europe, will influence the pattern of military spending - it will contain both elements of reduction and reallocation of resources. There are grounds to believe that the scaling down of military production will eventually lead to the decrease of military budgets in absolute terms. The UN matrix for military expenditures, albeit criticized by many, could serve as an indispensable instrument for comparing real quantities of resources dedicated to military purposes. One can only hope that more than the present 26 countries accept it.

The theme "disarmament and development" has been widely addressed, especially with regard to North-South relations. It is undoubtedly proper to consider that the easing of East-West tensions and disarmament should bring some benefits for economic development, including in the developing countries.

But it will not be easy to translate this just requirement into reality. Dynamic arms build-up in many countries of the Third World is motivated mostly by regional problems and facilitated by the prospering arms trade. It is difficult to foresee how this vicious circle can be broken. When, and if, the day comes that disarmament in the North can tangibly benefit the South, it could be very practical if some channels for the optimal use of any "peace dividend" were already defined.

Second Response

Keith Hartley

Let me raise three questions:

1. *Destruction Costs*
   How much do we know about the problems and likely costs to be incurred in disposing of, and destroying, nuclear warheads? Experience in the civil sector suggests that decommissioning nuclear power plants in the electricity industry is a costly process and that communities object to nuclear waste and material being dumped in their neighbourhoods.
2. *Future START Negotiations*
   Has any thought been given to the future expansion of START to include Europeans?
3. *Effective Agreements*
   Edward Kolodziej suggests that a successful START agreement will provide an incentive to expand bomber forces (e.g. B-2s). How can we, if at all, prevent such perverse effects of arms control agreements? Are they really effective in preventing modernization programmes? Or is it like squeezing a balloon: as soon as you squeeze one part, another part expands.

Third Response

Michael D. Intriligator

Both papers in this session focus on Soviet-US negotiated arms control agreements, that of Gennady Khromov on the 1987 INF Treaty and that of Edward Kolodziej on the prospective START Treaty. Three points should, however, be stressed in putting these papers into context in terms of the purpose of the conference, that of treating the economic consequences of disarmament:

1. *Revolutionary changes* have occurred in 1989 in Eastern Europe and over the last several years in the Soviet Union that have major effects on disarmament. These changes affect in a fundamental way the economics, the political organization and the military structures of the Warsaw Pact, and they have indirect effects on NATO;

2. A major factor in disarmament, with important economic implications, has been *unilateral initiatives*, such as those in Mikhail Gorbachev's UN speech of 7 December 1988. These initiatives are probably much more important in terms of arms reductions, defence cuts, etc. than negotiated arms reductions;

3. The *non-strategic* part of defence spending is much more important than the strategic part both in terms of its effects on the economy and in terms of economic conversion. National leaders and strategic analysts tend to exaggerate the importance of strategic weapons and, at the same time, to underestimate the importance of conventional forces. Yet, in terms of spending, employment and resource utilization, conventional forces are considerably more significant than strategic forces. Concern over the economic consequences of disarmament should therefore focus more on conventional than on strategic forces.

Fourth Response

Wally Struys

This presentation is divided in three parts, where the following aspects will successively be treated: the INF Treaty, the economic aspects of the disarmament treaties and the economic effects of the treaties on the European organization of the defence economy.

The INF Treaty: A Precedent

The Washington Treaty of 8 December 1987 between the US and the USSR on the elimination of their intermediate-range and shorter-range missiles and its Protocols on procedures governing the elimination of the missile systems and regarding the inspections relating to the Treaty are to be considered as an examplary procedure to follow.

The INF Treaty is an important precedent because it dictates not only the destruction of a large number of nuclear arms, but the *elimination of a whole category of weapons*, whereas previous disarmament agreements only put limits on the arms arsenals.

Its strategic importance cannot be denied because it questions:

- the employment doctrines of the weapons to be destroyed as well as of the other arms;

- the strategic competition between the Super Powers;
- the bilateral relationship between the US and Western Europe.

Professor Kolodziej's paper dealt with the first two points as well as with some cost-related aspects of planned or alternative nuclear force modernization.

Thanks to the Washington Treaty, the West learned to consider *arms control* and *defence* as two facets of the same global concept, which will favour a more consistent policy in the long run. The Treaty has to be considered as a first and important step leading away from previous disarmament agreements to new ones. Even if the INF Treaty has far from resolved all the problems, it has paved the way to other achievements. We know now that it is *possible* to reach agreements to START talks, on the elimination of chemical weapons, on CFE, on FOTL, on the suppression of nuclear artillery, etc.

Progress is slow, but if both parties show as much dedication to the cause as they did for the INF Treaty, there is no doubt that success will be at the end of the road ....

The Economic Aspects of the INF Treaty and of Future Disarmament Agreements

In the course of the last five decades, we have experienced a progressive evolution from a *"warm"* to a *"tepid"* and to a *"cold"* war economy, later to a *"defence"* economy and very recently to a *"peace"* economy, where the priorities assigned to military expenditure and to the armed forces are much lower.

In this context, defence economists must more than ever evaluate the economic effects of this evolution, such as:

- the macro-economic effects of reductions in defence budgets (on national and sectoral growth rates, on employment, on prices, on the balance of payments, etc.);
- the micro-economic effects of reductions in defence budgets (on the viability of specialized firms, on order books, on reconversion, on mergers, etc);
- the existence, the importance and the distribution of the so-called *peace dividend* (I personally prefer *détente dividend*); let me stress the fact that most politicians and newspapers not only discuss this détente dividend, but they even want to collect it and spend it immediately, whereas its existence is far from certain!

Before talking about the costs of the INF Treaty, one should not forget the costs which were involved in acquiring the intermediate- and shorter-range missiles. It has been established that the Pentagon spent US $3.45 billion on the Cruise missile produced by General Dynamics and US $2.46 billion on Martin Marietta's Pershing II. Taking into account the acquisition costs of the nuclear warheads (US $1 billion), training costs and minor expenses, the overall cost of these missiles can be estimated at more or less US $9 billion.

One should also take into account the infrastructure costs of the missile sites. In Belgium, for instance, where a flight of 16 Cruise missiles was located, these costs were estimated at US $140 million.

Now, since 1988, one has to take into account the costs induced by the Washington Treaty; they are far from being neglectable since the destruction and verification modalities are the most complex, thorough, detailed and coercive ever specified in an arms limitation agreement. Three methods are used:

- *On-site* inspections;
- Inspections *on formal notice*;
- *National technical means* of verification.

In its Article XI, the Treaty not only establishes the right to proceed to on-site inspections, but also compels both parties not to interfere with national technical means of verification and to implement co-operative measures in order to enhance observation (Article XII). It is thus not surprising that the Treaty costs are relatively high.

For each Super Power, the estimates are that the Treaty would cost US $200 million per year for the first three years (when the weapons are to be destroyed). For the following ten years, the annual verification cost is estimated at US $40 million. The entire process thus will cost US $1 billion over 13 years for the US and as much for the USSR.

One should also take into account the savings induced by the elimination of these weapons. In the US, the CBO (Congressional Budget Office) estimated that the Treaty would reduce long-term costs by about US $1 billion per year due to the fact that the costs of destroying weapons and treaty monitoring would be less than the savings from operating the weapons. These estimates assume that reductions do occur in funding for both personnel levels and other costs in all relevant budget categories (direct force operations and support, as well as indirect support).

In my opinion however, the following qualifications are to be made about these types of estimates:

1. The INF Treaty *itself* neither costs nor saves money, since defence funding is the subject of annual budget requests and appropriation bills!
2. The estimates are established partly in a *"ceteris paribus"* environment, which implies that "nothing else changes", and partly under the assumption that certain specified modifications will occur. However, real life is different from any set of assumptions, as we have learned the last few months;
3. One cannot accept as a "saving" the fact that, for example, the defence budget may be reduced thanks to the return to civilian life of a certain number of

military if they become unemployed; the social cost would not only remain at the same level, but would increase instead!

4. Total costing has to take into account not only direct and indirect costs, but also *induced* costs to the whole economy, by using dynamic Input-Output models. It should be underlined that it is difficult to have accurate figures in the field of defence economics due to the fact that detailed specific data are lacking;

5. Taking into consideration Professor Kolodziej's remarks about alternative strategic (or other) systems, we would not have any savings either if the destroyed range of weapons were to be replaced by another category. It should be stressed however that the current political trend in the US seems to point in the opposite direction: on Friday, 13 July 1990, the US Senate Commission of Defence voted a US $289 billion defence budget, implying the reduction of 100,000 military personnel (including 50,000 stationed in Europe). As a complement to Professor Kolodziej's presentation, I can also underline the fact that the Commission also decided to limit the expenses for the MX and Midgetman missiles to their R&D costs. According to certain sources, US $548 million were allocated to MX and US $202 million to Midgetman, which is US $2.2 billion less than asked for by the Bush administration.

The European Organization of the Defence Economy

I would like to end by referring to the possible effects of arms reductions treaties and disarmament on the European defence economy.

In my opinion, the INF Treaty initiated a political and strategic process that will have important economic effects in Western Europe: in addition to spending less for defence, the European NATO members will have to:

- increase their contributions to the common Atlantic defence;
- reduce their economic dependence on the US;
- realize a genuine co-operation in the field of R&D, acquisition and production of armaments.

Let us not forget that both NATO and the EEC have refused, in the past, to assume certain responsibilities: NATO with regard to the *economic* aspects of defence and the EEC in the field of *defence* economics, thanks to the alibi provided by Article 223 of the Rome Treaty. The latter might change in the near future since Article 30 of the Single European Act for the first time provides political and economic means for co-operation between its members:

> ... the High Contracting Parties are determined to maintain the technological and industrial conditions necessary for their security.

The EEC should thus pursue two goals:

- establish a *genuine European* industrial base; and
- enforce a *European* armaments acquisition policy.

Taking into account the new constraints, this would avoid duplication and would make financial means available for other social and economic purposes.

The disappearance of physical, technical, financial and institutional constraints in 1993 will also have an impact on the defence economy. The first signs of this popped up several months ago when important mergers started to take place in the European defence industry. Before the end of the century, the defence market in Western Europe will be dominated by two or three big conglomerates which will mainly be active in the civilian economy, but which will be solid enough to preserve their activities against important fluctuations in the demand for military goods and services.

I am a strong believer in this scenario of a Common Market which would also take up its responsibilities in the field of defence: the contrary would indeed be awkward. Defence expenditures take some 20 to 25 per cent of capital costs, the only ones to have a direct link with the acquisition of specifically military material, such as weapon systems. But defence expenditures represent an average of 3 to 5 per cent of GDP; armament acquisitions thus finally represent only some 0.6 to 1.5 per cent. Are we going to try to establish a single European market for "only" 98.5 per cent of production activities while continuing to apply a nationalistic policy for the remaining part?

Conclusion

New topics such as the détente dividend, reconversion and budget affectations problems must be analysed and discussed in a scientific, objective way. As a result, the political decision-makers will have to change their approach and use new lines of argument leading to an evaluation not only of the direct and indirect positive aspects of disarmament, but also its negative, often more induced effects. This is the only way to get rid of slogans and *idées reçues* and to identify in an objective way its economic and social constraints as well as the reluctance of the decision makers involved in the defence markets.

The economic factors will lead to a double challenge:

- In an environment of international détente, economic principles will lead decision-makers to choose in favour of economic and social goals other than defence. In this context, the economy will act as a natural military expenditure reducer and should be able to offer new alternatives in order to realize security at an acceptable level with lower social costs;
- The second and more difficult challenge will be to achieve rationalizations in the fields of demand and supply of defence goods and services.

Defence economics will become more and more civil, but we should keep in mind that any change will ultimately and merely depend on *political decisions, because there is no such thing as a spontaneous virtuous disarmament circle!*

Success will thus only be realized if political decisions create a propitious environment. Let us conclude, together with Seneca, that:

> It is not because things are difficult that we do not dare, but on the contrary, it is because we do not dare that things are difficult ... .

Part 2

**Economic Problems of Conventional
Disarmament in Europe**

Chapter 4

The Consequences of Conventional Disarmament in Europe on the Military Expenditure of the Countries of the Two Alliances

Keith Hartley

Introduction: The Policy Issues

The political and economic developments in Eastern Europe and the Soviet Union together with the prospects of successful arms control agreements between NATO and the Warsaw Pact raise a fascinating set of policy issues involving a variety of disciplines (e.g. science, technology, political sciences, strategic studies, etc.). This paper focuses on the economics and public choice aspects from a NATO perspective.

The prospect of substantial cuts in conventional defence spending has raised expectations of a large peace dividend. Predictably, substantial defence cuts will be opposed by those groups likely to lose from disarmament. The armed forces, defence ministries and defence industries throughout NATO are amongst the potential losers, together with those local communities and their economies which depend directly and indirectly on defence spending. Opponents of disarmament will stress the uncertain nature of the threat, potential instability in foreign governments, the prospects of cheating over arms control, and the losses of jobs and technology associated with cuts in defence spending. Clearly, the potential losers have every incentive to exaggerate the risks and adverse strategic, political and economic effects of disarmament. Special pleading, myths and emotion will abound which need to be subject to independent analysis, critical evaluation and an appraisal of the evidence.

In principle, if societies and their governments are to make informed choices about defence policy, they need information on the benefits and costs (or gains and losses) of different policies. However, since 1989, the pace of change in Eastern Europe, in the Soviet Union and in the arms control sphere has changed traditional relationships, requiring nations to undertake a radical reappraisal of their defence policies. This paper focuses on what we know, what we do not know and what we need to know if societies and governments in the NATO alliance are to make informed choices concerning their military expenditures in the 1990s and beyond. A conceptual framework is needed to enable governments to think about the major issues and to evaluate the effects of different policies.

A Conceptual Framework

Any reappraisal of defence policy for the 1990s and beyond requires choices to be made about the level of military spending and its allocation between nuclear and conventional forces, between manpower and equipment and between air, land and sea forces. To meet their national commitments, limited defence budgets have to buy costly new equipment and, in the UK and US, to recruit manpower for an all-volunteer force. Moreover, choices are constrained by arms control agreements (e.g. limitations on nuclear weapons) and have to be made in a world of uncertainty, where no one can accurately predict the future. In formulating policy, defence planners in NATO have to make assumptions about:

1. The likely future threat: who is the enemy?
2. The future of NATO, its membership and strategy;
3. Technical progress in defence equipment - e.g. a technical breakthrough might render the nuclear deterrent obsolete;
4. Future arms control agreements which will affect their choice of a force "mix";
5. The preferences of national governments and rival political parties for social welfare spending and lower taxation;
6. The ability to pay for defence as determined by a nation's economic growth and competitiveness and the relative scarcity of its factors of production (e.g. a nation with a small population might adopt capital-intensive force structures).

An assessment of the threat is an obvious starting point in determining defence policy and a nation's willingness to pay for defence. Nations have to take a view about likely future threats to their national interests. Table 4.1, which is illustrative rather than comprehensive, outlines various threat scenarios. Two broad threats are identified, namely, within Europe and in the rest of the world. Outside Europe, questions arise about the nature of any threat to NATO members, particularly its form and geographical location. Within Europe, a reduced threat is postulated and some of the associated assumptions and implications are presented. For example, will NATO remain in existence or be abolished and, either way, how will Europeans respond (Sloan 1988)? Presumably, NATO as an international voluntary club specializing in collective defence will continue to exist so long as membership is worthwhile (Olson and Zeckhauser 1966; Hansen, Murdoch and Sandler, 1990; Boyer 1990). On this basis, NATO will survive if it offers a reduced threat and more protection, and/or lower defence costs compared with complete independence. However, further questions arise about future NATO military strategy; the prospects of US troop withdrawals and whether they would return in an emergency; and whether Europe would respond by creating a common security policy with integrated defence forces and a European defence market.

Once nations have determined the threat and whether they will respond collectively (via NATO or the EC) or individually, they can formulate their defence policy, determine the size of the defence budget and its allocation between manpower and equipment and between air, land and sea forces. These choices will have major implications for the national economy (military versus civil trade-offs) and for the size, structure and composition of a nation's defence industries. Even these apparently simple assumptions conceal a variety of subsidiary assumptions and complex relationships. For example, the adjustment period (i.e. for re-contracting) has to be specified with costs varying for different speeds of adjustment; assumptions are needed about the operation of the national economy (e.g. a market or Keynesian view of the operation of the economy) and the possible role of government in assisting the adjustment process and the reallocation of resources from military to civil activities.

The Contribution of Economic Theory

In exploring the consequences of conventional disarmament on NATO military expenditure, it is useful to start from first principles, exploring the contribution of economic theory to policy formulation. Orthodox theory views government as maximizing a social welfare function containing civil and military goods and subject to an economy's resource constraints. With this approach, optimal protection is supplied from a military production function with inputs reflecting relative factor prices, the state of technology and regulatory constraints (arms control agreements). With this approach, a number of economic principles are relevant to the formulation of an efficient defence policy:

1. *Output and marginalism.* An emphasis on defence outputs in the form of safety, protection, security and the valuation of human lives shows the limitations of focusing on inputs and intermediate outputs such as a 50-squadron air force or a 600 ship navy (Jones-Lee 1990; McClelland 1990). Instead, the relevant question is what contribution do the inputs of aircraft, ships and soldiers make to a nation's protection and safety (i.e. a reduced risk of nuclear and conventional attack and the associated loss of life)? The prospects of a reduced threat in Europe will require nations to assess the effects on their safety of smaller defence budgets: what would be the effects on protection of reducing the defence budget by, say, 5 per cent or 10 per cent? Similarly, within a smaller defence budget, policy-makers need to assess the impact on protection of marginal changes in expenditure of, say, +/-5-10 per cent on air, land and sea forces: what would be the implications for security if the defence budget were cut by 10 per cent but expenditure on the air force increased by 10 per cent? Small annual cuts of 5-10 per cent become sizeable over, say, a five-year period.

Table 4.1 - Scenarios

A. Threat Scenarios

I. *A Reduced Threat in Europe* reflecting (i) the successful completion of current arms control agreements and (ii) possible follow-on agreements leading to further reductions in nuclear and conventional forces. All of which raise questions about:

1. *The future of NATO:*
   (a) Will it exist in the year 2000 and beyond?
   (b) Who will be its enemies - will the threat come from the USSR, or the Warsaw Pact or from increasing nationalism and adjustment problems in Eastern Europe and the Soviet Union?
   (c) If NATO is retained, what will be its:
      i.   Membership - e.g. the position of Germany;
      ii.   Strategy - nuclear versus conventional forces;
            - forward deployment or withdrawal of forces;
            - position of US troops in Europe: if they withdraw, will they "go for good" or return in an emergency?
            - role specialization and equipment standardization.
      iii. Future arrangements for sharing risks and burdens, particularly the role of the European Allies.

2. *The European response* might embrace the following:
   (a) A European or EC defence policy with or without Eastern Europe;
   (b) A European or EC procurement policy and the creation of a European defence market and industry;
   (c) An EC common market in defence equipment.

II. *The Threat in the Rest of the World*

   (a)   Will it remain unchanged?
   (b)   Where will it come from - e.g. Middle East; Africa; Asia; South America?
   (c)   What form will it take - e.g. international terrorism; chemical weapons?

B. Economic Scenarios

Implications of different threat scenarios for:

1. Defence policy;
2. Defence budgets - their size and allocation (e.g. manpower versus equipment; air versus land versus sea forces);
3. Defence industries: their size, structure, composition and performance;
4. National economies: is defence spending a burden or benefit?

2. *Substitution.* There are alternative methods of achieving protection. Examples include nuclear for conventional forces; aircraft for soldiers and ships; helicopters for tanks; and reserves replacing regulars. Cost minimization requires defence ministries and their armed forces to substitute relatively cheaper for more expensive forms of protection, regardless of the traditional property rights of air, land and sea forces. Here, technical progress is continually widening the range of substitution possibilities and rendering obsolescent existing force structures and equipment. Policy-makers can respond by investing in national R&D efforts or by buying new ideas "off-the-shelf" from foreign firms depending on their relative costs.

3. *Contestability.* Technical and allocative efficiency requires that markets be contestable. In principle, rivalry is required between:

   i. The armed forces, the aim being to reduce the traditional monopoly property rights of each of the Services. As a result, the defence budget would be allocated on the basis of each Service's comparative advantage;

   ii. The armed forces and private contractors, allowing firms opportunities to bid for activities traditionally undertaken "in-house" by the Services;

   iii. Firms seeking defence equipment contracts: for example, by opening national markets to foreign competition.

4. *Response to regulatory constraints.* Arms control agreements for one class of weapons or forces might encourage the search for new weapons leading to the continuation of the arms race in new and different forms. For example, an agreement limiting nuclear weapons might encourage an expansion of conventional forces; whilst restriction on manpower might lead to new developments which circumvent existing arms treaties. For defence budgets, such developments will lead to both income (scale) and substitution effects. Whether the income effect leads to a larger or smaller budget depends on whether arms control agreements are associated with a reduced threat.

5. *Specialization.* Within a military alliance, nations might be expected to specialize on the basis of their comparative advantage. Specialization would apply to both forces and to defence equipment industries and markets. Moreover, if arms control agreements restrict nuclear strategic weapons, then alliances relying more on protective and conventional forces are less likely to be characterized by free-riding (Hansen, Murdoch and Sandler 1990).

6. *Compensation.* Socially-desirable changes for an efficient defence policy require that the potential losers be compensated. These include members of the armed forces, defence contractors and communities dependent on defence spending. Society's preferred speed of adjustment will affect the size of compensation (e.g. rapid adjustment will require compensation for breaking contractual commitments).

Whilst these principles are persuasive and attractive to economists, they have to be implemented in real-world political markets where policy will be affected and determined by a variety of self-interested groups. As a result, actual policies often involve substantial departures from economists' concepts of efficiency.

A Public Choice Approach

A public choice view of government suggests that defence policies and budgets will reflect the behaviour of agents in the political market; namely, voters, political parties, bureaucracies, producer groups and other interest and pressure groups. An outline framework for identifying the various groups which will seek to influence public policies towards defence and disarmament is shown in Figure 4.1. For simplicity, the focus is on the government but a more accurate mapping would show a set of formal and informal linkages between the different agents which are assumed to be maximizing utility, votes, budgets or incomes (Hartley 1991). In this market, there are extensive opportunities for divergence between principals (voters) and agents. (See Figure 4.1).

Voters will seek the maximum benefit from the policies offered by rival political parties and politicians. But most voters have only limited information about specialized topics such as the future threat, nuclear weapons, NATO and the defence contribution of American and British forces in Germany. Where the collection of such information is costly and also restricted by national security interests, there are opportunities for producers and other interest groups with specialist knowledge to influence voters and political parties. Also, the limitations of the voting system as a means of accurately registering society's preferences on alternative defence policies, budgets and disarmament provide opportunities for governments, bureaucracies and other groups to interpret the "national will" and to influence defence policy.

Political parties are viewed as vote-maximizers with the winning party at an election capturing the entire market and forming the government. Its defence and disarmament policies will be implemented by the defence ministry and the armed forces, each with a desire to raise or protect their budgets. However, their preferences for a larger budget will be "policed" by rival government departments bidding for limited funds and by other interest and pressure groups. The various special interest groups will seek to influence defence policy in their favour through advertizing campaigns, consultancy reports, public meetings and demonstrations, lobbying and sponsorship of politicians. These interest groups will represent the potential gainers and losers from different defence and disarmament policies.

Figure 4.1

Defence, disarmament and the political market

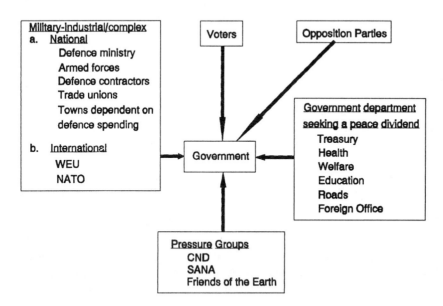

Public choice models suggest a number of predictions relevant to defence policies, budgets and disarmament:

1. In a two-party democracy, both parties agree on any issue strongly favoured by a majority of voters. The result is consensus politics with party policies being vague, similar to their rivals and less ideologically-based than in a multi-party system (Downs, 1957, p.297). On this basis, both parties will offer similar, vague policies on defence and disarmament. However, if the prospect of a large peace dividend appears to be a potential vote-winner, both parties will have an inducement to adopt similar policies favouring smaller defence budgets;
2. The policies of democratic governments tend to favour producers more than consumers (Downs 1957, p.297). Examples include support for a nation's defence industrial base and regulatory arrangements which benefit producers rather than taxpayers (e.g. negotiating "fair and reasonable" prices which guarantee the profitability of defence contractors);
3. Budget-maximizing bureaucracies are likely to be "too large" and technically inefficient (Niskanen 1971; Hartley and Tisdell 1981, chs.3 and 15). To raise and protect its budget, the defence ministry and the armed forces can exaggerate

the threat, under-estimate the costs of major new projects and offer programmes which are attractive to vote-sensitive governments (e.g. jobs, technology, etc.). After all, civil servants are monopoly suppliers of technical information on the military production function, with specialist knowledge of the possibilities for varying output and for factor substitution. They have an incentive to hoard valuable information, to erect a set of myths around their preferred policies and to offer solutions which are unattractive for vote-sensitive governments (e.g. closing military bases and plants in marginal constituencies).

Consider some of the applications of a public choice approach to the implications of conventional disarmament for NATO military expenditure. The approach identifies some of the agents most likely to oppose disarmament; the type of arguments likely to be used to protect defence budgets and to prevent change; and how the armed forces and defence industries are likely to respond to cuts and programme cancellations.

Disarmament will be opposed by those groups likely to lose from the policy, namely the defence ministry, armed forces, contractors, regions and towns which depend on military spending. Defence ministries and the armed forces will stress the need to maintain "strong defences" pointing to the continuing threat from the Soviet Union, political instability in Eastern Europe and the USSR, and the rapidly-developing threat from the rest of the world and from international terrorism. Scientists and trade unions will be concerned about the technological, employment and social consequences of cancelling major equipment projects and of closing military bases in remote rural areas lacking alternative job opportunities. To protect themselves against substantial cuts, defence ministries and the armed forces will promise efficiency improvements in the form of competition, civilianization, rationalization and international collaboration. They will also offer sizeable future cuts in planned spending, always hoping for a change in government or the emergence of a new threat. Similarly, the armed forces will try to protect their traditional property rights and their prestige, as well as their glamorous high technology weapons projects. Faced with cuts, the forces are likely to economize on training, support functions, stocks and civilian manpower rather than sacrifice their major new equipment programmes. For example, aircraft carriers, air superiority aircraft and tanks will be preferred to support ships, transport aircraft, helicopters and trucks. And, of course, the Services will demand a share of the peace dividend to ensure that their reduced forces are better equipped and more capable of protecting the national interest!

The Peace Dividend

In assessing the future prospects for defence budgets, history provides a useful starting point. Defence cuts are not new: we have been here before. The armed forces and defence industries in Europe and the US have substantial experience of cuts in defence spending. Examples occurred at the end of the First and Second World Wars, the

Korean and Vietnam Wars, as well as following reviews of defence policy and the cancellation of major new equipment projects. In addition, since the early 1950s, the defence share of national output in NATO nations has shown a long-run declining trend; within this trend, there have been variations in the share of the budget allocated to equipment and manpower. In the UK, for example, the level of real defence spending fell by almost 10 per cent between 1985 and 1990 and within this declining total, the share allocated to equipment fell from some 46 per cent to 41 per cent, with a corresponding rise in the manpower share of the budget. In other words, the armed forces, defence ministries and their supplying industries are both experienced at adjusting to change and are likely to include the prospects of cuts in their planning horizons.

It has to be recognized that the future is unknown and unknowable. Nonetheless, broad elements of a future framework can be identified from the 1990 agreement on conventional forces in Europe (CFE):

1. Future reductions in force levels in both NATO and the Warsaw Pact aimed at removing the threat of a Soviet surprise attack on Western Europe;
2. Reductions to be focused on the numbers of artillery, armoured combat vehicles, combat aircraft, attack helicopters, battle tanks and on American and Soviet manpower stationed in central Europe;
3. For NATO, the planned ceilings will mean reductions of the order of 10-15 per cent overall in its equipment holdings. These cuts will be shared among NATO members;
4. Further constraints on equipment in specific regions, limits on equipment stationed outside national territory and a limit on the proportion of the total holdings which any one country may possess;
5. Substantial transaction costs involved in arms control agreements associated with negotiating, bargaining, policing and monitoring the agreement and in the disposal of surplus equipment;
6. The adjustment period between signing and implementing the CFE agreement has been estimated at three years (SDE 1990, p.7).

In assessing future scenarios, uncertainty is complicated by the possibility of further arms control agreements. Some arms race models predict that disarmament could be dangerous, with a disarming race possibly resulting in war or preserving the peace (Intriligator and Brito, 1987). Nevertheless, the broad parameters of a CFE treaty have implications for future NATO defence spending and force structures which are likely to be characterized by the following features (some of which are speculative):

1. Cuts in defence budgets. With a CFE treaty, it seems reasonable to suggest initial average reductions in defence spending of 10-15(+/-5) per cent, with

larger cuts more likely for those NATO members bearing a greater share of the alliance defence burden (e.g. US, UK: Table 4.2). In addition, if NATO states perceive a considerable reduction in the threat, there is likely to be voter pressure for even greater cuts in defence spending; the pressure for cuts will be reinforced if nations enter into competitive cutting, responding to substantial cuts by other Member States (e.g. if A cuts by x per cent, then B will cut by x+y per cent and so on);

2. Arms control will create constraints on the factor mix, providing incentives to substitute unregulated for regulated and constrained inputs (e.g. basing of foreign forces outside of controlled regions; new technology);

3. Time will be required to readjust NATO forces to reduced budgets and a changed threat. Adjustment to the new situation will not be instantaneous, and re-contracting with military personnel and defence suppliers will not be without cost;

4. Within a smaller defence budget, there will be substitution effects with an emphasis on defensive rather than offensive forces and equipment. Examples include a greater emphasis on surveillance and early warning systems, rapid reinforcement capabilities for Europe and the rest of the world (e.g. transport aircraft, amphibious forces), helicopters, fighter aircraft and defensive missiles;

5. Cuts in manpower, especially in conscript forces, and a greater emphasis on equipment (substitution of capital for labour) and on reserve forces;

6. A reduced state of readiness which will reduce costs through less training, a reduced consumption of ammunition and the running-on of existing equipment (older capital stock);

7. With smaller defence budgets, there is likely to be even greater emphasis on increasing efficiency in defence forces and in equipment procurement (e.g. via contracting-out; competition in procurement and a greater willingness to buy equipment from abroad rather than supporting national champions). (See Table 4.2)

Implications for Defence Industries and Economies

The prospect of cuts in military spending and changes in the balance of armed forces will have major implications for the size, structure, composition and performance of national defence industries. Cuts in the size of armies, navies and air forces will reduce the demand for land, sea and air equipment, with adverse effects on the supplying industries. As a result, there will be even smaller national orders from each nation's armed forces and fewer new projects, with longer periods between re-equipment. Smaller orders mean further trends to higher unit costs (R&D and production) so making independence even costlier: hence the search for cheaper procurement methods such as co-ordinated purchasing (i.e. a number of nations pooling their orders to obtain a favourable transaction), international collaboration, reciprocal purchasing and buying-off-the-shelf. Whilst the volume of defence business will decline, there are also likely to be substantial changes in the type of equipment needed. For example, there will be less demand for equipment needed to fight an armoured land battle in central Europe and possibly more demand for reinforcement capabilities and forces able to fight outside of Europe.

Table 4.2
NATO Defence Spending

	Defence share of GDP (%)				
	1970-74	1975-79	1980-84	1985-89	1989
Belgium	2.9	3.2	3.3	2.9	2.7
Denmark	2.4	2.4	2.4	2.1	2.1
France	3.9	3.8	4.1	3.9	3.7
Germany	3.5	3.4	3.3	3.0	2.9
Greece	4.7	6.7	6.6	6.4	6.0
Italy	2.3	2.1	2.2	n.a	n.a
Luxembourg	0.8	1.0	1.2	1.2	1.2
Netherlands	3.1	3.2	3.2	3.0	2.9
Norway	3.3	3.1	2.9	3.2	3.3
Portugal	6.9	3.9	3.4	3.1	3.0
Spain	-	-	2.4	2.2	2.1
Turkey	4.4	5.7	4.9	4.3	3.9
UK	5.1	4.9	5.2	4.6	4.2
Canada	2.1	1.9	2.1	2.1	2.0
US	6.5	5.1	5.8	6.3	5.8

Source: NATO Review, February 1990, Brussels.

Defence contractors will respond to cuts in various ways. They will search for new military or civil business, or they will adapt to a lower output and await future new defence orders. Export markets are likely to become more competitive as European and US firms respond to defence cuts and the prospects of excess capacity by seeking overseas markets (e.g. with various forms of state support). However, export markets for new equipment might be reduced if arms control agreements cause NATO and Warsaw Pact nations to dispose of their surplus second-hand equipment to the rest of the world. Here, income-maximizing producer groups have an incentive to demand the destruction of surplus equipment resulting from arms control agreements! There is also a paradox: increased export sales to Third World nations might be destabilizing, thereby creating a new threat to Europe and the US.

Likely reductions in domestic and overseas market prospects will lead to job losses, plant closures, exits from the defence industry as well as to national and international mergers. During 1989-90, there were already signs of re-structuring in European defence industries, and further structural change is likely with the creation of the Single European Market. The trend is likely to be towards a smaller number of large defence contractors with a range of both military and civil activities. At the same time, contractors and other groups likely to lose from disarmament will lobby governments to oppose defence cuts and to modify their policies. They will seek to delay or revise the changes; they will demand state support for compensatory civil work (e.g. launching aid for civil aircraft); and insist that the government offer generous compensation to the losers, including an "active" conversion policy. All of which raises interesting questions about the proper role of government in disarmament policies.

At one level, governments have a role in formulating defence policies, determining a defence budget, and in negotiating and verifying arms control agreements. Questions then arise as to whether economic analysis can suggest any guidelines for a public policy for converting defence industries to civil activities; and, if so, whether policy should focus on assisting defence contractors to find new civil markets or whether it should assist resources, particularly labour and human capital, to reallocate from declining to expanding sectors of the economy (e.g. via manpower and/or regional policies). In formulating policy, problems immediately arise since this is a field suffering from a lack of adequate information. Little published data exist on the size, employment, structure, location and relative competitiveness of Europe's defence industries. For example, what is a defence contractor; what is the network of supplier relationships with prime contractors; how dependent are firms on defence contracts and how important are these firms in their local labour markets? Furthermore, there is a lack of information on how easily and quickly different types of defence contractors can switch resources from their traditional defence business to new markets. Certainly, there are cases of private firms in civil markets which have adjusted successfully to the loss of their traditional markets (e.g. diversification by tobacco companies). Similarly, there are examples of firms and industries which have failed to adjust to change (e.g. textiles, shipbuilding), as well as instances where governments have not been successful in "picking the winners" (e.g. Concorde). Nor are the problems of conversion necessarily any easier or simpler in centrally-planned economies. Whilst central planners can direct defence industries to produce scarce consumer goods, they are less likely to know which consumer goods are best suited to efficient production by defence industries which have been dominated by the pursuit of high technology (e.g. plants have to be re-equipped and workers retrained).

Finally, supporters of disarmament also claim that there will be beneficial effects for national economies. They claim that defence spending is a burden to an economy through its "crowding-out" of social welfare spending and valuable civil investment, with adverse effects on growth and international competitiveness. Also, nations with conscript forces bear an additional resource cost not reflected in the defence share of their national output. An alternative view claims that defence R&D is at the "leading edge"; it pushes forward the frontiers of technology and provides valuable spin-offs for civil use, so contributing to growth and competitiveness. Often such opposing arguments lack theoretical and empirical support, and the statistical results are sensitive to various factors including the tests undertaken, the countries included in the analysis and the time period chosen (Hartley, Hooper, Martin and Singleton, 1990).

Conclusion

Already a number of myths surround the peace dividend. It is reputed to be large (possibly not if restricted to the CFE cuts and if the armed forces succeed in obtaining a share); it will solve a nation's economic and social problems (it might help depending on whether the dividend is used for public or private sector consumption or investment); and that achieving the dividend will involve some adjustment problems and costs (these are likely to be substantial for those groups losing from the change; much more careful analysis and specification are needed of compensation issues and appropriate adjustment policies).

Major disarmament will be a shock to both the defence forces and to their national economies. Reduced defence budgets will mean greater pressure to improve efficiency in the armed forces and in equipment procurement. Substitution possibilities cannot be ignored. Equipment might replace manpower; reserves can replace regulars; and foreign equipment might be purchased instead of national equipment.

References

Boyer, M., 1990, "A simple and untraditional analysis of Western alliance burden sharing", *Defence Economics*, 1, 3, 243-259.

Downs, A., 1957, *An Economic Theory of Democracy*, Harper and Row, New York.

Hansen, L., Murdoch, J. and Sandler, T., 1990, "On distinguishing the behaviour of nuclear and non-nuclear allies in NATO", *Defence Economics*, 1, 1, 37-55.

Hartley, K. and Tisdell, C., 1981, *Micro-Economic Policy*, Wiley, London.

Hartley, K., 1991, *The Economics of Defence Policy*, Brasseys, London, chp.5.

Hartley, K., Hooper, N., Martin, S. and Singleton, J., 1990, "The economics of UK defence policy in the 1990s", *RUSI Journal*, 135, 2, Summer, 49-54.

Intriligator, M. and Brito, D., 1987, "Can arms races lead to the outbreak of war?" in Schmidt, C. (ed.), *The Economics of Military Expenditures*, Macmillan, London.

Jones-Lee, M.W., 1990, "Defence expenditure and the economics of safety", *Defence Economics*, 1, 1, 13-16.

McClelland, W.G., 1990, "Defence expenditure and the economics of safety: a comment", *Defence Economics*, 2, 1.

Niskanen, W., 1971, *Bureaucracy and Representative Government*, Aldine-Atherton, Chicago.

Olson, M. and Zeckhauser, R., 1966, "An economic theory of alliances", *Review of Economics and Statistics*, 48, 3, 266-279.

SDE, 1990, *Statement on the Defence Estimates 1990*, Cmnd 1022-I, HMSO, London.

Sloan, S., 1988, *NATO in the 1990s*, North Atlantic Treaty Assembly, Brussels.

Chapter 5

Economic Problems of Conversion in Hungary (A comparative case study)

Tibor Palankai

New European Scene

The revolutionary political changes in Central and Eastern Europe have not been limited to domestic affairs, but have also led to a strategic revision of basic principles of foreign policy and military doctrines. The Stalinist concept of class struggle in international relations has been gradually replaced by a recognition of growing interdependence, the tremendous advantages of international economic co-operation, and the urgent need for a common solution to the global problems threatening the world. More than 40 years of confrontation and hostility between East and West could now be replaced by friendly relations and co-operation.

In the past few years, several arms control proposals have been put forward, with the concept of "sufficient defence" emerging as one of the basic military doctrines of the Soviet Union. In May 1987 the Political Consultative Committee of WTO committed itself to a new defensive military doctrine for the whole alliance. The asymmetries in conventional arms were admitted on the side of WTO and beginning in December 1988 the Soviet Union, Bulgaria, Czechoslovakia, the German Democratic Republic, Hungary and Poland announced unilateral cuts in that field. This created a better atmosphere and prospects, not only for the Vienna negotiations, but also in other areas. Now WTO is dissolving and NATO is looking for new defence structures and concepts.

Economic difficulties - due to growing structural weaknesses, the shortcomings of planning and management systems and increasing indebtedness - are leading to serious budgetary deficits in many Eastern European countries. Therefore in recent years most of the WTO countries have made either smaller or greater cuts in their military expenditures. In 1989 the Soviet defence budget was reduced by 14.2 per cent, which was accompanied by a 19.5 per cent cut in production of armaments and military hardware. The Polish government announced a 4 per cent cut in military spending in 1989, which reduced its share in the State budget from 7.7 per cent to 5.5 per cent. In the same year the GDP decided to cut its military budget by 10 per cent, Bulgaria by 12 per cent; Czechoslovakia announced cuts of 15 per cent by 1991.[1] As a result of these decisions and political changes, it seems that the size of armies and armaments

---

[1]   *ADIU Report*, Vol.10, No.6, 1988.

could be reduced substantially in the coming years. In light of NATO discussions it can be assumed that the role and the military potential of both alliances could be drastically changed in the near future.

In January 1989 the Government of Hungary announced unilateral cuts of 9 per cent in forces and armaments for the years 1989 and 1990. The cuts affect 9,300 soldiers. As regards armaments, 250 tanks, 430 artillery pieces and mine-throwers, nine MIG-21 fighter interceptors, six tactical rocket launchers and 30 armoured personnel carriers will be withdrawn. As a first step, a tank brigade was disbanded in Szabadszállás on 11 August 1989 and another was transformed into a motorized rifle brigade. In November 1989 a new army reform was announced by the Hungarian Government and further unilateral cuts of 20-25 per cent were decided on. As a result of these measures, the number of Hungarian troops will be decreased from 106,000 to 70,000 by the end of 1991. Due to the Vienna negotiations, further reductions of 20-25 per cent may be expected, which would bring down the peace-time Hungarian troop level to 50,000-55,000. In August 1990 compulsory military service was reduced to 12 months.

As a result of budgetary problems, the Hungarian army had to face budgetary restraints as early as 1986. Since then, in fact, military expenditures in the country have been frozen. Originally, a gradual increase in military expenditures was foreseen in the five-year plan for 1986-90, but under the worsening budgetary conditions this was postponed each year. According to army sources, increases of about 47 billion Hungarian forint were simply deleted from the budget as a result of annual revisions. Owing to cumulating budgetary deficits, the Hungarian Government was compelled to make nominal cuts as early as 1989. According to government decisions in the summer of 1989, these cuts would amount to about 5.5 billion forint for the years 1989-90. For 1990 the parliament approved a budget of 40.4 billion forint for the military (35.8 billion budgetary support plus 4.6 billion forint supposed army incomes), which according to estimates represents about a 30 per cent reduction in real terms as compared with 1989.

In the circumstances outlined above, it seems no exaggeration to state that Hungary is facing probably the greatest conversion of its economy in its peace-time history. This time the question does not arise simply as a result of political proposals or decisions: the call for conversion is based on deep-rooted and fundamental political, social and economic changes in the region and in the international environment. The conversion will be wide-ranging and substantial in size and will probably go on for many years.

It does not simply mean cuts in military expenditures; on the contrary, in accordance with the new defence status and structures of the country, cuts of one sort may be combined with substantial and costly developments of another (a credible air force and communication system supporting the territorial defence forces). In any case the broad conversion would have wide-ranging effects on society and on the economy, raising the need for adjustment in government policies, institutions, companies and of course individuals.

Some Micro-Economic Consequences

Ten large Hungarian companies responsible for the bulk of the country's military production have been most affected by the cuts in military budgets. Contrary to some other WTO countries, Hungary has no closed military industry; these companies are largely involved in civilian activities. Arms production is relatively marginal compared to other WTO countries (Czechoslovakia or GDR), and the military-related industries mostly concentrating on telecommunications and electronics. Hungary has no "military-industrial complex" in a broad sense. The military industries of Hungary are mostly suppliers of arms (and space) industries of other WTO countries, particularly the Soviet Union. This has resulted a high and unilateral dependence on external partners and led to high vulnerability of companies involved. For instance the Hungarian electronics industry, was adversely affected and suffered big losses as result of large and sudden cuts in orders from WTO partners.

The military cuts have really only been felt since 1988, becoming severe in 1989. The first public admission of trouble was given by the general director of Videoton, János Kazsmer, in a radio interview in December 1988. He revealed that his company might suffer a loss of about 2-3 billion forint because of military cuts in 1989. Other companies then voiced similar problems. Orders to industry fell by about 20-30 per cent, and some companies had to face even larger cuts (see Table 5.1).

There are about two dozen other companies, involved in military production (mostly as subcontractors and component suppliers), but the above share is under 5 per cent.

Of course, the companies are not only affected by cuts in different ways: they also face different conversion problems. In some cases where the products are strictly for military use, the companies have to try to find a completely different kind of production. Some specialized machinery cannot be "converted" to civilian use, and in some cases very expensive machines have had to be put out of service. The same may apply to certain materials, which were sometimes stocked in large quantities. Even the shift to similar products requires new developments, reconstruction and retraining of the labour force. Not only must the capacities and products be "converted", but in parallel, new markets have to be sought and the products sold at profitable prices. The shift may be particularly difficult when a company has to turn from undemanding East European partners to competitive Western markets. In this case, the conversion may be helped by international co-operation or joint-venture agreements with Western firms. Some companies are in fact involved in promising negotiations.

The very different performance of companies indicate that the inventiveness and flexibility of management are important in changing to new products, in exploring new markets and also in solving employment problems. The following examples are illustrative.

Table 5.1
The share of arms and military equipment
in the total production of leading Hungarian manufacturing companies[2]
(in per cent)

	1988	1989
Videoton	35.3	28.8
FMV	79.4	73.9
Mechanikai Laboratorium	82.2	68.9
DIGEP	29.3	18.9
Gamma	26.2	9.8
Pestvideki Gepgyar	59.7	40.6
Labor NIM	49.1	n.a.
FEG	17.5	11.2
Godöllö Gepgyar	100.0	--

Videoton, one of the leading manufacturing companies of the country, mainly produced computers and radio equipment for the military, with a great proportion of the products going to Soviet markets. In 1988 the value of military production was about 7 billion forint which, according to estimates, will be reduced to about 4.5 billion forint by 1991. Videoton is one of the enterprises most badly affected by military cuts. Besides consumer electronics (colour television sets and radios), in which the company has a long tradition, it is turning to telecommunications (telephone centrals). Some of the machinery may be used for manufacturing car components, either for prospective Hungarian car assembly plants or for major vehicle manufacturers of Western Europe. Videoton has already begun to manufacture compact disks in co-operation with Thomson, and VCRs with Japanese companies. It is, however, facing serious financial and employment problems, and of the 7,000 employees in military production, about 3,000 may not be retained. The company was modernized and transformed into a joint stock company, giving substantial managerial autonomy to its 10 independent branches.

FMV is in a more difficult situation, because it has mostly produced long-distance radio transmission equipment, used 80 per cent by the military. Being extremely

---

[2]   *Magyar Hirlap*, 15 June, 1989 (in Hungarian).

expensive, only governments can afford to buy them; the main consumers have been the WTO countries. In 1986 FMV still hoped to expand sales and invested accordingly. But sales dropped by 1.8 billion forint (10 per cent) as early as 1988 and by about a further 30 per cent in 1989. The company is looking for television transmission techniques and co-operation with foreign firms.

DIGEP also has serious conversion problems. Though military output is only about one-quarter of total sales, producing artillery equipment and ammunition, the structural change is more complicated. From 1988 to 1989 the orders for military products were halved, and the company was unable to adjust to the sudden changes. One option was to take part in production of car components for future car assembly plants in the country. The company has about 1200 employees in addition to the 600 are have been put on pension under an early retirement scheme.

FEG, which has been making guns for about a hundred years, managed to maintain normal utilization of its capacities throughout 1988. It is thought that there will be sufficient demand for this type of product in the future also. On the whole, however, according to the estimates, the company may be forced to cut its military production to one third in the next two years. The company has decided to develop and manufacture gas apparatus which it hopes will be marketable in Western Europe. So far no personnel have had to be laid off.

The Machine Factory of Gödöllö is a military company, involved mainly in the production of parts and components and in the repair of military vehicles. Orders from domestic sources dropped by 30 per cent in 1989 and exports shrank even more. In 1990 a further 10 per cent reduction of orders was expected. One of the options for conversion is manufacturing tractors or heavy machinery. Among other things, the company produces mobile army service cars, which can easily be transformed for civilian use on highways or for mobile repair service units for agricultural machines in remote places. The company has contacts with Citroen and there are some possibilities of co-operation or participation in assembling ambulances in Hungary. The company has so far managed to avoid laying off any personnel.

In many companies, the conversion problems are complicated by serious financial difficulties. Under the assumption of favourable future market possibilities between 1982 and 1988, most of the companies in military fields made substantial investments in research and development and in new production capacities. These investments were based on miscalculation of future needs and were undertaken to compensate for bleak market prospects in civilian fields. The ratio of investment of a company's own sources to State investment subsidies (credits and also free transfer of government funds) was about 1:2, but considerable credits were also drawn from commercial banks. The government funds were for the most part extended by the State Development Institute, but some commercial banks also found it attractive to join in giving credit for military development and investment. Now, with shrinking sales, many companies are facing serious difficulty in servicing these debts. As most of the companies now need further funds for conversion, the situation is particularly difficult and complicated.

The financial problems are further aggravated by the difficulties of the civilian sections of these companies. In fact, along with the military business, which was for the most part lucrative, numerous inefficient and unprofitable civilian activities were often maintained. They could be "subsidized" from the high military profits, and the company management often did not care too much about improving them. The secure military markets allowed monopolistic attitudes towards civilian fields, and in closed national economies there was no challenge of external competition. Now, with the military cuts, these problems have to be faced and an overall adjustment can hardly be avoided. Owing to similar difficulties in civilian sectors, the problems relating to debt servicing and the need for new development funds arise in many cases and have to be tackled in parallel in both sectors. The negative "symbiosis" of military and civilian sectors has long been pointed out, and several Hungarian economists considered the "militarization" of some leading companies to be an obstacle to reforms. From 1990 on, because of the breaking down of CMEA markets and growing competition of Western companies, the sector has to take serious adjustment measures.

Some Macro-Economic Aspects

Conversion is a complex process and may be conceived of as an adjustment in different fields. The agents of economic life face new challenges and changing conditions from time to time, and they always need to react to them in order to avoid problems and maintain normal and efficient operations. In most cases, this means not only changing policies, but also transforming internal structures and organization. This organic approach also applies to conversion, with structural and policy aspects needing equal attention.

The uses of resources for other than military expenditure are widely analysed in terms of opportunity costs. In a typical approach to budgetary opportunity costs, a certain number of tanks or submarines are calculated in terms of the number of hospitals or power-plants that could be built with the same amount of money; these productive investments or consumptions are often defined as "peace dividends" of conversion. Of course it is generally recognized that national security and defence are also important and indispensable public goods, but the relation between actual military potential and the real national security needs of a given country, as a function basically of political factors, usually remains highly controversial and scarcely identifiable. While it is widely believed that military expenditures are excessive, there is no doubt that the arguments set forth above may be taken as true.

The recent cuts in Hungarian military expenditures were directly enforced by the serious and cumulative deficits in the budget. These deficit- and debt-financing military cuts, however, are considered with some reservation in the conversion literature, particularly because it is assumed that the "peace dividends" of conversion do not accrue in such cases. Of course, the opportunity cost analysis of the cuts can still be applied, but these cuts must be put in special perspective.

In a difficult economic situation such as that in Hungary, the military spending cuts may be seen as the least bad solution. One possibility (other than not touching military expenditure) would have been to increase taxes. There is however wide agreement among the experts that, owing to the servicing of the country's heavy indebtedness the Hungarian economy is already overtaxed. Therefore a further increase in profit or other corporate taxes could cut or worsen those investment possibilities, which are desperately needed from the point of view of structural and technological modernization of the economy. A rise in income taxes would have no less negative effects inasmuch as increasing taxes on low incomes could lead to further undesirable income reduction and equalization, thus contradicting the Government's transformation philosophy.

Another possibility would have been cuts in health, education or other social services, but this was considered a no less undesirable option inasmuch as these fields had already been the subject of budgetary freezes and cuts in earlier years. In certain fields further cuts would endanger even the mere functioning of the services (such as the supply of necessary medicine or working of schools).

Direct cuts in military expenditures however do not mean equal budgetary savings. In fact, net savings can be much lower in many respects, and such unsatisfactory calculations raise controversies and problems. First of all, the State can suffer losses in tax revenues; because of the relatively high volume and profitability of military production, these lower budgetary incomes may be substantial. According to some expert estimates, about 50-60 per cent of Hungarian military budgetary cuts may be lost because of these missed tax revenues.[3] Sometimes there are also unfounded illusions about the extent of possible direct savings in expenditures. It is increasingly realized however that the costs of conversion are far from negligible, and a certain part of them must be directly financed from the central budget.

The question of conversion, in physical terms, arises first of all as regards armaments and equipment used by the military. Some of the equipment and products can be used in civilian sectors, and their sale could be a direct contribution to the budget. In other cases, it is difficult to find markets and users for them because they are usually technically outdated and physically outworn. This applies especially to military equipment and armaments, which in most cases have no value for civilian use and therefore cannot be sold at all or can only be utilized as spare parts or components. Such arms and equipment have to be disassembled and at best sold as junk, and even in that case the cost may far exceed the possible revenue. According to army sources, for example, the cost of disassembling a tank is about 250,000-750,000 forint which at the present official rate of exchange means about US $4,000-12,000, and only after that can it be refounded.[4] For 250 tanks, that is a substantial amount of money. The

---

[3]   *Figyelo*, 13 April 1989 (in Hungarian).
[4]   *Magyar Hirlap*, 22 May 1989 (in Hungarian).

storage of these products or materials may also be costly and must be covered by the budget.

The conversion of buildings and other military objects is also not without problems. Many of them are designed and built for special military functions and their "conversion" to some other use is either physically impossible or expensive. They require functional rebuilding; as they are often in very bad condition, they would also require costly restoration. The simplest case is that of apartments, which can be directly transferred to local councils and used to ease otherwise serious housing problems. The question of reconstruction and renovation arises mostly with regard to military barracks and other buildings, but in most cases these are beyond the capacities of the local councils to which they are usually transferred.

Sudden budgetary cuts usually lead to difficulties for companies and institutions, and only part of the costs of conversion can be transferred to them. In many respects, they need a different kind of support (often unforeseen) from that provided by the central budget. These costs may arise in connection either with conversion investments or with the retaining of personnel.

The army has often taken various welfare and communal functions upon itself in the areas near which troops are stationed. This could be of great benefit to the local community and could ease the budget of the local council. As the President of the City Council of Szabadszállás said at the farewell ceremony for the tank brigade:

> It is impossible not to remember them, because they by their support and presence greatly contributed to the development of our city. They helped us to build water and gas supplies, roads and a culture house.[5]

This could be conceived of as a sort of "hidden conversion" of certain resources and human effort. On the whole, this type of "conversion" has been marginal, although for the budgets of some local communities it may be irreplaceable and taken as the cost of military cuts.

The military cuts also raise conversion problems as regards employment, both in the army and in the arms industries. The first planned cuts of 9 per cent in the army will probably not cause any substantial unemployment as they mainly affect conscripts who can return to their families and their jobs. In the future, fewer people will be drafted which is a very positive development in both human and economic terms. The possibilities of "conversion" have long been taken into account in the training of officers; therefore, in military colleges and academies, so-called "dual diplomas" are issued, acceptable also in civilian professions (as engineers, teachers or economists). Since there is a shortage of trained officers in the country, those who want to stay in the army are simply transferred from the units that have been eliminated to others where they are needed. Taking into account possible future cuts, the number of

---

[5]   *Magyar Hirlap*, 12 August 1989 (in Hungarian).

persons enrolled in military colleges has already been reduced by about half. This makes it possible to improve the selection and, eventually, the quality of the new students. The new defence doctrines and strategies envisage new concepts in training and also the need for retraining of existing army officers. At the same time, a great many officers are near retirement age. For the most part, the structural changes in the army will cause only some redistribution of functions, the overall effects on employment still being marginal. The de-politicization and de-ideologization of the army, for example, has meant the elimination of the post of political officer; according to army sources, such officers were transferred to other jobs (social, education or welfare). The number of border guards will also be reduced by 60 per cent by 1995 but this will only affect the drafting of guards. Hungary introduced the possibility of "alternative" military service in the summer of 1989. According to army sources more than 600 persons applied for that course, most of whom will be called for non-military public service. These people will work mainly in social services, a new option which can also be conceived of as a form of "conversion".

As the Szabadszállás case showed, difficulties have so far arisen only with respect to civilian employees of the army. It is difficult to find jobs for them in nearby areas, and owing to serious housing problems, it is almost impossible for them to move elsewhere. In reality, however, army cuts will not contribute significantly to unemployment rates. According to estimates of the new Hungarian government, due to the possible bankruptcy of inefficient companies and necessary structural changes, the number of unemployed may reach 100,000 in the future. The recent reduction of military service from 18 to 12 months will further increase the numbers on the labour market.

For those employed in weapons industries, the problems are different. In general, cuts in military expenditure and the transfer of resources to civilian sectors do not cause unemployment. "Long historical series for the US and the UK and pooled post-war data for eleven countries do not suggest that the share of military expenditure is a significant influence on the unemployment rate".[6] In fact, the opposite may occur: the transfer of development and investment resources from military to civilian industries may create more jobs because of the generally higher labour intensity of the latter. In the US a recent study by the Council on Economic Priorities estimated that "for every $1 billion spent on military procurement, roughly 28,000 jobs are created. The same expenditure on public transit would create 32,000 jobs, on education 71,000".[7] In cases of deficit financing cuts and closing factories, of course, the results are different. In view of the present difficulties of Hungarian companies, the jobs of about 5,000 to 6,000 persons are in jeopardy. This number does not, seem too high, and according to some official views, the central unemployment facilities

---

[6] Paul Dunne and Ron Smith, "Military Expenditure and Unemployment in the OECD", *Defence Economics*, 1990, Vol.1, p.70.

[7] *International Herald Tribune*, 9 March, 1990.

(compensation payments, unemployment benefits and retraining) can cope with the problem. In light of prospects of rapidly increasing unemployment in the economy in general, however, this optimism is not at all warranted.

The conversion of productive capacities and the changing of products implies the need for retraining those who remain. Large numbers of highly specialized workers and technicians not only have to be retrained, but may suffer a loss in salary. According to the Center of Arms Research and Production in Massachusetts, American wages in the military sector in 1987 were 23 per cent more than average incomes in the private sector.[8] The same applies in Hungary, particularly for the highly skilled. The difficulty of moving from one place to another also arises. These personal problems can be met only through planned and comprehensive measures at the company level.

Planning of Conversion

It is almost axiomatic that conversion must be based on comprehensive advance planning.

> Despite the fact that persistent, high levels of military spending tend to be fearsomely damaging to any economy, a simple-minded policy of sharply cutting back military expenditures would create considerable economic distress. Not only would the workers who lose their jobs in military industry suffer, but their loss of income would cause a drop in consumer spending that would also generate further job loss in industries supplying consumer goods. Similarly, reduced purchases of equipment and the like by the military industrial firms whose projects are cut back would generate job loss in producer goods industries. Advanced planning for conversion on a contingency basis can avoid such problems by preparing military-serving facilities and their workforces to move efficiently into productive and profitable civilian-oriented activity".[9]

Professor Seymour Melman of Columbia University is even more specific and categorical with regard to conversion problems in the United States:

> Without a highly decentralized and mandatory two-year planning requirement, conversion to a civilian economy will fail.[10]

In case of deficit financing cuts, the peace dividends of military savings can melt away in the central budget. The desirable priorities can be achieved only through proper conversion planning.

---

8   *New York Times*, 15 April, 1990.
9   Lloyd J. Dumas, "Economic Conversion: The Critical Link", *Bulletin of Peace Proposals*, Vol.19, No.1 (1988 Special issue), p.5.
10   Seymour Melman, "What to do with the Cold War Money", *The New York Times*, 17 December 1989.

This worries many scholars and some politicians, who fear that without forethought, the windfall will be frittered away. After the Vietnam War, unplanned and unrestrained social spending gobbled up the dollars saved by the American withdrawal.[11]

In fact, in a message to the United Nations International Conference on the Relationship between Disarmament and Development in 1987, Soviet President Gorbachev proposed that every country should work out a national conversion plan.

The problem of conversion policy and the need for forward conversion planning have only arisen in recent years. The Hungarian government made the first warning signals about possible restraints in military spending as early as 1984 when the Planning Office tried to caution companies about their over-ambitious development plans in military fields. Unfortunately at that time they had only limited success. In November 1987 these official warnings became serious and in February 1988, at a joint meeting of authorities and companies, it was announced that Hungarian industry would have to prepare for a substantial reduction in military demand, both domestically and from abroad.

A more comprehensive conversion policy was worked out by the Hungarian government in the summer of 1989. The Economic Consultative Council of the government discussed the possibilities of a conversion programme and made several proposals. On the basis of these proposals, the government took a number of decisions with the result that closer co-operation between the authorities and the companies seems to be developing. The government measures concentrate on the financial difficulties of companies but try to make a strategic compromise between defence interests and the economic capacities of the country.

From the point of view of easing financial difficulties, the most important step was granting the companies a moratorium for 1989 on repayment of credits drawn from the State Development Institute for military production; the transfer of some State funds was not excluded. Similar arrangements were suggested with the commercial banks. The export credit schemes promoting hard currency export can now be extended to these companies. The commercial banks are encouraged to give development credits to these companies too, but strictly on commercial grounds. In fact, one of the basic principles of these government measures was that the former special preferences given to military projects have been abolished; arrangements now have to correspond to those relating to the civilian sectors of the economy.

As a condition of the above-mentioned financial support, the companies were obliged to work out their own development plans although they may join government programmes to help with adjustment. Under certain conditions a part of their cumulated stocks can be transferred to central State reserve funds or sold. Some stocks can be calculated as costs, reducing the tax obligations of the company. The Government decided that the so-called "M" capacities (comprising mainly capacities,

---

[11]   *New York Times*, 25 March, 1990.

units and stocks that are idle in peacetime but which can be mobilized for military use in case of emergency) would have to be revised and reduced, easing the financial burden on companies and on the central budget. In the future companies will have the possibility of negotiating with foreign (CMEA) partners, whom they can contract direct at their own risk. The liberalization measures on imports are also considered to be helping these companies in their adjustment.

From the experience of recent years, several conclusions may be drawn with regard to the planning of conversion. It must be stressed that as the result of important reform measures from 1968 onwards, the Hungarian economy has been widely marketized compared with other WTO countries. The central planning targets have been abolished; prices have been increasingly liberalized; companies have had growing autonomy; the central distribution of resources has been largely reduced, and recently the capital market was gradually introduced. On the other hand, military-related spheres have remained the "most planned" sector of the economy. While in civilian fields marketing was combined with the transition to indicative planning, in the non-civilian economy classical directive administrative central planning has been maintained almost unchanged. The military sphere was kept under central control and the five-year planning practice, including also physical targeting, was further applied. The sector worked to a large extent with calculated prices, which in most cases not only covered costs but also secured high profits. In foreign trade the State monopoly was preserved; special State foreign trade companies were required to sell and buy these products, and the bilateral balancing of trade was strictly practised.

There has been a general belief that unlike conditions in the civilian economy, the classical "planning" models have been successful in military fields. The experience of the past decades, however, seems to contradict these assumptions. The false motivation of bureaucracies has been no less detrimental in military fields, and the system has proved to be too rigid to meet sudden changes. Prices and profits have in fact been guaranteed, while the monopolistic market positions of companies have made them insensitive to efficiency and innovation. The "success" of the sector seems only relative as all of the deficiencies of a central planning system (low efficiency, waste of resources, quality problems, sluggish innovation, etc.) have continued to prevail in military sectors of the economy.

There is now broad agreement that market-oriented planning has to be extended to military fields, and recent measures are aimed at putting these companies on a commercial basis. The importance of the time factor in conversion planning must also be stressed. In fact, some companies have complained - quite rightly - that as the result of sudden budgetary cuts, they received only two months' advance notice about the postponement of some long-planned contracts. Of course, it is impossible to adjust under such circumstances. The time factor has to be taken into account particularly in the case of long-term developments and new investments. The close co-ordination of interests and co-operation between partners are also of the utmost importance. In recent years the companies and the Government have been blaming each other which has proved to be counter-productive and of no benefit to either side. The views and complaints of companies were summarized in an article in the following way:

> We have been obliged to produce under the defence legislation, we had to draw credits for that and we have substantial stocks and production capacities which can be used only for military ends. We have been pushed into this situation by the government; therefore, now the budget must bail us out from this mess.[12]

On the other hand, Gyorgy Doro, the former deputy president of the Planning Office, pointed out that the companies had been warned about future cuts in advance and that they had called for adjustments in time. As was noted by him:

> The companies have been very much content with that centrally steered situation until it had brought secure and substantial profits.[13]

The "democratization" of planning is urged in these remaining fields. It has been broadly pointed out recently in the press that behind the "iron curtain" of excessive military secrecy there have been good opportunities for lobbying; sometimes even the economic policy-makers have had no clear picture of the real situation. Secrets have to be guarded in the national interest, but effective democratic parliamentary control over military budgets and industries is widely considered to be desirable. In the coming years, Hungary faces the difficult and complex tasks of completing fundamental transformation and consolidating a debt-burdened economy. A comprehensive programme of further conversions can contribute greatly to the solution of these problems.

---

[12]   *Magyar Hirlap*, 15 June 1989 (in Hungarian).
[13]   *Magyar Hirlap*, 14 June 1989 (in Hungarian).

Chapter 6

Responses

First Response

Anguel Anastassov

Over the past two years the Parliament of Bulgaria has twice taken decisions to reduce national military outlays, once in 1989 for a 12 per cent reduction of its military budget. This reduction included expenses on weapons, combat vehicles, munitions, military facilities, food for armed forces personnel, clothing and other items. Total army strength was reduced by 10,000 troops. Bulgaria does not produce nuclear weapons or weapons for mass destruction, nor does it have any such weapons on its territory. This does not, however, mean that in Bulgaria the conversion of military production is proceeding without problems. Recently, several companies working for the military industry and related organizations have devised a programme for military conversion entitled "Programme for Conversion of the Defence Industry till 1995". The main goal of this programme is to guarantee that the production potential of military facilities is switched rapidly to civilian production including basic industrial goods, specialized technological equipment, modern equipment for the food-processing industry, the textile and metal processing industry, electronics, medical devices and others. To implement this goal the following steps are envisaged:

- Maximum use of the technological capacities of the defence industry and the experience of its personnel for civilian output;
- Bringing adequate changes to the civilian industry in order to increase its compatibility with the civilian output of consumer goods;
- Optimizing the resource and energy cost of the civilian output of converted military potentials through modern technologies and new products under licence;
- Retaining present market positions and opening up new markets for civilian output.

The concrete statistics regarding the conversion of military potential in Bulgaria are just one of the features illustrating the consistent intention of the Bulgarian Government to guarantee national security at ever lower levels of military confrontation. At the United Nations Bulgaria is co-author of the resolution on the conversion of military potential. This resolution elicits the active support of the world organization in the promotion of military conversion as an issue of prime importance for all nations. It is expected that the United Nations will now make a survey of this

71

matter, creating also a common data bank for specific ideas and proposals in the field of military conversion. This data bank could be used by all UN Member States, inter-governmental organizations, NGOs and others.

Bulgaria has completed its preparatory work on the announcement of its military expenditures. It has submitted to the United Nations the relevant documents on the standardized accountability of military outlays for 1988 and 1989. The relative share of Bulgaria's military expenditures versus its total national income and state budget has been decreasing constantly over the past few years. Thus, in 1986 they made up 6.38 per cent of the national income and 8.78 per cent of the state budget. For 1987 these figures were 6.06 per cent and 8.36 per cent respectively. For 1988, 5.82 per cent and 7.62 per cent. For 1989, 5.05 per cent and 6.36 per cent.

Bulgaria strictly observes the commitments it has undertaken under the Concluding document of the Stockholm Conference on Security Confidence-Building Measures and Disarmament in Europe. It submits in due time its annual plans for military activities and meets all the agreed conditions for carrying out inspections on its territory. Our country participates actively in the Vienna negotiations on the reduction of conventional arms and armed forces in Europe. It strives sincerely for a sizeable limitation of armed forces and conventional weapons, cuts in military budgets, elimination of existing asymmetries and imbalances. It insists upon a gradual inclusion in the Vienna negotiations agenda of the rest of the military power components of participating States, such as naval and air forces. In doing so Bulgaria proceeds from the understanding that the continuing omission of these issues from the negotiating agenda will lead to new imbalances and asymmetries.

Bulgaria considers conversion of military production as a logical contribution to the process of disarmament. National approaches in determining and implementing various conversion measures ought to be in close relationship with the implementation of partial disarmament. This is, indeed, the best way to guarantee national security, which in turn is a condition *sine qua non* for the existence of an international legal order in the field of disarmament. Another very important attribute of military conversion is that it would actually make the process of disarmament an irreversible one. It would also deepen and expand it. Conversion should break the vicious circle of just changing the material means of waging war.

In Bulgaria the practical implementation of conversion of military potential has met with a number of problems. First of all, the transition from a centrally-planned to market economy complicates to a certain degree the conversion of military potential. This is so because such conversion in many ways requires centralized management at government level. For instance, without government control it is very difficult to organize adequate compensation measures to ease economic and social hardships. At the same time centralized planning may in some cases sustain unimaginative administration and management. International experience to date has defined two major difficulties that are already being felt in Bulgaria. First, a sharp increase in prices in the output of civilian products. Secondly, difficulties in having this new civilian output absorbed by the market.

The economics of disarmament requires ever greater objective information about military activities in general and conventional weapons in particular. Of course, as far as Bulgaria is concerned until last year it was out inconceivable to imagine such transparency and openness in military matters. But we have now identified with greater precision what potentials to convert: 200 tanks, 200 artillery systems, 20 military aircraft and five navy vessels. It would not be totally correct, however, to say that the expenditures made on these weapons have been senseless from an economic point of view. Such military products have a specific military use. They do not fill any production or personal needs. But if sold, such products may bring profit that would fill such needs. The issue of profits from trade in armaments also has its moral and political side which is not, however, a subject of analysis in this paper.

Some politologists and economists support the thesis that resources invested in military production stimulate national economies in general. Such conclusions, however, can hardly be accepted at face value. The viewpoint that military industry stimulates the economy is probably based on the fact that officers' corps of the armed forces and the personnel employed in the military industry are composed of highly qualified and experienced people. At the same time, the impartiality of scientific analysis requires us to distance ourselves from the totally negative assessment traditionally given to the influence of military production on the economy as a whole. A massive investment of financial and human resources in military industry often leads to rapid results in fundamental scientific research and technological breakthroughs.

Some sources show that disarmament will cost a lot, for it is linked with additional expenditures and an inefficient redistribution of existing military production potentials. These shortcomings of military conversion may be overcome in different ways. For instance, it is hardly sound economic policy simply to substitute new government contracts for old military ones. Better to announce the basic data of the respective production facilities, including personnel, means of production, profit rate and others. On a competitive basis the most efficient civilian production should be determined for a given military production facility. There can be various forms of conversion, but perhaps the smoothest one could be, in the view of my delegation, to convert not just individual enterprises but whole technologies and scientific knowledge. Redirecting advanced military technologies to the civilian sector would have a beneficial impact upon the whole of society.

The feeling in Bulgaria is that the results of military conversion should be most beneficial for the whole of society. For the period 1990-95 companies working for the military sector will turn out civilian products worth nearly US $19 billion. The share of civilian output of these companies will rise from 30.6 per cent in 1988 to 70.7 per cent in 1990, and will reach 85.5 per cent in 1995.

Converted military facilities will produce equipment for the food processing industry, consumer goods and others.

The national conversion programme provides for expanding the list of spare parts and different components produced for the automobile industry. Another promising avenue for converted military facilities in Bulgaria is the production of infrared medical equipment and related items.

Naturally, not everything is satisfactory with the conversion plans in Bulgaria. In the conditions of a deepening economic crisis, military conversion causes difficulties for the companies involved. At some places it has led to a deterioration of the social climate among affected personnel. Nevertheless, the Bulgarian Government is firmly intent on pursuing military conversion for the well-being of all citizens.

Second Response

Louis Pilandon

There is a universal truth that:

- disarmament can only exist on the basis of trust;
- a decision to arm can be taken in a national context, but decisions to disarm are possible and capable of being envisaged only in a multilateral context.

For this reason, knowledge of actions taken and choices made by partners in the area of defence, and hence in budgets, must be the first stage in any disarmament effort. The United Nations clearly understood this principle, since a little over a decade ago it put forward a system of joint accounting for military expenditure. The effort was not a success - only a very small minority of States accepted the principle.

Knowledge of true military expenditure is of fundamental importance for any progress towards genuine disarmament, which should go beyond the mere counting of equipment (tanks, aeroplanes, ships, missiles and so on). The scope for cheating is such that a definition, followed by an inventory - hence complete and thorough knowledge of the real amounts budgeted for the military sector - are vital. Many opportunities exist for substitutions and transfers within national budgets. An exhaustive study is therefore indispensable. This must be accompanied by total transparency in the national accounts.

If we wish to ascertain what scope there is for shifting certain elements of military expenditure under other budget items, the most urgent task is to draw up an inventory of the latter. This can be done in parallel with other investigations, notably in the field of the conversion of industry to new types of production, and so on.

Knowledge of real military expenditure is also essential in order to evaluate what is called the "peace dividend" as precisely as possible.

An accounting system which makes international comparisons possible and also allows us to determine the cost prices of various items of equipment for the arms industry would undoubtedly be a fundamental and therefore decisive step in the field of mutual understanding.

As has been said, the current trend in market economy countries to place a growing share of the burden of armaments manufacturing costs on the private sector cannot lead to radical changes, since in each country the State is the sole customer at the national level. The State's outgoings, if they are properly known, can thus give a precise idea of the investment effort in the same way as if the industry were in State hands.

However, two specific problems deserve mention:

- Firstly, State aid for industrial R&D (research and development) is in most cases channelled through military expenditure. Will this sector be affected in the event of a decline in such expenditure, or will the State find a palliative by using other channels, such as the space industry?

There is no doubt that the consequences of technological progress are of greatest significance in the field of armaments, and hence of disarmament. Such progress has made it possible to bypass each of the agreements so painstakingly reached in the field of arms limitation.

Hence State aid in this area can have major consequences, and hence the positions of countries must be viewed differently depending on their level of development.

- Secondly, the main difficulty must stem from the categorization of items as civilian or military. Often, the categorization can be carried out only on the basis of destination (traditional vehicles, for example), or the linking of two substances that it is by no means unusual to produce (chemical weapons, for example). For this reason there is a risk that identification of these items will raise serious problems, stir up suspicion and thereby destroy the trust without which there can be no disarmament.

The goal of any negotiator must be to avoid surprises and the destabilization they can cause. For that reason knowledge of military expenditure in the greatest possible detail is indispensable - in fact an essential prerequisite in my view.

Third Response

Christian Schmidt

Economic Prospects Versus Conventional Forecasting

Assessing the economic impact of CFE and other negotiations for the countries involved in the disarmament process is a difficult and unusual exercise. Indeed in order to provide forecasts, three different kinds of uncertainties must be calculated:

1. *A political uncertainty* about the content and the time schedule of an expected final agreement;
2. *An accounting uncertainty* as regards the evaluation of the net savings tentatively provided by the agreement;
3. *A theoretical uncertainty* concerning the consequences of these economies on the main macro-economic variables (internal as well as external) of every country.

Each kind of uncertainty can be briefly characterized in the following way. (a) is dominated by the international climate, internal politics and principally by the tacit linkage between CFE talks and the others arms negotiations (START, Chemical Ban, etc). The existence nowadays of four simultaneous disarmament negotiation processes is a new feature of this political dimension. In any case, (1) is mainly outside the sphere of economics. For (2) the uncertainty is partly the result of a lack of information. At this preliminary stage, two main difficulties are to be underlined: the net result will be the combination of heterogeneous aggregates of savings on one hand (military manpower, troop deployment, arms reductions of different types, etc.), and new unknown costs on the other (direct and indirect costs of verification and control). The knowledge to be gained from past experiments is very limited, because most took place post-war in a quite different environment. (3) underlines weaknesses in economic theory. Indeed many econometric studies have been undertaken on the topics but, until now, no general principle has emerged regarding the relationship between macro-economic variables and variations in military expenditures. Furthermore, as for (2), the historical material provided by past study series is not very illuminating. Indeed most of them are concerned with the arms race; the assumption of a symmetric linkage between military expenditures and economic trends in the case of arms reduction is not supported by any serious argument (Schmidt, 1987).

So the question to be explored by economists provides a useful case study which can be summarized as *"prospect versus forecasting"*. The emphasis must therefore be put on preliminary methodological reflexion in order to propose a relevant analytical framework.

Common Fallacies and Illusory Approaches

First of all, several common fallacies due to confusions are to be avoided in the preliminary step of this task. Three familiar approaches must be reconsidered according to the specificity of CFE negotiations today.

1. *The cost benefit analysis.* There is, of course, an economic cost for conventional arms reductions via verifications and inspections and even a ticklish problem of its importation and sharing. However, a direct comparison between such a cost and the economies induced by troop limitations and arms reductions seems economically irrelevant for many reasons. A large disparity of knowledge exists with regard to these two components. Firstly, the indirect cost of inspecting INF is largely dependent on the final protocol; moreover, the initial information from the Washington Treaty's application cannot be applied to the CFE case. Secondly, the time schedule appears quite different for costs and economies (delay, horizon, etc);

2. *The peace dividends.* This budgetary approach assumes a substitution relationship between defence and socio-economic budgets (such as for education and health) with significant elasticity coefficients. Not only does the budgetary allocation process vary from one country to another because of various institutional systems, but also empirical studies do not generally confirm the existence of such a substitution effect (Russet, 1982; Schmidt, Pilandon, Aben, 1990). In Western economies during peace time, the relationship between military and civil expenditures appears to be determined by the increase of public expenditure and the ratio of PE/GNP. Such macro considerations must have a place in the present context;

3. *The industrial conversion.* An important indicator of the economic impact of a CFE agreement would obviously be the industrial one. This does not mean that conversion is the only or even the most fruitful avenue to scrutinize the industrial consequences of CFE agreements. Certain facets of the problem cannot be reduced to the conversion forumula. Let us note some of the most important. From a strategic point of view, CFE talks do not only induce quantitative reductions in military arsenals, but also and more deeply, qualitative changes in defence and security concepts. Schematically, one can expect a certain shift from offensive and threat to defensive and protection postures, with their consequences on unit costs (Macguire, 1987). The relationship between military and civil purposes is not the same for the latter as for the former. In most Western countries (US as well as European countries), the major armament companies are simultaneously civil and military. Such duality is often a key to arms industrial management (Gansler, 1980; Dussauge, 1985; Kolodziej, 1988). Then the problem is not to convert from military to civil activities in the same structure, but to identify correctly civil

sectors developing the same kind of synergy as armaments through public high-technology programmes.

Nevertheless, in spite of the critical points mentioned above, specific studies relating to (1) and (2) can provide data and figures to complement research programmes designed from an alternative starting point.

A Multilevel Analytical Framework

According to preliminary observations, the proposed analytical framework is not based on past observations of time series or cross sections, but definitely future oriented. In order to take the different kinds of uncertainties into account (cf. P.1) and in the absence of precise information about their inter-relationship, it is preferable to compute them analytically as independent problems. Therefore, three steps will be successively described below.

Step 1 - From CFE to Strategic Options

The goal of this step is to provide possible scenarios relevant for economic and industrial investigations (cf. step 2 and step 3). Starting from the first kind of uncertainty, its background can be summarized by two main assumptions:

  i. The economic impact of the CFE agreement will be the consequence of the agreement itself plus the strategic option which will determine its application;
  ii. The technical content of the various talks in the CFE and the time profiles developed will be independent of the alternative strategic options open to the countries participating in the negotiation.

Combining (i) and (ii) leads to a first list of scenarios whose details can be found in recent studies (Epstein, 1989). Their main determining features for economic purposes can be listed as follows:

  • The magnitude of troop reductions (defence budget);
  • The number of types of weapons relevant to the negotiation (arms industry);
  • The protocol of control and verification (economic costs);
  • The time schedule of the agreement's application (economic time lags).

Each of these features will be compared with alternative strategic options (alliance's revision, national reallocation among defence components) in order to build an operational matrix.

Step 2 - From Strategic Disarmament to Defence Economics

The basic idea of this step will be to direct the information gathered from step 1 into three independent fields of research corresponding to the impact of the scenarios on: (1) the current defence budget (manpower and related effects), (2) the price of their realization and the allocation of the consequent burden (disaggregations of the different cost components of the agreement) and (3) the organization of arms production (arms industry regulation at different levels, companies, government and international). Note that the three different fields do not necessarily follow the same methodology. (1) and (3) will be briefly analysed.

Current defence budget

The final consequences of troop reductions in national military budgets are to be studied through various national models of public expenditure allocation. The peculiarities of the institutional dimension in each national allocative decision process must be taken into account (for example: France versus US; for US, see Kanter, 1979; Tubbing, 1986; and for France, Schmidt, 1990b). Furthermore game theory and more precisely, Nash, and Stackelberg models provide interesting tools for such examinations (Intriligator, Brito, 1983; Schmidt, 1987).

Arms industry

Two poles dominate the question. The first is the arms procurement process; the second, the economic management of the arms sector. Public choice methodology offers clarifications to investigate the former and leads to various conclusions (Hartley, 1989). It must be supplemented by specific models which explain some of the bias relative to military sectors (for instance, quality versus quantity, Rogerson, 1990). The economic management of the arms sector is to be understood by reference to long-term trends in world arms transfers and investment cycles which are largely independent of the scenarios. Rather than having a direct impact, the economic consequences of the selected scenarios would be the combined result of such autonomous trends with the CFE strategic agreements. Therefore, a matrix coupling both series of independent factors, in the same spirit of step 1, would be a preliminary task necessary to appreciate the whole set of alternative possibilities.

Step 3 - From Defence Economics to National and International Economy

The last step is dependent on steps 1 and 2. The weakness of the accounting system *vis-à-vis* the concept of military expenditure has a negative effect on the quality of macro-economic forecasting (cf.P.1). The opportunity to improve the statistical definitions of defence expense (Pilandon, 1989) and to integrate them into different national accounting systems may then be assessed (cf. UN propositions).

Beyond these well-known methodological limitations, some figures tend to emerge from the first wave of studies completed in Western countries, mainly in the US from the beginning of the CFE negotiation process. According to them, four statements may be put forward which can be summarized as follows:

- The macro-economic impact of expected changes in defence economics will be relatively small on the macro level but more significant on the micro and sectoral levels (Gold, 1990; Adam, 1990). Such an appreciation is supported, on one hand, by the weak econometric relationship observed between macro variables and military expenditures, and on the other by the dominant role of home politics in the budgetary decision-making process (cf. step 2);

- The cuts in defence spending due to the expected change in defence economics will have mainly regional and local consequences, especially in terms of unemployment and commercial activities. A proportion of these situations will stem from the localization of active-duty military personnel, and others from the local concentration of the defence industry. Basically, the manpower problem envisaged by the studied scenarios must be set in regional terms;

- The final effect of the expected changes in defence economics on global industrial investment would be relatively small because of possible compensation between two contradictory effects: substitution and complementarity (Gold, 1990). Thus, no negative effect is expected, at least in the short and medium terms, in major Western European countries in this direction;

- The expected changes in defence economics will not necessarily involve a significant average reduction of military R&D. Firstly, quantitative reductions restate a process of a technological race. Secondly, R&D military programmes would probably be the last to be revised in certain countries such as the US. On the other hand, important shifts are to be expected among programmes with resulting consequences for industry. For example, the long-term forecasts in the electronics industry sound relatively optimistic for the future (more than 1.5 per cent growth rate every year in real terms after 1993, Schmidt, 1990a), contrasting with the anticipated decline in military aerospace companies. In any case, costs will be the determining factor related to the reshaping of military scales in industrial countries.

Fourth Response

Katarzyna Zukrowska

Although the accuracy of officially published statistical data on the level of military expenditures, values of arms transfers and military production has always been criticized by scientists dealing with defence economics, it must be said that much more is known in this field in the Western alliance than in the Eastern one. This fact could be clearly seen in the two papers presented by Professors Keith Hartley and Tibor Palankai. The first paper focused mainly on the economic effects of conventional reductions in NATO countries, while the author of the second paper dealt with only one of the Eastern countries - namely Hungary. This could lead to a certain disproportion in the vision of what is really happening in this very specific field in East Central Europe. In my remarks I would like to throw some light on the changes occurring in defence economics in the whole of East Central Europe.

The current process of restructuring political and economic systems (which is leading progressively towards democratization in most East Central Europe countries and the Soviet Union) is conducive to making public most of the matters that were formerly kept secret in the economic sphere. In such circumstances it would be wise to put forward some of the problems which are occurring in defence economics in the Soviet Union and East Central Europe and which can be considered as direct or indirect effects of the contemporary phase of disarmament.

This issue is interesting not only because our knowledge about defence economics in the Warsaw Treaty Organization countries (WTO) is so limited, but also because there are remarkable differences in this field as compared with NATO countries which I would like to discuss further in this paper.

Obviously it is rather difficult to be precise in predicting future developments in this rather complex field in which so many variables are in flux at the same time. Despite that it may be possible to show some general trends common to all those complicated processes which are underway in the Soviet Union and in the countries of East Central Europe. Another task in this paper is to show linkages that exist between different factors and processes, as well as some positive and negative direct and side effects which they have on the economy as a whole.

What are the New Conditions for Military Production in the WTO Countries?

It is easy to list several factors which are not only tightly interconnected but, in contemporary conditions, also have a direct or indirect impact on arms production in the countries of East Central Europe. These factors vary in their nature since some of them occur on the national level, while others manifest themselves more widely in the international environment. Moreover, the latter can be considered either as global factors or only regional ones depending on their scale of influence. Since most of these factors are widely known, I will concentrate on eight of the most important issues.

- At the global level, on a *macro* scale, the improvement in East-West relations caused by disarmament (INF Treaty as well as troops and conventional reductions in Europe) has led step by step from the cold war through *détente* towards *entente*;
- Countries grouped in NATO and the Warsaw Pact are together trying to work out a concept which will allow them to replace the *deterrence doctrine* with a concept of *sufficient defence*;
- Attempts are being made to replace a *bipolar security system* with a new *multipolar* one, which would not only be able to ensure security, but would also oversee most of the specific national interests of the smaller and medium-sized European countries which were subordinated in the past to the interests of the two Super Powers. Such a goal in the transitional period introduces a new role for NATO, as this organization unexpectedly works to stabilize change in East Central Europe. At the same time, despite many efforts to reshape the WTO, its role is diminishing as a result of the bloc's disintegration process;
- A tight network of economic ties is developing which will not be limited as in the past to the exchange of goods, but will also embrace direct investments and concepts of stabilization of East-West relations;
- Growing costs of arms races and their social and economic consequences can be considered as one of the reasons to enforce cuts of military expenditures and to promote the process of rationalizing of the structures of military budgets;
- On a regional level *perestroika* and *glasnost* in the USSR mean the rejection of Brezhniev's doctrine, with its direct and indirect consequences;
- On the national level of most East Central European countries, the democratization of both policy and economics, will bring about qualitatively new conditions for the operation of plants which are specialized in arms production;
- Countries in East Central Europe are attempting to end the period of autonomous and separate development and to join the mainstream of the world economy. This means that attempts are being made to replace the distribution-command economy with a market mechanism which brings competition into all sectors of production, breaking down ineffective structures and stimulating enterprise.

All these factors individually or combined lead not only to reductions of the military potentials of the Super Powers and their allies grouped in the Warsaw Pact and NATO, but they also diminish pressure to increase the rate of growth of military expenditures and the demand for arms supplies. Despite some similarities in the general trend of adjustments to the new conditions, some divergent reactions of individual countries can be noted which are the natural result of policies introduced by the countries in question, taking into account their specific conditions. Moreover, the process of adjusting military industries in East Central Europe will also vary to a certain extent in comparison with the same industries in the West. This fact requires some additional explanation as:

- First of all, it can create certain suspicions that things are not going the right way;
- Secondly, most Western specialists see the difference between the East and the West in the organization of the economy as a whole, but do not take this fact into account in the field of defence economics.

Differences in Organization of Arms Production between NATO and WTO and their Impact on Adjustments to the New Conditions

The arms industry has to adjust to the new conditions and this adaptation will be achieved in different ways, in different countries according to their specific *macro* and *micro* conditions. The biggest divergences in this field will be seen between medium or small Eastern and Western countries and the two Super Powers.

One can also foresee big differences between the Eastern and Western countries since in the past their patterns of military production developed very differently. In the West most of the countries are trying to switch from relative self-sufficiency in military production towards closer co-operation with allies in the same military alliance, while in the East, the arms production which used to be based on close co-operation with other WTO countries seems to be collapsing in contemporary conditions.

In both cases (WTO and NATO) the process of adjusting to new conditions of military production, with cuts in military expenditures, will lead to greater international co-operation but this will be achieved in slightly different ways. In the case of NATO a new stage of co-operation in this field will simply mean an acceleration of the process which was deeply rooted in the past but did not develop effectively as each country naturally preferred to produce almost all its needed arms at home. Putting the idea of closer co-operation in arms procurement into practice can bring about meaningful savings in R&D expenditures since most of the countries concerned (especially US, Great Britain, France and to a smaller extent West Germany) have devoted enormous resources to military R&D. Long ago it was clear that R&D expenditures in NATO countries were not being utilized effectively, as most of the countries were financing the same or at least similar programmes.

Savings on a similar scale in R&D cannot be made in the WTO countries. It is clear that the biggest savings in this field can be achieved in the Soviet Union as it possesses the biggest military-industrial potential and has carried out most of the R&D

work of the WTO. East and Central European WTO members devoted relatively few resources to R&D, mainly in order to upgrade weapons produced under Soviet licence.

In other words, East Central European countries were to a very small degree self-sufficient in their arms production; they did not have the needed R&D potential nor the necessary resources to carry on their own work on a wider scale. Moreover, in the name of standardization and unification of the utilized equipment, most of the countries in East Central Europe had to curtail their own weapons production in the post-war period. Such a solution was not only supported by economic and strategic reasoning, but also by political arguments.

How will this fact influence the future development of military production in East Central Europe? First of all one can argue that in such conditions conversion of arms-producing plants in these countries will be relatively easier to achieve than in the West. But it is not so simple since most of these countries will try to save some of their arms-producing potential, a natural reaction taking into account their internal and external security needs. In such circumstances one can expect that only some of the plants will be assigned for conversion to civilian production; others will have to convert to new military technologies or continue their production without spectacular changes.

Other differences in organization of military production between the East and West lie on the level of integration of military and civilian production. It is no secret that such integration is developed to a much higher degree in Western companies than in the Eastern ones. Moreover, the deep technological gap between civilian and military production which exists in the Eastern countries can be considered a serious obstacle for future integration of these two sectors.

One could easily list many more factors which constitute specific obstacles to the process of adapting the arms industry in the East which do not occur in the West. It is enough to mention some of them, namely:

- Growing integration in the West and disintegration in the WTO (economic, political and military);
- The existing technological gap between the East and the West, which in case of the East means fewer possibilities to adapt military technology for civilian purposes even in case of universal (electronics) technologies since the costs of such processes are higher than in the West and resources more limited;
- The degree of militarization of the economy is much higher in the East than in the West (even in case of medium and smaller countries) as civilian industrial production capacities are comparatively limited;
- Dependence of the economy on arms exports, which in most cases seem to be the East's only relatively competitive industrial goods on the world market;
- Deep economic crises in the East and destabilization in the political sphere resulting from the transitional period of systematic restructuring *versus* political

and economic stability in the West. Lack of a market mechanism which is just starting to be constructed;

- Differences in flexibility of the economies towards changes in demand or innovations and fashions;
- Differences in supply of capital, labour and other factors of production, etc.;
- Deficit in the East *versus* surplus in the West.

In conclusion it could be said that, in the case of the West, conversion can create two problems:

- First, lack of resources needed for retooling plants and re-education of specialized labour;
- Second, the growth of unemployment rate in areas where arms industry is concentrated.

In case of East Central Europe, in addition to those problems mentioned above many more obstacles exist since the whole environment of industrial production is in turmoil. Also the problems of conversion will be much bigger and thus more difficult to overcome in the Soviet Union than in the rest of the members of the WTO since the scale of militarization of its economy is incomparably greater.

Differences in Arms Production within the WTO Countries

It should be mentioned that within the group of the WTO countries big differences exist in this field. This is especially so between the Soviet Union, with its military potential and economic environment which was largelly subordinated to arms production, and the small and medium countries of East Central Europe with their marginal needs and capacities in this sphere. The differences can also be studied from the point of view of the advancement of economic and political reforms which are underway in this group of countries, which create new qualitative conditions for the development of military production.

The main disparities in this field can be found between the Soviet Union and the rest of its WTO allies as the scale in each of those countries defined different needs of arms procurement, resulting in differently developed industrial capacities. Data illustrating this problem still have to be studied on the national level and are not yet widely public. An indirect way to surmount this obstacle is to compare military expenditures of those countries given by one of the international agencies such as ACDA, SIPRI or IISS. National data on military expenditures are difficult to compare as most East European countries do not have realistic exchange rates for their national currencies. Moreover, after a period of extreme secrecy about Soviet military expenditures, there are still great difficulties in estimating their level accurately.

The differences in scale and scope of military expenditures within the WTO countries had a direct and indirect influence on arms production, purchases, imports and exports as well as on the industrial, labour and scientific potentials which were engaged in arms procurement by individual countries. This can be partially illustrated by the Polish example.

The industrial base contributing to arms production is rather small in Poland. It consists of 80 companies which have the status of "enterprises belonging to the defence industry" or in other words are participating in so-called "special production".

According to Polish law the status of a "special production" supplier is given to a company which sells at least 20 per cent of its production on the military market. Including their civilian output, those companies supply 8.1 per cent of total production organized by the Ministry of Industry. The share of total "special production" in Polish industrial output is 3 per cent and the share of those 80 companies amounts to 2 per cent. The remaining 1 per cent is delivered by other companies which do not have "special production" status.

Table 6.1
Military Expenditures of WTO countries (1985-89)
(current prices, local currency and in constant prices in $)

Country	Currency	1985	1986	1987	1988	1989
Bulgaria	m. leva	1,127	1,404	1,547	1,751	1,605
	m. $	800	1,071	1,180	1,337	1,225
Czechoslovakia	m. korunas	25,512	26,435	27,362	28,374	28,193
	m. $	3,838	3,962	4,097	4,241	4,027
German DR	m. marks	13,041	14,045	15,141	15,654	14,871
	m. $	6,181	6,565	7,176	7,419	7,048
Hungary	m. forints	23,700	38,800	41,500	49,200	49,200
	m. $	2,375	2,321	2,285	2,343	2,006
Poland	m. zlotys	37,700	38,800	41,500	49,200	49,200
	m. $	4,730	5,945	5,863	5,657	5,431
Rumania	m. lei	315	466	576	889	2,154
	m. $	1,470	1,483	1,407	1,402	1,426
USSR	m. roubles	n.a.	n.a.	n.a.	n.a.	n.a.[a]
	m. $	n.a.	n.a.	n.a.	n.a.	n.a.

[a]   Data on USSR military expenditures are not published by SIPRI as this source is waiting for an official statement from the Soviet government. According to Soviet sources, military expenditures in 1989 amounted to 70 billion roubles but Western estimates are higher (120-140 billion roubles).
Source: SIPRI Yearbook 1990, pp. 187-92.

The majority of Polish arms-producing companies are engaged in civilian production, a fact which gives them a greater chance of utilizing some of their capacity for supplies to the civilian market. This opportunity is fully exploited by most of the plants which have seen a meaningful drop in orders from the Ministry of Defence. It should be said that most of arms-producing plants are utilizing only 20-30 per cent of their production capacities as a result of cuts in Polish military expenditures, cuts in exports to other WTO countries and troop reductions.

Sales from most of the arms industries in the WTO countries are highly dependent on arms exports. Moreover, as was mentioned earlier, arms exports seem to be the only industrial goods which are able to compete on the world market. As most of the national currencies in Eastern Europe are not convertible, the arms industry creates the opportunity to earn hard currency which can be used for imports badly needed by their backward economies. The scale and scope of arms exports of the WTO countries - though also very limited - shows to a certain extent the differentiation in military production capacity which exists among countries belonging to this organization.

Table 6.2

Values of Arms Exports of selected WTO countries
(figures are in US $ m., at constant 1985 prices)

Place on the list of world exporters	Country	Year 1985	1987	1989	1985-89
1.	USSR[a]	12,795	14,718	11,652	66,209
7.	Czechoslovakia[b]	497	570	546	2,658
16.	Poland[c]	-	-	-	596
25.	German DR[d]	-	-	-	167

[a] USSR - largest world weapons exporter.
[b] Only example of a smaller East European country which is in the first ten of world arms suppliers.
[c] Poland 7.
[d] GDR - data not available for previous years, only aggregate data for 1985-89.
Source: SIPRI Yearbook 1990, p. 221.

Apart from the Soviet Union the share of arms exports of countries from East Central Europe is rather limited (US $3,421 million) if compared with world turnover in this field (US $172,816 million). In the five-year period of 1985-90 it was 1.9 per cent. Thus export will not create a special problem in the process of adjustments to the new conditions stemming from disarmament and reductions of military expenditures as this kind of production will be totally driven by the demand of importers. Production has to react to the shrinking demand of importers as export transactions are concluded for purely economic reasons.

In conditions of shrinking demand for arms deliveries on national markets, most East European countries have made efforts to increase their exports. This fact seemed to be a natural reaction of the arms producers. It gave a possibility, at least in short term, of saving some of their military-industrial capacity especially when such production was also endangered by economic reforms. It also gave the management time to reach decisions about what to do in the future with excess labour and unutilized production capacities. At the same time exports brought in exchangeable currency which because of the decentralization of the economy was used by some of the plants to increase, at least in part, their civilian production capacities.

Arms Production in the Environment of Political and Economic Reforms

Future possible changes in military production and arms transfers cannot be studied in isolation from the political and economic background of East Central Europe, especially when things are changing so rapidly. In such circumstances it is necessary to show the main tide of developments even in a schematic manner. Military production is usually a specific part of the national economy but has direct and indirect connections with the whole economic performance of a country.

Repeating the fact that political and economic reforms in East Central European countries are tightly linked with the new stage of *détente* seems to be obvious but true. Changes in national politics and economy in most of Eastern Europe would be much slower if *perestroika* and *glasnost* had not transformed the international climate. All past efforts to reform made by Hungary and Poland in 1956, Czechoslovakia in 1968, and in Poland in 1980-81 were stymied by a hostile political environment.

Now the political and economic systems in East Central Europe are in flux, the stage of transformation varying from country to country. Moreover, the national and international situation can be considered as a stimulus which works with different strengths and effectiveness in each particular case. Despite some clear similarities which can be found in this group of countries, varying conditions of change are dictating different models. Those differences can be seen not only in changes in political systems, but also in the economic field. Among the different models are the following:

- The GDR model which is tightly interlinked with the FRG, mainly in the political sphere (similar political structures) and strongly supported as far as organization and financial help are concerned in the economic field;[1]

---

[1]   R. Watson & others, "The New Superpower", *Newsweek*, 26 February 1990, p.8-13; W. Grabska, "Ekonomiczne konsekwencje Zjednoczenia Niemiec", *PTE*, 28 March 1990.

- The Polish model, often called "big bang", has some weak political structures from underground. There is no other political force with an alternative programme which could replace the contemporary one. Economically this model is linked with the programme worked out by the World Bank;[2]
- The Soviet model which embraces political reforms within the old structures and in the economic field hesitates between the Polish model and a less drastic J.K. Galbraith solution;[3]
- The Czechoslovak model, similar in political ideas to the Polish or Hungarian one and still undefined in the economic field. First attempts are being made to overcome the imbalance between demand and supply by the regulation of prices.[4]

Despite major differences there are four common elements in the above-mentioned models:

- Coexistence of some elements from the old model with the new ones in the transitional period;
- Necessity of controlling inflation;
- Privatization; an organic increase in private ownership;
- Definition of the goal of transformation.

There is also a fifth similarity which does not fit two of the "pole models", namely Soviet and the GDR, but does fit the other ones: it is the lack of political power to enforce the desired changes. Usually in all revolutionary movements there is a driving political force; in the case of Poland or Czechoslovakia the changes were mainly supported by voters through the rejection of previous political actors. Solidarity, New Forum or Charter 77 are civic movements, not political parties. They can be considered as laying the groundwork for the future development of political parties, but have actually split into smaller political organizations.[5] It is necessary to understand that under current circumstances East European countries may not be considered to

---

2   K. Zukrowska, "Philosophie realer Preise, Horizont", *Zeitung für Internationale Politik und Wirtschaft*, No.3, 1990, p.11.

3   M. Gorbachev proclaimed himself in favour of the Polish economic solution but there are strong voices supporting the J.K. Galbraith idea about keeping subsidies for agricultural products, housing, transportation, heavy industry but allowing market forces to reign in the rest of light industry (*Literaturnaya Gazeta*, 14 February 1990). Final decisions in this field were taken at the beginning of September 1990.

4   According to Ivan Havel, member of the Executive Committee of the Civic Forum, Czechoslovakia will follow Poland in the economic field.

5   Such a split took place in Poland in July 1990 with the creation of CENTRUM and ROAD. It is too early to evaluate such developments on the Polish political scene but it can be said that despite the fact that a shadow cabinet is needed, division in Solidarity came too quickly, when too many problems are still not solved or even noticed.

have the proper background for real parties as they exist in traditional democracies, since there is no middle class. Such a class can only be developed as a result of further political and economic changes, in the first instance, of privatization.

To conclude, we know the direction of developments in the countries in question, but the results of the on-going processes have to be treated as largely unknown. What can be said in these circumstances about future developments in military procurement? An attempt to predict precisely the developments in different countries with their specific models is quite impossible, especially given the volatile nature of contemporary events on the national and international level. I will therefore try to draw a general framework, establishing the current background for arms industries in East Central Europe.

Generally the conditions for development of military production in East Central Europe are not friendly. The economies are in bad shape; co-operative links have broken down and new patterns need to be worked out in this field. Budgets have been reduced in a way which mainly affects military expenditures. Moreover, the strict economic policy of "difficult money" which have been introduced in most of the East European countries does not make concessions for military production. In Poland, for instance, all the privileges for military production such as tax reductions and subsidies have been cancelled. In other words, the "good years" for the industrial complexes in the East seem to be over. Most of the arms-producing plants have to face such new realities as less money, and growing problems with selling their production, and having to look for every possible means of adjusting to the new conditions. Clearly this process will take time, and military industries will go through different stages before they reach the phase of total conversion from military to civilian production. Moreover, those industrial capacities left within the military industry of most Eastern countries will also require some additional investments and structural changes in order to face new challenges defined by qualitatively new conditions.

Adjustments of Military Industry in the WTO Countries

In accordance with the existing differences in the arms industry between the Soviet Union and the rest of its allies, the pattern of adjustments in both cases will be different. In the Soviet Union a considerable proportion of arms-producing plants have to be converted in the first stage of adjustments which will happen with the support of resources from the central budget.

The possibilities of using military technology for civilian purposes are in this case rather wide. Some of them were shown in the exhibition called "Conversion 90", organized in Moscow. Specialists say that most of the machines used for arms production cannot be utilized for peaceful purposes without additional investment. With some technological changes, they can often be successfully utilized for the production of market goods, but unfortunately at higher cost in comparison with the civilian conditions of production. Some solution to this problem can be found in the price reform which has been planned for introduction in the autumn of 1990.

Other Soviet military plants will go through a similar pattern of adjustment as that experienced in other East European countries. The time required for this transition will be conditioned by two factors:

- On the one hand, by the level of integration of military into civilian production;
- On the other hand, by the availability of resources which can be devoted to retooling the plant and retraining its staff.

Close connections with civilian procurement, which exist in most of the East Central European countries, offer some prospects for effective adjustments into civilian production of part of the industrial capacities constructed for military use. Moreover, they also offer some chances to lower costs of production in both sectors. But as practice shows, all such adjustments require new investments which often are rather costly. This means that the management has to make every possible effort to look for resources for retooling and restructuring production.

It is necessary to take into account all available resources which can cover the costs of adjustments and further conversion since the expected "peace dividend" will not occur immediately after arms reductions and is also questionable over a longer period. Specialists say that in the short and medium run we should expect only indirect effects of arms reductions and reductions of military expenditures. Since reductions are often equivalent to an increase of costs, and since financial resources cannot be transferred for conversion activities, the arms industry has to look for other sources in order to cover its costs of reconversion . Moreover, in the case of "post-communist" countries which have had or still have unbalanced markets (demand exceeding supply), financial resources are allocated in different areas than for conversion purposes, as it is often easier and cheaper to build a new plant than to convert the old one.

The needed capital can be received from different sources:

- Sales of manufactured goods on the domestic market;
- Credits obtained from a bank or other manufacturer;
- Reprivatization of the factory by selling shares to the workers, management and on the market;
- Fund-raising organized by a special foundation;
- Co-operation with a foreign investor;
- Exports of previously manufactured goods should there be a demand for them on the world market;
- Utilization of mixed sources.

Limited possibilities to retool machinery in order to increase civilian supplies push producers to seek markets abroad or face increasing difficulties and even bankruptcy. Lack of capital and modern technology limit the flexibility of most companies operating on the market.

Producers try to survive this transitional period in four ways:

- By increasing exports of weapons to Third World countries;
- By increasing production for the civilian market, utilizing the existing capacities of the plant;
- By retooling the plant and reconverting its production from military supplies to civilian;
- By closing plants down temporarily or for good.

Conversion

In order to prepare a complete programme to convert military plants, it is necessary to answer several questions. Some of these are formulated below:

- The scale of the future demand of defence ministries;
- The future pattern of international co-operation in arms reduction;
- Future possible exports of arms production;
- Technical and technological possibilities of conversion of unutilized military plants;
- Costs of the conversion (retooling and labour) and financial resources for covering them;
- The future structure of the military industry in individual Eastern countries (ownership, share in the industry as a whole, organization, etc.);
- Future military production, conversion and environment; and
- Demand for the goods which can be produced after conversion, their competitiveness.

It is clear that national programmes of conversion can only be prepared after specification of these matters. This requires political decisions which can be taken only by leading politicians in individual Eastern countries, not by arms producers.

For instance in Poland a special group consisting of civilians and military is working on this issue in the Ministry of Industry. It aims to work out frameworks on the macro scale which will be tested in the next stage, with plans for the conversion of specific plants. Some of the arms-producing plants are trying to work out their own strategies which are based on what little information comes from the infant market mechanisms replacing the command-distribution mechanism. At this stage of transformation it is difficult to say how effective those individual changes might be and how they will fit in to the centrally prepared strategy.

Also it should be emphasized that the introduction of a market mechanism can not be treated as a panacea in the process of adjustments and conversion of the military industry. If the market does not solve the problems which occur in the course of converting the arms industry in countries which have a healthy economy and fully developed democratic political systems, it cannot solve them for those trying to restructure their policy and economy. The market, by increasing competition, can help to break down existing monopolies, stimulate innovation or heighten the effectiveness of production, but all this needs time during which infant tools, infant institutions and infant structures can develop into a strong and well-functioning mechanism.

Despite the fact that the plans for conversion are in a preparatory phase, it is clear that plants will have great difficulties in obtaining resources which will enable them to cover all the costs of this process. International co-operation in technology transfer and direct investments could help to overcome this bottleneck which could seriously hamper the transformation of military plants in East Central Europe.

Part 3

Economic Consequences of East-West Disarmament for Developing Countries

Chapter 7

Economic and Security Consequences of the East-West Arms Control Process on the Third World

Saadet Deger

Introduction

During 1989 and 1990 the political map of Europe has undergone a remarkable transformation. The Super Powers are now embarked on a phase of entente. Negotiated and spontaneous arms control has led to possibilities for real disarmament. The old military alliances, NATO and WTO, are facing an identity crisis. The Soviet Union has begun, probably for the first time in 20 years, a demilitarization of society and a major reduction in military expenditure and capability. The Cold War is over and peace is breaking out.

However, this rosy picture is clouded by various problems. Naval arms control remains a major irritant to Super Power relations. Regional conflicts are far from being solved. Indeed, after the Gulf crisis in 1990, the burden of major power military involvement has shifted towards the Third World. Growth of subnationalism could have grave implications for domestic and foreign policy. Non-military threats to security remain as powerful as ever. The debt crisis threatens the lives of millions. Environmental security must become a major priority in the 1990s. As has been stated succinctly: "The decade of the 1990s may tell us whether the North is heading for both a new political and security structure in Europe and a considerably improved understanding of its responsibility to attend to the non-military dimensions of security, as they trouble the Third World - political stability in the 1990s will greatly depend on whether the North manages to reconstruct economies in Europe and rescue Third World economies from bankruptcy. *It is no small agenda that is ahead of us*" (emphasis added).[1]

The purpose of this paper is to analyse the North-South implications of the major transformation that has taken place in the international politico/security system. I will try to analyse these issues in the framework of the defence, disarmament and development debate. Discussions within this framework have ebbed and flowed during the last decade based on the Thorsson Report[2], named after Inga Thorsson, which the United Nations sponsored in the early 1980s. The basic concept, that security is multi-

---

[1] Stützle, Walther, "Introduction: More questions than answers - how to manage the change", *SIPRI Yearbook 1990: World Armament and Disarmament* (Oxford, Oxford University Press, 1990).

[2] *Study on the Relationship between Disarmament and Development*, UN document A/36/356, 5 October 1981; henceforth referred to as the Thorsson Report.

dimensional and must encompass economic and political factors as well as the usual military ones, has taken on new meaning in the context of changes in Eastern and Central Europe.

The following analysis will be based on facts and figures but, given the nature of structural and systematic changes, will need to be of the 'crystal gazing' type. As old certainties disappear and new concepts are slow to emerge, it is possibly the most difficult time ever to analyse the future. We will have to be speculative as well as brave to take up the challenge of research in a fast-changing world.

It is well recognized that there are three dimensions to this problem: military, political and economic. However, each of these dimensions is becoming increasingly more complex and specialized. To study the economic or political or military aspect alone of security and development is difficult enough. At the same time, to emphasize the implications of the inter-linkages makes the research more complex indeed. Our theoretical models and conceptual framework must be both 'widened' and 'deepened' at the same time. This is a formidable task, yet there is no alternative. We should be aware of all three dimensions simultaneously even though we may concentrate on only one.

The questions that are being raised all reflect the interdependence of the triad of security concepts. Can international military security be preserved without economic development? How does military expenditure affect economic growth under different political structures? How is military expenditure affected in the face of budgetary austerity under alternative political regimes? Is there a link between economic development and political pluralism, and what role does the military have in fostering such links if they exist? What is the effect of certain types of developmental policies on internal and external security? Can regional economic co-operation succeed without corresponding security co-operation? Should foreign economic aid be used as a means towards arms control?

This interrelationships between defence, disarmament and development are complex. It is not just an issue of whether military expenditure has positive or negative effects on growth and development of the international economy. It is not simply a matter of transferring resources from the international military to the civilian sectors, though this is of some importance. Nor is it a matter of creating a world economy of disarmament from an economy of armaments (to paraphrase a statement of President Gorbachev). It is all these and more. The fundamental point to understand is that the whole concept of security, on which national welfare so crucially depends, must be redefined. We can no longer think of security as a military problem alone. Security should now become all-encompassing to include military, socio-economic, political and even environmental dimensions. In some instances, particularly in the Third World, there is an overlap between these three aspects of security. For example, food scarcity, famines and refugees in Africa are a product of wars, the debt crisis and ecological disasters. Some East European countries are worried about the decline of military security and stability in the face of the possible disintegration of the

USSR and the withdrawal of the military umbrella of the WTO; yet developmental failures and political unrest make it difficult to tackle defence problems. In this paper I will concentrate on the triad of security concepts, as related to underdevelopment, armaments and political problems. The issue of environment, even though extremely important, cannot be adequately discussed in this short presentation.

The international economy has passed through a period of unprecedented economic turbulence over the last one and half decades. In the industrial economies, rapid inflation in the 1970s gave away to stagnation, with high unemployment and unutilized capacity. Even now, with high growth rates, the average unemployment rate in the EEC countries is around 10 per cent; in 1960 it was around 2.9 per cent. External imbalances are growing. The trade deficits of only two countries - the US and the UK - are enough to absorb all the world's trade surplus which itself emanates from only six countries[3] (Japan, Germany (Federal Republic of) and four Asian NICs). The developing countries have seen a collapse of commodity prices, an intensification of debt service burdens, a recurrence of famines and a loss of basic needs for significant parts of the population. The former socialist non-market economies are faced with low growth and declining productivity, as well as a total collapse of their economic model. Yet there have been exceptional success stories as in South East Asia. The newly industrializing countries have shown how high growth is possible even in a world of debts and deficits.

One of the few "growth" areas of the global politico-economic system has been in military expenditure. Annual worldwide defence spending was at least $950 billion in 1989 according to SIPRI estimates. Though most of it is spent in developed economies (both East and West), less developed countries (LDCs) have also seen exceptional rises in milex until at least the mid-1980s.

In spite of determined efforts, both by governments in developing countries and international agencies, to reduce poverty and spread the benefits of growth to larger sections of the community, the record remains patchy. It is estimated that around one billion people in the Third World exist in absolute poverty;[4] half the world's population may not have access to safe drinking water; three quarters of the developing world have no adequate sanitary facilities; and about 200 million people exist without minimal shelter.

The developed countries (both East and West) spend around $800 billion per year on defence. On the other hand Official Development Assistance (ODA) is about $50 billion.[5] If the developed countries cut down defence expenditure by 10 per cent, then there would be a potential resource fund of about $80 billion. If even half of this were transferred to the Third World, the ODA would be almost doubled i.e. rise by about

[3]   Sen, Somnath, "Debt, financial flows and international security", *SIPRI Yearbook 1990: World Armament and Disarmament* (Oxford, Oxford University Press, 1990), Ch.6.

[4]   *World Development Report 1990*, Washington D.C., World Bank, (Oxford, Oxford University Press, 1990).

[5]   *Development Co-operation, 1990 Report* (Paris, OECD, 1990).

100 per cent. In other words a 10 per cent cut in defence spending, partially transferred, could raise foreign aid by almost 100 per cent - a truly significant sum.

It is tempting to believe that an *automatic* link exists between armaments and underdevelopment or between military expenditure and the global economic crisis - that disarmament must stimulate development for the world economy. As we shall see, the linkages are much more complex; there may not always be obvious relationships between guns and butter. However, a substantial volume of research over the 1980s by analysts in the development research community has shown that disarmament and development are conceptually interconnected and that one may lead to the other, but only with careful preparation, planning and political will.

The impact of East-West arms control and disarmament will have many types of effects. For analytical convenience these can be grouped into two basic categories. The first relates to structural changes. Within this category two different types of impact can be isolated: North-South relations and what the South can do for itself. The second category relates to the so-called peace dividend whereby resources utilized for the military and arms trade are diverted towards socio-economic development with special reference to the Third World. The next four sections deal with these issues. The final section discusses military expenditure in the North and resource transfer.

Structural Changes: North South Relations

Recent events, particularly in Europe, have developed so rapidly and remarkably that their implications for the Third World are unclear but need to be analysed very carefully. In addition, there are certain systemic factors which are operating more slowly but surely in shaping the international security and developmental order. These must also be accounted for.

European Disarmament

Ever since Gorbachev's speech at the United Nations[6] in December 1988, promising unilateral Soviet troop and arms cuts, there has been a flurry of activity on the arms control front in Europe. The Conventional Forces in Europe (CFE) Treaty has been signed and the reductions in weapons and troops ratified by treaty. The process of multilateral disarmament should begin in earnest in Europe. Hopes are running high and there are now tentative discussions about CFE II. In particular, procurement budgets of the European powers are expected to be reduced as purchases of new weapons stagnate.

The optimistic prognosis is that disarmament in Europe will therefore have major implications for itself and the rest of the world. Political tensions will be reduced.

---

6   *Statement by Mikhail S. Gorbachev, President of the Presidium of the Supreme Soviet of the USSR, at a Plenary Meeting of the United Nations General Assembly*, 7 December 1988.

The scale of militarization will decline. There may be resource transfers to the domestic economy as well as the Third World. If Eastern Europe can replicate the growth performance of its Western counterpart, then the omens for the rest of the world are good. On the other hand, the pessimistic prognosis is that major problems and uncertainties exist particularly the problems of political and economic stability. The Soviet Union is the classic example of the forces of destabilization that are characteristic of the region, but Eastern Europe is also torn by economic and political dissension. The reduction of confrontation has increased security. But it has also reduced stability which could precipitate further crises.

North-South Relations in Military and Economic Affairs

There is both an optimistic and pessimistic scenario when contemplating North-South relations in the coming decade. The former stresses the fact that reductions in European confrontation will release more positive interest, resources and involvement of the developed countries (West and East) towards the Third World. There will be much more active co-operation between North and South on mutually beneficial exchanges - be they economic or political. To take a simple example: if either the United States or the Soviet Union cut its military expenditure by 1 per cent, the amount of resources released could increase their own Official Development Assistance (ODA) by over 30 per cent. If the amount of annual military expenditure required to sustain European confrontation were reduced by only 10 per cent, then total ODA by the West could be doubled every year. Such is the potential transfer!

The alternative point of view emphasizes that Europe will become inward-looking as a result of current changes. The debate about the 'widening' or 'deepening' of European structures will dominate all other interests. The United States will play an increasingly important role in democratic Eastern Europe. Possibly it will transfer its economic assistance from the South to European countries. The Soviet Union will need to cope with its massive domestic problems and ultimately could lose both its internal structure and external interests. This will make it isolationist. Hence, instead of a benevolent cycle, one can expect a much worse deal for its Third World allies.

Debt Crisis

There is no need to stress the developmental failures that have plagued the Third World overall during the decade of the 1980s. South East Asia is one of the few growth areas where per capita income has consistently risen during this period. But even here there are major problems of inequality and poverty in certain areas. There are too many issues in terms of growth retardation to be specific in a short paper. But certainly for Latin America and Africa, the 1980s have been a lost decade due to the debt crisis.

The amount of debt service payments (interest and principal) for the Third World as a whole is now approaching US $200 billion per year. Its nominal value has increased steadily every year from 1982 onwards. In 1988 there was a negative resource transfer of over US $50 billion; that is, the poor countries paid back to the rich US $50 billion more than they actually received in new loans. Semi-concessional transfers or Official Development Assistance was about US $48 billion in 1988 - insufficient to cover the negative resource movement. Table 7.1 indicates the nature of this problem. The data is for long-term debt alone; in addition, there is also the burden of short-term debt. Once again, future research must concentrate on the fact that military and economic security inevitably go hand-in-hand. If the debt problem degenerates into a debt crisis, then international security will be threatened even in the absence of direct military threats.

Table 7.1
Third World Long-Term Debt and Financial Flows (billion US $)

	1984	1986	1988	1989
Total debt	686.7	893.9	993.2	988.5
Debt service	101.8	116.4	142.4	129.8
Net transfer	-10.2	-28.7	-50.1	-42.9
ODA	28.7	36.7	48.1	46.7

Source: Sen S., "Debt, Financial Flows and International Security", in *SIPRI Yearbook 1991*, Chapter 6.

Structural Changes: Within South Effects

If the North loses interest in the South, except as providers of raw materials or as markets in the case of some large countries (Brazil, China or India), then the South will have to acquire more resources domestically. In addition, a more searching evaluation of their defence spending and arms imports will be made by all donor countries who do provide assistance. No longer can the East-West confrontation be used, except in special cases like that of Egypt and Israel in the recent Gulf crisis, to invoke large amounts of military and economic assistance for political reasons. Either way, a more rapid decline in LDC military expenditure is needed to release resources for socio-economic needs. Even though overall military expenditure has fallen steadily since the mid-1980s, in the Third World the decline is slow. In 1989, it was estimated that over 4 per cent of GDP in the developing world was expended on the military - a defence burden higher than in most European countries.

There is a large literature and much heuristic evidence that shows the adverse effects of defence spending on social and economic development.[7] Yet, arms control is not a first priority in many Third World countries. Where reductions are taking place it is simply because the countries cannot afford arms any more. Thus, a reversal of the current economic decline could prompt an upward movement of military expenditures.

There are many reasons for the failure of arms control in the Third World. Since this paper concentrates on the economics of security, we deal with two specific aspects that are relevant. The first arises due to the time dimension of the problem. Here we can distinguish between the long-run and the short- (or medium) run effects. In principle they are difficult to define precisely, but in practice the concepts are clear enough. We will now consider, in some detail, how the time dimension affects our understanding of defence, disarmament and development.

Disarmament at the national level will reduce military spending and release additional resources to the civilian economy. A lot of research has shown that the long term effect will generally be favourable in terms of growth, capital formation, income distribution and overall development. However, in the short run, there are bound to be adverse consequences of reduced milex. Even if conversion is well planned, and there are reasons to doubt such a well-ordered transformation, there will be major economic problems associated with structural change. The fall in aggregate demand needs to be fully compensated for elsewhere in government budgets, otherwise there will be negative multiplier effects on national income. Demobilization of personnel will create unemployment at least initially. Military de-industrialization will have adverse linkages with the rest of the manufacturing sector until civilian industries pick up the slack. If the resources available from the defence sector are transferred to human capital formation in the form of health, education, nutrition and so forth, once again the beneficial effect will take a long time to be apparent. Overall, the positive developmental role of disarmament will only be manifest after a considerable period of time.

National security needs, on the other hand, are essentially short term in nature. This is particularly true for arms races which seem to be so prevalent in the Third World. Unilateral disarmament will look particularly unattractive in term of security risks. But even bi(multi)lateral reductions will have inherent tensions, particularly if one country is small and the other large.

This analysis therefore points out one major difficulty with disarmament in its relation to development. The gains are essentially long run. The losses (costs) are basically short run. Further, there is no clear-cut answer to the question - how long (short) is long (short)? It is not possible to predict when the short-term costs will start to decline and the long-term advantages become apparent. Thus there is little incentive

---

[7]   Deger, Saadet, *Military Expenditure in Third World Countries: The Economic Effects*, (London, Routledge and Kegan Paul, 1986).

for current policy-makers to support disarmament since their perspectives are incompatible with the implicit cost-benefit process. In a sense this is an inter-generational problem: the current generation may have to bear the costs of disarmament while future generations will gather the fruits of development.

The second problem arises from the non-linear nature of the relationship between defence and economic growth. For some countries, and at certain stages of development, military expenditure can have positive effects on the economy. From the early 'military as modernizer' theories to the econometric studies done in the 1980s, a considerable literature has accumulated on such positive effects.

I myself have discussed elsewhere, in some detail, the various channels through which military expenditure positively affects economic growth and development.[8] There are essentially four such channels. First, military expenditure creates effective demand which, in a macro-economy with unemployed resources, can raise aggregate output. Higher resource utilization can also raise profit rates and thereby increase investment and growth. Second, the military can provide stability and thus help to create an environment in which growth can take place. Third, defence industries stimulate inter-industrial linkages and create industrial output through 'backward' and 'forward' links with other sectors. Finally, there is a whole host of 'spin-offs': training, modernization, discipline, infrastructure and so forth.

Yet after a while, these positive effects begin to fade away. The negative effects of military expenditure seem to dominate. My econometric studies, with large data sets, can be summarized as follows:

> The empirical evidence goes against the findings of Benoît and others regarding the positive effects of defence and growth -- defence expenditure allocates scarce resources away from productive civilian investment and fails to mobilize or create any additional savings.[9]

Even for highly developed countries the military-industrial complex, which usually has lower productivity due to government protection, competes with the more competitive civilian industrial sectors for the same stock of capital, technology and skilled labour. There exists a potential trade-off between military expenditure and investment in the economy. This has serious negative growth effects. Thus, in the post-war period the high military spenders (US, UK) tended to have lower investment shares (in GDP) and growth rates than the low military spenders (Japan, Germany).

All this analysis suggests a systematic relationship. At early stages of development, military spending has a negative effect as the defence sector absorbs very scarce resources (for example in Vietnam). After a threshold, with relatively higher levels of development, military expenditure may stimulate growth through the positive channels mentioned above (consider South Korea). Finally, as countries reach the fully

---

8   Deger, Saadet and West, Robert (ed.), *Defence, Security and Development*, (London, Frances Pinter Publishers, 1987); also see note 7.
9   See note 7.

developed stage, defence spending is inversely related to growth (UK, Germany as the two polar cases).

The existence of this non-linearity makes it difficult to convince governments of the imperative towards disarmament. Since defence can have a potentially favourable impact, it is not easy to reduce it, particularly in face of specific military security threats. Yet it must be realized that there is a limit to this beneficial process. Ultimately, military security can only be bought at the expense of other forms of security.

Finally, we must emphasize a different issue which has become a major problem in recent years. This is the decline of national authority and the related growth of sub-nationalism. This problem will have a direct impact on security spending in general and make it difficult to release resources for socio-economic needs. Nor is it confined to developing states alone; witness the situation in the Soviet Union's Baltic states and in the Caucasas. A combination of developmental failures, of erosion of governmental control and legitimacy, as well as systemic inefficiency, has increased the propensity of minorities to rebel against national authority. In South Asia, Israel (occupied territories of the West Bank), the Philippines and many other areas of the world, the major threat is not only from external sources. The 'enemy within' has become a central threat, irrespective of the moral cause behind it.

The growth of sub-nationalism has contributed directly to the erosion of the legitimacy of the nation-state which has traditionally been the foundation of national security. In addition, a whole host of factors - military, political and economic - have contributed to this decline of what traditionally constitutes legitimate authority: refugees moving across state boundaries; drug traffickers flouting international law; resource conflicts for water or land which obey no national boundaries; and so forth. These tendencies are contributing to an upward pull on defence spending as the armed forces and paramilitary are being utilized to protect the government and even the state.

East-West détente will increase international security but will not increase stability, particularly in the Third World. Developing countries will have to do more for themselves to stem the impact of developmental failures. But rapid military expenditure reductions will not be easy. Even a reasonable target such as reducing the military burden (share of military expenditure in gross domestic product) to 2 per cent by the end of the 1990s, instead of the current 4 per cent, seems at present to be beyond the reach of the Third World.

Military Expenditure in the North and Resource Transfer

Over the last four decades and more, vast resources have been spent on maintaining the conflictual antagonism in Europe. All European countries, as well as the two Super Powers, have expended huge amounts of money, technological resources and manpower in this conflict. Some claim that 'peace' was maintained; however, there is little doubt that the costs were high. The best way of measuring this cost is to look at the evolution of military expenditure (such as the opportunity costs of conscripted manpower or research personnel) even though other more qualitative factors are also vital.

Trends

In 1989, according to my latest estimate, a sum of about US $511.3 billion (in 1988 prices and exchange rates) was spent for military purposes due to the European confrontation. This sum includes expenditures by European NATO and non-Soviet WTO countries, as well as apportioned amounts from Soviet and US military spending. The sum represents over 50 per cent of world military expenditure.

It should be noted that WTO domestic value expenditures have been converted to dollars by using purchasing power parities. Thus they represent opportunity costs i.e. what value of goods and services could have been purchased at US prices. Since official exchange rates have little value, the use of PPP is recommended. In addition, 50 per cent of total US military expenditure has been taken to represent costs for Europe. This is based on figures presented by the Department of Defence to which modest adjustments have been made. For the Soviet Union, the relevant share is 75 per cent of my estimate of that country's aggregate military expenditure. The USSR had a greater commitment to European defence, for obvious reasons. In addition, the majority of its armed forces and weapons stocks were based in Europe (west of the Ural mountains) in 1989.

Table 7.2 gives my estimates of military expenditure, from 1980 to 1989, spent *on Europe* by all the powers that have been involved in the confrontation. It rose continuously from 1980 to 1987 and then began to fall.

This remarkably large sum of money and financial resources were regularly being expended for the European region. Equally important is the unprecedented growth rate of defence spending on Europe during the decade of the 1980s. It rose by 4.2 per cent per annum from 1980 to 1987, when it peaked. There has been a modest fall between 1987-89 of around 1.6 per cent per year. The decline has been slow but hopefully will accelerate in the coming years.

Disarmament Dividend

The maximum potential size of the peace dividend will be determined by this sum of over US $511 billion that the major military powers have been spending on Europe. Even if 10 per cent is diverted to foreign aid, then ODA to the Third World will rise by over 100 per cent. Therefore, if defence reductions of the major military powers, most of whom are also the rich developed countries, could be translated into greater foreign aid, then LDCs would perceive tangible, short-term benefits to the process of disarmament and development. The sums involved are large, hence the incentive element is high. An alternative way of looking at the problem is to note that the negative net transfer from the debt servicing burden of the Third World is of the order of US $50 billion. This is the amount that LDC debtors are paying back (in interest and principal repayments) over and above the new money that they are receiving every year. The poor are subsidizing the rich. A 10 per cent reduction of defence spending on Europe transferred to the South would be enough to eliminate this burden.

Table 7.2
Military Expenditure on Europe,
for all Major and European Powers Combined
(billion US 1988 dollars)

Year	Military Spending
1980	396.1
1981	412.4
1982	434.6
1983	454.0
1984	471.8
1985	493.9
1986	515.0
1987	527.8
1988	524.9
1989	511.3

Source: Author's estimates.

But even here a cautionary word is in order. Currently, economic and military aid are often entwined, with the recipient country receiving both from the same source. If global disarmament leads to a reduction in military growth, then it might also encroach on development assistance. Resource transfers from the disarmament levy might not therefore compensate some developing countries. The donor countries might also wish to renege on their other aid commitments. What is really required is the setting up of a multilateral disarmament and development fund, created from the money released from military expenditure reductions in the developed countries, which will channel resources towards the Third World.[10]

The United Nations has repeatedly called for the establishment of such a fund, but the response has been muted partly due to the intransigence of the United States. At the International Conference on Disarmament and Development the issue was raised by numerous countries but the final resolution failed to mention it due to the objection of the major Western powers.[11] The United States did not attend the Conference. However, with recent changes in the world security system, the time has come for such global funding mechanisms to be put back on the agenda for renewed discussion.

It should be clear that the permanent benefits of disarmament and development are strong, but the transitory difficulties of achieving long-term gains are also substantial. There can be little dispute about the moral and economic advantages of reducing defence spending and channelling resources to increase growth and enhance the quality of life. But practical policy making is rarely conducted in terms of such ideals. When a short-run cost-benefit analysis is conducted, the advantages of disarmament and development look less attractive; this is probably the major reason why there have been so few concrete, practicable and operational suggestions as to how disarmament and development are to be achieved in practice. We need simple policy rules within the current international institutional framework. These are not easy to derive given the conflict between the short and long run.

Peace Penalty

Recently, the question of the so-called 'peace penalty' has surfaced. What if the beneficial effects of peace and disarmament are overwhelmed by certain negative features? There are four areas in which doubts have been raised as to whether the costs of disarmament might be excessively high.[12]

1. The expenditure involved in implementing arms control measures could be high. These include: verification costs, particularly if satellite-based systems need to be utilized; elimination of weapons called Treaty Limited Items (TLI), particularly for certain categories and countries (for example tanks belonging to the Soviet Union); closure of bases, particularly as foreign troops withdraw; provision of social security for communities disadvantaged, particularly those wholly dependent on military services; granting subsidies for industrial restructuring, particularly for companies most vulnerable to defence cuts; major

---

[10]   Fontanel, Jacques and Smith, Ron "The creation of an international disarmament fund for development", *in:* Deger and West (eds.), note 8.

[11]   Deger, Saadet, "The United Nations International Conference on the Relationship between Disarmament and Development", *SIPRI Yearbook 1988: World Armament and Disarmament* (Oxford, 1988).

[12]   Deger, Saadet and Sen, Somnath, *Military Expenditure: The Political Economy of International Security* (Oxford, Oxford University Press, 1990).

new investment for conversion, particularly for the Soviet Union where the defence industrial complex has asked for over 60 billion roubles - almost equivalent to the annual official military budget; coping with unemployment, particularly in specific regions like California or Moscow where employment dependence on defence output is high.

    As yet no detailed analysis has been conducted on the financial expenses involved in these areas. But one point needs to be stressed repeatedly. These costs, however high, are once and for all. Permanent benefits should outweigh temporary problems. However, the tension discussed earlier between long- and short-run advantages remains;

2. The major powers will lose interest in the global community and become more inward looking except in relation to their immediate neighbours. Thus, any resources saved will be spent on domestic economic problems - of which there are many - and nothing will be left for the rest of the world. For both the United States and the Soviet Union, reduction of military expenditure will be immediately swallowed up by many other social needs, as well as to balance the huge budget deficits which both countries bear;

3. There will be greater competition for global resources as East European countries enter international financial markets and also demand more foreign aid. Thus resources currently destined for the Third World might be 'crowded out' and economic development suffer, causing conflicts to increase;

4. As arms procurement in the industrial economies declines, there develops an incentive to export. This 'export version' of the peace penalty could be particularly pernicious and will be dealt with in the next section.

Arms Trade and the Conflict Between Politics and Commerce

In any discussion of North-South relations within the framework of economic security, the arms trade figures prominently. Most of the sellers, and the overwhelming proportion of the value of the trade, emanate from the developed countries of both the East and the West. A major proportion of the world total of arms imports continues to be received by the Third World. The supply-demand nexus still follows a North-South division, even though there are significant exceptions, including China as a major seller and Japan as a major buyer. The six biggest exporters, during 1985-89, were the USSR, US, France, UK, China and Germany. The six largest importers, during the same period, were India, Iraq, Japan, Saudi Arabia, Syria and Egypt. The structure of the arms trade, in the new North-South environment, is therefore important.

Trends

Third World arms imports rose rapidly in the 1970s, faster than the growth of merchandise trade. In the 1980s arms imports levelled off for developing countries as a whole, even though in some regions growth continued to be positive. In 1989, arms imports fell dramatically to their early 1970s level, although one statistical observation cannot establish a trend.[13] There was evidence of some large-scale arms purchases after the recent Gulf crisis, although the embargo on Iraq exerted a downward pull. Overall, Third World arms trade can be said to have reached a low plateau after a decline in the late 1980s.

The decline in the growth of arms and the recent fall can be explained by economic factors affecting the purchasing countries rather than any conscious effort at trade controls from the suppliers. Much of the expansion took place due to the oil boom and the recycling of petro dollars. The fall, where it occurred, has been a consequence of economic misfortunes related to expanding debt, collapse of the terms of trade, and the general decline in merchandise imports that Third World countries have faced in the 'lost decade' of the 1980s.

Arms imports will not remain permanently depressed until supplier controls are firmly established. IF and when economic growth begins again in LDCs and export earnings start rising, the demand for arms will also increase. The new international climate requires co-ordination among the major powers to stop the trade from the supply side. The Soviet Union has officially announced that it will put stringent controls on foreign sales. The United States is also worried about proliferation, particularly in ballistic missiles, and will therefore be more cautious. However, in practice, few countries have exercised very much control over exports; they have left the market to operate relatively freely within broad guidelines. Weapons in excess of those allowed after the CFE Treaty is in force, for TLIs, have already reached Third World countries and more may be transferred.

Commercialization

During the 1980s the arms industries in developed countries of the West became increasingly commercialized.[14] Until then most national industries, except in the US, were operated and owned by the State. In recent years, privatization has increased dramatically. Taking the larger national suppliers of arms exports: in the US, UK and Germany, the armaments industry is concentrated in the private sector; in France, the call for privatization is increasing; in China, relatively independent companies have been set up to promote exports; in the Soviet Union the defence enterprises, though controlled by the government are also expected to be self-financing and earn profits.

In terms of the motives that dominate nations' arms exports, there is an incipient conflict between economic and political factors. Arms are never sold to enemies, of

---

[13]   See Chapter 7 in *SIPRI Yearbook 1990: World Armament and Disarmament*, (Oxford, Oxford University Press, 1990).

[14]   Deger, Saadet, "Regional Conflict and Recent Trends in the International Arms Trade", *in: Arms and Defence in Southeast Asia*, Chandran Jeshurun (ed.), Institute of Southeast Asian Studies (ISEAS), 1989.

course, but the distinction between allies and adversaries is sometimes not clear-cut nor permanent. As a general rule, the Super Powers have been concerned predominantly with political motives, though some economic gains have been made. The next four 'majors' - France, UK, Germany and China - have been more concerned with making economic gains though they have implicit political motives too. All other countries (including many Third World nations) have been overwhelmingly interested in profits from arms sales. Table 7.3 provides the market shares among these three groups of countries. Clearly, the share (wholly economic) of the group risen over time. During 1975-79, the second and third groups in the Table had one-quarter of the arms exports; a decade later they had increased their relative share to one-third. As more countries with dominant economic motives enter the market, the political consensus may break down. The size of the market and its growth will be determined by demand factors alone. This creates potential for conflict and economic losses to the Third World. Equally ominously, even the Super Powers are paying more attention to 'market forces'. An export version of conversion has been discussed in the Soviet Union, and large corporations are expected to make high sales in situations like the recent Gulf crisis.

Table 7.3
Shares in Arms Exports
(percentages)

Group	1975-79	1985-89
Mainly political (2 Super Powers)	73.2	64.0
Mainly economic (4 majors)	19.7	25.0
Wholly economic (Others)	7.1	11.0

Source: Author's estimates from SIPRI data base.

Individual corporations, mostly in the private sector of the West, have become very large during the 1980s, partly as a result of mergers and acquisition and partly because of the increase in procurement orders. Procurement expenditure[15] on major weapons increased from US $40.3 billion to US $79.4 billion (in constant 1988 prices) between 1980 to 1987 in the United States. For European NATO the corresponding rise was

---

[15]   Deger, Saadet, "World Military Expenditure, *SIPRI Yearbook 1990: World Armament and Disarmament*, (Oxford, Oxford University Press, 1990).

from US $27.2 billion to US $33.7 billion. In 1989, NATO spent over US $106 billion on major weapons purchases alone. Table 7.4 gives data on Western government procurement of major weapons for the years 1980, 1987 and 1989. Arms sales of McDonnell Douglas, estimated to be US $8.5 billion in 1988, exceed the gross domestic product of many Third World countries. The business is highly concentrated. The top ten American companies in 1988 sold over US $61 billion of arms - almost the whole procurement budget of the US Defence Department. When domestic demand is booming, there is little incentive for companies to face governmental restrictions in selling abroad.

As arms control succeeds, domestic weapons procurement will decline drastically. A modest reduction is already underway, as the data for 1987 and 1989 shows. Faced with such a decline, consequent to the changing political climate, arms-producing companies and enterprises will have an incentive to sell abroad and earn profits if they fail to diversify or convert. Increasing commercialization will therefore threaten the political framework within which the market currently functions. If the laws of supply and demand operate alone, then the Third World will be the recipient of the peace penalty provided they can pay for it. During the Cold War arms transfers were used to 'win friends and influence people'. In the post Cold War period, arms transfers may be facilitated by the 'merchants of death'.

Table 7.4
Major Weapons Procurement Expenditure, NATO
(billion US $ at constant 1988 prices)

	1980	1987	1988	1989	1990
US	40.3	79.4	71.8	73.2	66.5
European NATO	27.2	33.7	32.4	33.4	30.0
Total NATO	68.6	116.8	108.8	108.5	98.4

Source: Deger, S., "World Military Expenditure" *in: SIPRI Yearbook 1991*, Chapter 5, Oxford, Oxford University Press, 1991.

Conclusion

At a time of systemic and structural change it is difficult to predict the future from past experience. This paper has summarized some of the implications for the Third World of the current transformation in the international security order. There is both a 'pessimistic' and an 'optimistic' version of the future. It is difficult to provide a 'realistic' version which will probably be a mean of the two extremes. There is reason to be hopeful, but there is also reason to be cautious. Arms control and disarmament can potentially bring great benefits. But in the absence of political will and policy co-ordination, the development effects will be minimal. The potential for conflict will then rise and the new international order may not be as peaceful and prosperous as we might expect or hope.

Chapter 8

Effects for Developing Countries of the East-West Disarmament Process

Jacques Fontanel

The disarmament procedures entered into voluntarily or involuntarily by NATO and the Warsaw Pact are bound to have important consequences for developing countries.[1] Many efforts are being made, even if the results still remain extremely disappointing and in any event not sufficiently decisive to ensure, even in the short term, a situation favourable to the emergence of a society at peace.[2] A number of questions have been raised:

1. Does this progressive disarmament process stem from the considered desires of the States concerned or is it the result of a particularly alarming economic situation liable directly to challenge the very conditions of international security?[3] In fact, public opinion in most States is favourable to disarmament procedures. In a situation of economic crisis, discontent grows and it becomes even more difficult

---

[1] There is some ambiguity over the concept of developing countries, despite the existence within the United Nations of a political consensus for empirical decisions on which countries may be so designated. It should be recalled that the Third World is not a homogeneous entity and that it has many embodiments. However, as regards the study to be undertaken here, this economic heterogeneity does not precisely correspond to the varied political conditions of the security of each State, even if the petroleum-producing and exporting countries retain a special status that greatly complicates their analysis. See Jacques Fontanel, *L'armement et la santé dans les pays du tiers-monde* (Grenoble, Etudes et Travaux, Cahiers de la Faculté des Sciences Economiques de Grenoble, 1990).

[2] Brief summaries of all these negotiations are to be found in the publications of the United Nations Department for Disarmament Affairs (*Disarmament, Disarmament Newsletter, Yearbook of the United Nations*) and of the United Nations Institute for Disarmament Research (*Conventional Disarmament in Europe* by André Brie, Andrzej Karkoszka, Manfred Müller and Helga Schirmeister, Geneva, UNIDIR, 1988) and research papers such as *A Legal Approach to Verification in Disarmament or Arms Limitations* by Serge Sur, September 1988, etc. *La revue ARES, Défense et Sécurité* also makes an annual review of developments in these negotiations; see Jean-François Guilhaudis and Jacques Fontanel, "La vérification du désarmement", *Course aux armements et Désarmement* (Grenoble), Vol.XI, No.1, December 1989.

[3] On this matter, it would be of interest to go back to models of the arms race. See Jean Christian Lambelet and Urs Luterbacher, "Conflict, Arms Races and War: A Synthetic Approach" in *Peace, Defence and Economic Analysis*. Proceedings of a Conference held in Stockholm jointly by the International Economic Association and the Stockholm International Research Institute, Christian Schmidt and Frank Blackaby, eds. (London, Macmillan Press, 1987); Dagobert Brito and Michael Intriligator, "Arms Races and the Outbreak of War: Application of Principal-Agent Relationships and Asymmetric Information", *ibid.*

to run a heavily militarized economy. The present disarmament situation, which finds its expression more in the political than in the military or the strategic context, is highly exceptional and cannot really be interpreted on the basis of historical examples. It appears to be extremely original, as was the uninterrupted period of the arms race that has lasted for more than half a century. It may even be said that it is a novel situation for the Great Powers, one that is liable significantly to modify the whole of their foreign policy. It has been said that United States' foreign policy will lose the sextant by which the ship of State has been navigated since 1945, and that the dividends of peace will not be fully embodied in the money that will be freed, but will also include the categories of thought that will ultimately flourish.[4] In that context, there are three different interpretations of disarmament:

- First, it may be concerned with the reduction of excess armaments; consequently it turns out to be necessary, at some point or other, to define the concept of excessive stocks of weapons. It is likely that, under those conditions, economic factors will not be the tools best suited to be reliable indicators. On the one hand, with respect to the international agreements in force and to the technological features of the weapons, some types of systems, such as nuclear missiles, are decidedly more effective than conventional armaments, having a relatively low cost in terms of the strategic, military and political advantages that they confer. On the other hand, the balance of power is often expressed in terms of thresholds, yet a scaling down of military expenditure does not necessarily result in the previous balance of power being maintained. At the present time the principal expression of disarmament is in the destruction of existing stocks (that is to say 4 per cent of all nuclear forces), but also in the practically unilateral limitation of military expenditure. Destroying missiles is a costly business and the saving of a billion dollars on the budget of the Pentagon immediately leads to the disappearance of 38,000 jobs.[5] In other words, disarmament, taking the form of the destruction of military materials, appears as a cost and any possible transfers of resources should initially serve to offset the costs inherent in this collective decision;

---

[4]   *US News and World Report*, 14 May 1990.

[5]   Jacques Decornoy, "Sortir du Bourbier Militaire, rebâtir une économie civile", *Le Monde Diplomatique*, July 1990.

- Next, disarmament can be imposed by disastrous national economic conditions. Governments are beginning to ponder the economic effectiveness of the arms race and, particularly, the adverse long-term effects that it may have on the amount of resources available to maintain adequate military forces.[6] In other words, if the effect of today's armament on the national economy is to produce a recession, that may be a hindrance for tomorrow's armament and, consequently, for tomorrow's defence. The dynamics of military expenditure progressively sap the economic foundations of the Great Powers, above all when the international political and social climate is an obstacle to economic use of the possible effects of domination through the power developed by the balance of power of national armed forces. It has been stated that national security can no longer be analysed in purely military terms; economic security must also be taken into account.[7] Furthermore, public opinion is less and less willing to put up with the restrictions on private and public non-military consumption brought about by the military effort. This is probably the prevailing situation as we enter the 1990s. Under these conditions, it is less a matter of seeking disarmament for disarmament's sake than of finding new resources capable of promoting the struggle against an economic crisis that is deemed intolerable. Strategic tensions between the Great Powers then tend to decrease, to the advantage of an international "climate" conducive to economic development. The countries responsible for the arms race, having previously extolled the merits of military investment for their development, begin to ponder the existence of an economic dead end with which their military and strategic power is threatened in the fairly short term. Each State, while keeping generally to its position, seeks to obtain a reduction of the military effort of the other, not so much to acquire a strategic advantage but rather to be in a position to combat effectively the discontent of its own population or to be able to further new economic conquests liable ultimately to strengthen the country's strategic power;

- Lastly, disarmament presupposes a real process of the reduction of opposing forces, without reference to massive stocks of weapons, but with the idea of establishing a lasting peace able to overcome the ideological, political and religious differences that sometimes lead to situations of armed crises. This is the situation most favourable to true disarmament. However, the question that

---

[6] Louis Pilandon, "Quantitative and Causal Analysis of Military Expenditures", in *The Economics of Military Expenditures. Military Expenditures, Economic Growth and Fluctuations.* Proceedings of a Conference held by the International Economic Association in Paris, Christian Schmidt, ed. (London, Macmillan, 1987).

[7] Charles William Maynes, "America without the Cold War", *Foreign Policy*, Spring, 1990.

remains unanswered is knowing whether the conditions for peace have really been established or whether it may not rather be an historical stage of breathlessness in the arms race after several decades of uninterrupted effort.

At the present time States remain extremely distrustful in general. It does indeed appear that the second interpretation may be the correct one. However, a disarmament procedure is capable of giving rise to new situations of mutual confidence, which prompt a real awareness of the need to maintain the effort to reduce military expenditure so as to perpetuate this essential "breathing space" in the interests of international civilian consumption. The reduction of military expenditure, if negotiated, does raise problems of international comparisons and comparisons in time that are difficult to resolve, but for which it has already been possible to find some interesting solutions.[8]

2. Is not this disarmament the premise for an economic rapprochement between West and East capable of further reducing the scale of economic flows between North and South? When we analyse the speed with which the monetary unity of Germany, followed by economic and political unity are being carried out, we may note that the poles of exchange and development that have been dominant since 1945 are on the way to being displaced principally in favour of the countries of the East, which appear to be more dynamic and richer in high-quality human resources than the countries of the South. Under these conditions, this process of disarmament heralding new economic exchanges is modifying the map of countries that constitute risks in favour of the European socialist countries. There is undeniably a considerable danger that countries of the Third World will be supplanted even should disarmament measures have largely positive effects on the whole of the world economy. Conversely, the developing countries have to set about acting and attracting capital unless they wish to be the ones overlooked at the end of the twentieth century. There is a risk that aid to Third World countries will be diverted to the countries of the East that offer better prospects of development;

3. What are the specific economic costs of this disarmament and what will be the reactions of enterprises concerned with military activities, especially in their search for new outlets? The conversion of arms industries to other economic activities

---

[8]   Hans Christian Cars and Jacques Fontanel, "Military Expenditure Comparisons", *Peace, Defence and Economic Analysis*. Proceedings of a Conference held in Stockholm jointly by the International Economic Association and the Stockholm International Research Institute, Christian Schmidt and Frank Blackaby, eds (London, Macmillan Press, 1987); Jacques Fontanel, "Les Comparaisons des dépenses militaires dans les pays de l'OCDE", *ARES, Défense et Sécurité*, Vol. XI, No. 1, 1989 (Collection "Course aux armements et désarmement", eds. Guilhaudis and Fontanel).

may have obvious positive effects on the well-being of the populations of countries, but may also exhibit some undesirable effects that ought not to be overlooked in the short term.[9] When faced with the strengthening of international competition, converted industries may seek, in particular, new outlets that presuppose competition with products exported or sold locally by developing countries. Under these conditions, unless the poorest countries take real measures to protect themselves, the result may be that their national companies lose their competitiveness. This may lead either to economic collapse or, at best, to the establishment of foreign industries and a drastic reduction in the amount of freedom that the State has in the management of its economy;

4. Will this disarmament be effected in the context of assistance to the countries of the Third World or will it be confined to a regular reduction of military expenditure, the expected economic benefits of which over a period of more than one year will be re-invested in the country itself, without international transfer? The United States appears to be interested mainly in limiting of the deficiency of public revenue, restoring national savings and reducing interest rates.[10] The social problems facing the Soviet Union are sufficiently serious to limit its ambitions to the restoration of its own economy. France and the United Kingdom have not yet decided to make a significant disarmament effort. These countries together account for more than two thirds of world military expenditure. In other words, at least in the short term, it appears unlikely that transfers to developing countries will ensue even given the existence of a potential disarmament situation;

5. Will this disarmament affect the poorest countries, which are generally heavily penalized by the problems of international debt and famine? On first analysis it is clear that reduction of the national armament effort is bound to have positive effects, especially when armaments are imported, other things being equal. However, a reduction of military outlay is capable of eliminating all concern for national defence and of leading to a gradual resurgence of regional wars, owing to the weakness of the opposing forces. It should be recalled, moreover, that some States have sought to use their armaments industry to favour policies of import substitution, growth through exports and industrializing industries.[11] In that context, the manner of coping with the existence of technical and manpower resources rendered obsolete by a new decision and a new international situation,

9 Wally Struys, *Défense et économie. Mythes et réalités* (Bruxelles, Centre d'Etudes de Défense), No. 26, May 1989.

10 Charles Schultze, "Use the Peace Dividend to Increase Saving", *Challenge*, March-April 1990; Lawrence R. Klein, "The Economics of Turning Swords into Plowshares", *Challenge*, March-April 1990.

11 Jacques Fontanel and José Drummond-Saraiva, *Les industries d'armement comme vecteurs du développement économique des pays du tiers-monde* (Paris, Etudes Polemologiques, No. 40, 1986).

even if heavy investment has already been committed in this sector, will be revealing of the intentions of the developing countries and even perhaps, more broadly, of the real potentialities of lasting disarmament. Lastly, a disarmament procedure almost invariably involves the opening of economic frontiers. This situation produces results that are the subject of great controversy between those who commend the impetus generated by the liberalization of trade and those who fear the rapid expansion of new effects of domination that are favourable to the developed countries and are responsible for the continuous bogging down of the economies of Third World countries.

The impact of a disarmament procedure on the economies of Third World countries is a question that needs to be approached on two levels:

1. The reduction of military effort permits the development of new economic activities and is favourable to international exchanges. Third World countries will benefit from this context conducive to international economic growth;
2. Third World countries will also be led to disarm, which should make it easier to use currency for civilian purposes, to reduce unproductive expenditure and to promote redeployment of military activities that are not very profitable (when they are profitable at all) and are in any case economically highly risky.

International Economic Growth Brought about by the Disarmament Process as an Instrument for the Development of Third World Countries

Disarmament is a procedure that very rapidly improves the international economic situation even if it is capable of producing some problems over economic conditions and some regional problems. This general proposition is confirmed by recent history, especially in the interpretation of the events that followed the last world war, the Korean war and the Vietnamese war. The first question is to determine whether the current disarmament of the United States and the Soviet Union is capable of creating new opportunities for growth. Most economists consider that countries that disarm will reap the benefits of new growth potential. The second question is to know whether all developing countries can effectively benefit from this economic upsurge, having regard to the interdependence of national economies.

Current Disarmament and World Growth

It is of interest to analyse the nature of disarmament, since that nature may modify its expected economic impact. Moreover it is of interest to give prominence to the foreseeable economic activity of the Great Powers, principally the United States and the USSR, in order to understand the economic consequences of a reduction of their economic defence effort on Third World countries.

1. *The economic forms of disarmament.*

Current disarmament is taking two forms: on the one hand, negotiations on the (highly) partial destruction of existing stocks of weapons and, on the other hand, a generalized trend towards restricting the economic defence effort that finds expression in a reduction in the national ratios between military expenditure and Gross Domestic Product. From an economic standpoint the two forms of disarmament have different consequences:

i. The first form implies additional costs at the outset for the elimination of excess stocks, followed by a decline in expenditure in the handling and possibly the monitoring of particularly hazardous equipment;
ii. The second form of disarmament leads to a reduction of military might. It may be effected in the short term without necessarily implying any process of reduction of the opposing forces, particularly by strict control of possible waste, restriction on commitments to carry out research and development, the introduction of conscription at a lower cost than an army of regular soldiers and strategic options that have the effect of favouring more cost-effective weapons, in particular nuclear weapons.[12]

Let us consider the existing conditions of the relationship between economic growth and disarmament and principally the driving force behind current developments. In other words, is disarmament a consequence of the economic crisis or vice versa; is it impossible to find a solution to the economic crisis other than through a procedure of disarmament? It is probably impossible to give a peremptory answer to this question. Nevertheless, at least for the countries of Eastern Europe, it does appear that the priority given to the military sector has had rather adverse effects on their economies, although it is difficult to calculate the effective cost, partly because of the existence of planned prices that are, to say the least, only a limited reflection of economic "reality".

---

[12] Jacques Fontanel, "Le coût du nucléaire militaire dans le monde", *Le désarmement pour le développement*, Fontanel and Guilhaudis, eds. (Grenoble, ARES, Collection *Désarmement et course aux armements*, 1986).

Economists have no doubt in their own minds that a reduction of military expenditure tends to have a positive effect in the long term on the economy of a country, obviously provided that there are no potential armed conflicts. With the new strategies of dissuasion it is quite difficult to know how useful defence forces actually are since, given that history never repeats itself in exactly the same way, it is impossible to determine with certainty what actual contribution the defence effort of a country makes to the decision of another country not to stir up a conflict from which it could derive politico-economic advantages. It is therefore of more interest to raise the question of disarmament in the context of hypotheses on excessive levels of armaments and on the status quo of the opposing forces, it being understood that no decisive strategic modifications are to be expected, at least in the short term, from the Great Powers, even if the treatment of military R&D is capable in the longer term of bringing about a new balance of power. Disarmament ought not to be thought of exclusively as a transfer of resources to the benefit of the civilian economy; it must also be analysed in a dynamic context of the reduction of opposing forces and of the maintenance of balances that are essentially of a precarious nature when once the major strategic and economic variables become the subject of appreciable modification.

In furtherance of our argument we shall therefore hypothesize that the present procedures of disarmament are taking place in the context of a struggle against excessive levels of armaments, but that the major strategic equilibria will be maintained with a considerable likelihood of success at least until the end of the 20th century. However, it is relatively difficult to accept this latter proposition regarding the considerable changes that have arisen during recent years, particularly with the unification of Germany and the degeneration of the Warsaw Pact. Nevertheless, the strategic military forces of the countries of the East remain completely dominated by the Soviet Union and consequently the hypothesis retains an adequate degree of realism, for the present.

2. *The economic activity of the great powers in the present context of disarmament*

As far as Lawrence Klein and Charles Schultze are concerned, a procedure of disarmament will necessarily have a positive effect on the American economy.[13] The production of civilian capital goods is extremely useful when it replaces military output, because the former gives rise to new earnings flows, whereas the latter is used to destroy or to be destroyed without any economic return. Thus, the usefulness of a motorway will extend far beyond the expenditure period and will be conducive to other uses. As regards military equipment, the first condition is not always obtained, and the second is hardly ever ensured. All conversion from the military to the civilian leads, *a priori*, to an indisputable economic gain, even if some problems of economic or regional conditions

---

[13]   Charles Schultze, "Use the Peace Dividend to Increase Saving", *Challenge*, March-April 1990; Lawrence R. Klein, "The Economics of Turning Swords into Plowshares", *Challenge*, March-April 1990.

may occasionally be admitted. The reduction of military expenditure ought not to lead to a restriction on overall demand, however, and the government ought to engage simultaneously in a policy of compensatory public expenditure or reduction of the budgetary deficit.

For the United States, Klein recommends progressive reduction of the public deficit, the effect of which would be firstly to reduce the rate of interest, then to limit the cost of debt servicing, and ultimately to improve export positions. There would in effect be a renovation of heavily indebted economies that would receive a true subsidy from the reduction of interest rates and would then be in a position once again to become importers of American products. In the short term some major American enterprises would experience a considerable reduction in their public orders, in particular McDonnel Douglas, General Dynamics, General Electric, Tenneco and Raytheon, which together hold more than US $130 billion worth of Pentagon contracts. In the medium term, lower interest rates will lead to more investment, a situation that will be favourable both to international trade and to a reduction of the public deficit. It is noteworthy that a change in interest rates would be bound to have important effects on foreign exchange markets.[14] Lastly, military expenditure exerts undeniable inflationary tensions, because the economy provides salaries without a flow of goods being produced in exchange.

Under these conditions, the reduction of defence expenditure furthers the competitiveness and productivity of American enterprises,[15] the more so because the technological spin-offs of the military sector are regarded as inefficient and costly. The LINK model posed the question of what the economic impact of a 3 per cent reduction in military expenditure combined with a more flexible monetary policy would be. The main reply was that there would be an appreciable reduction in interest rates, of the order of 2 per cent. Charles Schultze of the Brookings Institution is putting forward a plan for a progressive reduction of military expenditure of the order of $50 billion over five years (falling from $287 to $237 billion between 1989 and 1994); the "economies" thus made would be set aside, one-fifth to be used for federal civilian expenditure on high-priority programmes and the remainder to reduce the public deficit.

A few years ago when the United States caught a cold, the Western countries went down with bronchitis. At the present time Europe is progressively becoming the economic centre of the world and its regular process of integration should lead to important positive effects for the whole of the world economy. The Government of the United States no longer plays the dominant economic role it has held since the last World War and the effects that the developing countries may expect from a reduction in the military

---

14 Christian Schmidt, *Revue d'Economie Politique*, 1987.
15 This idea had already been developed by Seymour Melman in *The Permanent War Economy* (New York, Simon & Schuster, 1974).

expenditure of the United States are only indirect, mainly through the channel of the progressive reduction of interest rates. It should be added that a procedure of disarmament by the United States has global (and certainly non-structural) significance only if its allies do not increase their own military efforts in the framework of an agreement to share the burden of defence.[16] Furthermore, a changing economic situation is sometimes the source or the cause of new potentialities for conflict and rearmament.[17]

Two fundamental problems are currently being raised in the countries of the East, namely the restructuring of their economies and the reduction of military expenditure. The USSR for long carried out a process of "paradoxical militarism",[18] under which the strategic emphasis was laid on the ostentatious aspects of force, the politico-strategic purpose of which was often realized even at the expense of the real effectiveness of the armed forces. At present the Soviet Union desires a disarmament procedure because the economic impact of military expenditure is too heavy for a stricken economy. Mikhail Gorbachev clearly expressed this willingness when he stated that "development and international relations have been distorted by the arms race and militarization of the way of thinking".[19] This is an essential point of the new Soviet strategy. Klein considers that a 5 per cent reduction in military expenditure in Poland is associated with a 3 per cent expansion in expenditure for civilian consumption. Allowing for the fact that the armament markets were highly controlled by quotas, this is a new opening for international trade which should strengthen relations of interdependence and solidarity. However, there are no known econometric or quantitative studies to demonstrate the economic interest of a disarmament procedure in the countries of Eastern Europe. Reconversions scarcely seem to pose problems in the short term in the context of a planned economy, even though the urgency of the action that needs to be taken to stimulate the economy makes most modifications both tricky and necessary. Moreover, conversions should raise fewer problems than in Western countries because many military enterprises already work in the civilian sector. In the opinion of Cooper,[20] half the

---

[16]   Todd Sandler, "NATO Burden-Sharing: Rules or Reality?", *Peace, Defence and Economic Analysis.* Proceedings of a Conference held in Stockholm jointly by the International Economic Association and the Stockholm International Research Institute, Christian Schmidt and Frank Blackaby, eds. (London, Macmillan Press, 1987).

[17]   Bruce Russett, "Economic Change as a Cause of International Conflict", *Peace, Defence and Economic Analysis.* Proceedings of a Conference held in Stockholm jointly by the International Economic Association and the Stockholm International Research Institute, Christian Schmidt and Frank Blackaby, eds. (London, Macmillan Press, 1987).

[18]   Jacques Sapir, "URSS. La conversion de l'industrie militaire vers le secteur civil", *Informations et Commentaires*, No. 68 (July-September 1989).

[19]   Cited in the article by Jacques Decornoy, *op. cit.*, p. 16.

[20]   J. Cooper, "The Scales of Output of Civilian Products by Enterprises of the Soviet Defence Industry", *SITS Paper*, No. 3 (CREES, University of Birmingham, 1988).

electric steel, a quarter of railway equipment and more than a fifth of consumer goods are already being produced by the military sector, which points to good prospects for reconversion in a country in which private consumption still remains limited and open to good development prospects.

Logically, the flow of international capital to the countries of the East ought not to come from the United States, but rather from France, Germany and Japan. The United States will be led initially to deal with its internal economic problems, especially the ill-considered lowering of the rate of national saving. There are few economic studies on the impact of disarmament on the economies of France[21] and the United Kingdom,[22] and those there are do not relate to the current situation. This is actual proof that, despite some statements to the contrary, the two Governments do not really wish to commit themselves to the path of disarmament. Moreover, it does not appear that either Germany or Japan has decided to reduce its armament effort, at least in the short term.[23] However, the debates are becoming increasingly contradictory and it is probable that these two countries will in the end follow the disarmament trend to which the two Great Powers have given impetus.

Will the World Growth Instigated by Disarmament also Affect the Developing Countries?

The impact of the disarmament of the Great Powers on the economies of Third World countries is a question that is in general not much debated. The prevailing idea is that the improvement in the economic situation of the rich countries is bound, in the long term, to have only positive consequences for the developing countries. That analysis is probably not very satisfactory in fact, because it omits the emergence of new balances of forces capable, at least in the medium term, of substantially modifying the relative economic development conditions of the countries of the whole world.

1. *The fundamental question of the passing on of economic growth and development*
   Economists traditionally ponder the interdependence of States and the international spreading of economic growth. In the view of classical and liberal authors the least

---

[21] Jacques Aben, "Désarmement, activité et emploi", *Défense Nationale*, May 1981.

[22] Keith Hartley, "Reducing Defence Expenditure: A Public Choice Analysis and a Case Study of the UK", *Peace, Defence and Economic Analysis*. Proceedings of a Conference held in Stockholm jointly by the International Economic Association and the Stockholm International Research Institute, Christian Schmidt and Frank Blackaby, eds. (London, Macmillan Press, 1987).

[23] Jun Nishihawa, "Note on the Impact of Military Expenditure on the Japanese Economy", *The Economics of Military Expenditures. Military Expenditures, Economic Growth and Fluctuations*, Christian Schmidt, ed. for the International Economic Association (Paris, Macmillan, 1987).

well-off countries are absorbed by the richest countries and therefore benefit from their development. Socialist, Marxist and mercantilist authors find this analysis inadequate because it fails to consider the balance of power. Two questions must then be raised in the context of disarmament liable to lead to accelerated development in the industrialized countries:

- Will the Great Powers lose the advantages of their effects of domination which also find expression in the economic order? It is probably too soon to ask this question because, despite the willingness to disarm, the disparities that exist between the forces of Third World States and those of the industrialized countries are so great that nothing would appear to have to change in the immediate future;
- Is the strengthening of the economies of the developed countries conducive to development in the least well-off countries? This question invites several replies. In the liberal view the opening up of trade gives the less well-endowed countries the best advantages; on the understanding that there is competition between producers, there are not really any effects of domination, at least in the economic order; a reduction of military expenditure reduces international tension and limits the existence of the captive markets developed through conflict. The theory of underdevelopment as a product of development opposes this thesis and considers that the economic situation of Third World countries is likely to deteriorate if, for example, the converted enterprises enter into competition with national products or if they no longer purchase the raw materials that were the greater part of the export resources of the developing countries. We shall not here consider in any depth this fundamental debate, which would merit lengthy consideration on its own. We shall merely consider that a reduction of military expenditure in the developed countries will have nothing but positive effects for the countries of the Third World provided that this disarmament procedure is not accompanied by serious reforms affecting international economic organization, which is rather too favourable to the major economic powers.

> Basically, the economy of these countries has been made totally dependent on the developed countries. Consequently, the Western countries must make restitution and most international organizations are calling for the establishment of a New International Economic Order. In any case, we may reject two myths, that of the important part played by colonial outlets for Western industries, and that of Western development based on raw materials coming from the Third World, even if there was an epoch when these relations could have favourable effects for the countries of the North at the expense of the countries of the South. Colonization is both undoubtedly responsible for the underdevelopment of many regions of the world (the phenomena of cultural integration, political inequality and

economic exploitation) and a scapegoat invoked to explain all mistakes in the management of the national economies of Third World countries.[24]

The economy has become an occasion for and an effective means of making war. Insecurity is not maintained merely by the arms race, but is also dependent on social and international inequalities and domination. The contemporary world of the coexistence of two economic systems that are by nature antagonistic presupposes the existence of a continual conflict, ranging from armed peace to the threat of nuclear war, and taking in local wars, economic retaliatory measures and, more generally, indirect strategies of dissuasion. Economics is one weapon, but it is difficult over a lengthy period to create the conditions of national security without a strong economy capable of bearing the strategic costs and of deploying them. The countries of the Third World are greatly disadvantaged by their weak capacity for economic and military defence. Military men are obliged to take into account the balance that must be maintained between defence expenditure, which is often impoverishing, and ultimately the maintenance of national security. A choice has therefore to be made between security today and tomorrow. Economic and military power confers certain advantages on those that have it, particularly in the field of commercial negotiations. The contemporary economy is a battlefield, and a process of disarmament may lead to a progressive change in the world geography of the satisfaction of needs.

Under the Charter of the United Nations, demilitarization implies respect for the sovereign equality of its member States, prohibition of the threat or use of force against the territorial integrity of any State, recognition of the inviolability of frontiers, renunciation of any action against independence and national unity, non-intervention in the internal affairs of other States and refraining from giving assistance to terrorism. These principles could be respected by systematic exchanges of military information, the publication of military expenditure, the withdrawal of troops from frontier zones, and the establishment of systems of rapid and direct communication between civilian and military authorities.[25]

2. *The short-term economic interest of the Western industrialized countries for the Third World*

Historically, the Western countries used their military strength to further their political and economic conquest of the world. Colonization, a by-product of militarization, is often regarded as the essential reason for underdevelopment, because in particular it led to:

---

[24] Jacques Fontanel, "Aspects économiques de la militarisation et de la démilitarisation dans l'hémisphère sud", *Colloque "Géostratégie dans l'hémisphère sud"* (Ile de la Réunion, June 1990).

[25] Jacques Fontanel, "Aspects économiques de la militarisation et de la démilitarisation dans l'hémisphère sud", *Colloque "Géostratégie dans l'hémisphère sud"* (Ile de la Réunion, June 1990).

- the extension of export crops at the expense of food crops;
- mining activities;
- worsening of the terms of exchange;
- the construction of specialized communications routes turned towards the metropolitan country;
- the destruction of local craft industries through the competition of manufactured products; and,
- the establishment of nonsensical national frontiers.

Despite the idea of disarmament, which had been in mind for some years, there is no question of the Great Powers lowering their guard and putting a stop to the modernization of weapons systems or of discontinuing all preparation for possible intervention in the countries of the Third World. There is a balance of power that has not really been questioned, as is shown by the continuing relative equilibrium in the most underprivileged regions that are largely dependent on spheres of influence inherited from the antagonism of the two economic systems. At present the expression of power has been unusually transformed. It has become less militarized, at least in the daily life of dominated countries. On the economic level, however, the balance of power is maintained and we only have to note the disputes to which major international economic negotiations give rise to be assured that these relationships of conflict are of a lasting nature.

Within the context of present international economic structures, the rapprochement between East and West may lead the industralized nations to become even less interested in Third World countries. Thus, in view of the urgency of reforms in the countries of the East, we may wonder what motivation the western countries may have to continue to give assistance to heavily indebted poor countries just when new, more exciting and probably more lucrative outlets are likely to develop in the socialist states.

Both Klein and Leontieff consider that disarmament will benefit everybody by virtue of the reduction in interest rates that should stimulate world economic growth by increasing the incentive to invest. If the countries of the East are increasingly involved in international trade, all countries are then in a position to benefit from these new markets.

In the absence of any real international will to assist the poorest countries, their economic situations will scarcely be able to improve. Henceforth the attention of most Western countries will be turned towards the countries of the East since they do not wish to miss a major change in direction that could allow them to expand their markets and to stimulate their national economies. Under these conditions, and with the exception of a few special countries, it is difficult to conceive of major investment in regions whose economic potential is heavily burdened by debt or by a chronic low level of productivity.

Furthermore, we ought not to overlook the dangers of maldevelopment arising from aid coming from developed countries. The latter always seek to derive benefit from any kind of aid and, in so doing, they may lead States in a weak situation to follow policies that are more in line with the interests of the donor country than with their own interests. Furthermore, some forms of transfer may ultimately prove to be costly, at least in operating costs, and political constraints are rarely excluded from such a commitment by rich countries. The result is that although developing countries do of course have to seek assistance, they must also be able to refuse it when it is not obviously of ultimate benefit to the whole of their national community. Furthermore, "aid to developing countries may be devoted to prestige expenditure, to the enhancement of social inequalities, and to promoting the expansion of societies in which the rights of man are not necessarily respected. Transfers may also be the subject of sordid motives of self-interest that tend to accustom peoples to a type of consumption that makes them dependent on industrialized countries ...".[26] Disarmament will be a stage on the road to development provided that it is the source of a reduction in inequality and in effects of domination because it increases the level of satisfaction of human needs (the "entitlement").[27]

Analyses of the tensions, the conflicts and even the trade or economic wars that countries are led to provoke or to undergo scarcely figure at all in liberal ideas.[28] The opening up of economic frontiers is not the panacea to generalized economic development, because there are undeniable effects of domination that may reduce or block the development potential of the weakest countries. In the absence of a real international organization laying down rules for protection, the complete liberalization of markets leads inescapably to a power struggle similar to that existing in enterprises and one that may bankrupt countries.

Can the Present Disarmament be made General and does it Offer New Scope for Development to Third World Countries?

In the medium term the progressive disarmament of Third World countries will probably be one condition of the accelerated disarmament of the Great Powers. In fact, it is scarcely conceivable that it should be otherwise, unless one considers that the present disarmament is no more than a temporary fruit of the economic crisis, it being understood

---

[26]   Jacques Fontanel, "L'économie des armes", *La Découverte* (Paris, Collection Repères, 1984).

[27]   Amartya Sen, "Public Action and the Quality of Life in Developing Countries", *Oxford Bulletin of Economics and Statistics* (November 1981); "Development: Which Way Now?", *Economic Journal*, Vol. 93, December 1983.

[28]   D.A. Baldwin, *Economic Statescraft* (Princeton University, 1985); Lachaux, Larcorne, Lamoureux and Labbe, *De l'arme économique* (Paris, Fondation pour les Etudes de Défense Nationale, Collection les Sept Epées, 1987).

that Third World countries are the objects of permanent conflict between the United States, the USSR, France and the United Kingdom.

Is Disarmament Immediately Desirable in the Countries of the Third World?

In his last book, Robert Looney[29] considers that the effects of military expenditure are dependent on whether developing countries are producers or importers of arms. We shall therefore distinguish between the general effects of military expenditure and the specific effects of national armaments production, two economic variables that are also affected by national and international disarmament.

1. *Military expenditure and economic growth of Third World countries*

It is assumed in United Nations reports that the arms race reduces world growth potential and limits the scope for economic development through the squandering of scarce resources. Nevertheless, some economists have argued that in certain specific economic situations, the armed forces could provide an impetus for development through their capacity to develop new techniques; their sense of order and discipline has also been considered useful for the organization of social labour. Benoit[30] considers that military effort is conducive to industrial modernization, to improvement of the infrastructure, and to the training and information of people. He does not point out any effect of competition between the civilian sector and the military sector, especially at the level of the hiring of key staff and the selection of modern technologies. However, most empirical studies do reveal the effect of sectoral substitution (the choice between civilian or military industrial activities), the effect of temporal substitution (the choice between the present and the future) and the effect of the squeezing out of investment exerted by military expenditure. Under these conditions, military expenditure does have an adverse effect on economic development, even if, as public expenditure, it may contribute to an upsurge of demand. Thus, it is likely that the increasing of military expenditure is made possible by the increased growth rate of the economy and not vice versa.

Augusto Varas[31] considers that the impact of military expenditure on the growth of developing countries is not the same as its impact on developed countries because it initially affects material well-being rather than growth. Whereas a change in the relationship between military expenditure and material well-being may have only

---

[29]   Robert E. Looney, *Third-World Military Expenditure and Arms Production* (London, Macmillan Press, 1988; foreword by Robert L. West).

[30]   Emile Benoît, "Growth and Defense in Developing Countries", *Economic Development and Cultural Change*, No. 2 (January 1978).

[31]   Augusto Varas, "Military Spending and the Development Process", in *Disarmament*, Vol. IX, No. 3 (New York, Autumn 1986).

secondary effects in developed countries, the outcome is different in developing countries because the military effort seriously worsens a standard of living that is already very low for the majority. As far as Varas is concerned there are no stable and significant correlations between military expenditure and economic growth. Jwabena Gyimah-Brempong[32] considers that the military expenditure of African countries is prejudicial to their economic development potential because any the possible positive effects are largely offset by the reduction in investment resulting from defence outlay. Ron and Dan Smith[33] consider that the militarization of developing economies is not favourable to their economic development in the long term, even if there may be some positive effects from it, in particular the mobilization of the surplus. The theory of the division of resources, represented in developed countries by the thought of Seymour Melman,[34] argues that an economy in which large amounts of critical resources keep on being allocated to unproductive activities is one in which the capacity to produce efficiently is considerably reduced, either because the industry of the country ceases to be competitive, or through corruption of the behaviour of economic agents. Under these conditions, the end effect of disarmament is to improve the average national standard of living and to increase the world economic development potential.

It is fairly generally recognized that there is a relationship of substitution between investment and military expenditure.[35] However, there are three factors that may invalidate this:

- Social acceptance of the financial outlay on defence;
- The structure of military expenditure (expenditure on personnel as a proportion of capital or infrastructure expenditure); and
- The level of economic growth (in a period of economic stagnation military expenditure is in more direct competition with investment).

If the population is prepared to accept the outlay on defence, in particular in a situation of heavy and identified international threats, it may also accept a reduction in its consumption. If the increase in military expenditure is currently leading to a reduction in global investment, that is because citizens still do not clearly apprehend an imminent threat of war. There is therefore a divergence between the needs expressed by economic agents and the attitude of States; moreover such divergence may be essentially due to the

---

[32] Kwabena Gyimah-Brempong, "Defense Spending and Economic Growth in sub-Saharan Africa: An Econometric Investigation", *Journal of Peace Research*, No. 1 (1989).

[33] Ron Smith and Dan Smith, *The Economics of Militarism* (London, Pluto Press, 1983).

[34] Seymour Melman, *The Permanent War Economy* (New York, Simon & Schuster, 1974).

[35] Jacques Fontanel and Ron Smith, "Analyse économique des déspenses militaires", *Stratégique* (Fondation pour les Etudes de Défense Nationale, 1985).

availability of different strategic information. In the short term, disarmament that finds its expression in a reduction of military expenditure may be offset by an increase in investment, even though in developing countries consumption is liable to be strongly boosted.

2. *Disarmament and arms-producing developing countries*

The arguments put forward to justify the establishment of national arms production are national security, strategico-economic independence and economic growth. The choice between imports and armaments production is a difficult one to make when there are established ideological constraints. It is possible to reduce armaments production in a disarmament situation, even though there is a threshold effect from which an enterprise becomes increasingly costly to the community. In other words, the conditions of generalized disarmament are such that enterprises may be led to produce rather unprofitable and extremely expensive goods, thus altering the conditions and even the relevance of production. Even when its immediate aims are relatively slight, disarmament is capable of having adverse effects on the productivity of arms manufacturers and of leading to a real cessation of local military activity on account of inadequate productivity. Under these conditions the international armaments market would be less saturated. It is now asserted that arms industries have weak industrializing effects, in particular because military technologies have relatively limited spin-offs for civilian sectors and because the arms exports trade war is probably as costly for the community as it is lucrative for the numerous intermediaries.[36]

Economies are still very heavily militarized.[37] This militarization is defined as a situation in which war, the threat of war or preparation for war are a major collective concern, which implies a higher degree of legitimacy, considerable political influence in government decisions and a significant allocation of national resources. Many countries have based their industrialization on arms production, which is dangerous from the economic point of view, in particular when the international arms market becomes stagnant, and is a reducing factor on account of the politico-military constraints that inevitably emerge and that restrict the freedom of action of civilian and military governments regarding disarmament.[38] A serious economic study could also show that

---

[36] Christian Schmidt, "Industrie d'armement et endettement dans les pays en voie de développement: les exemples d'Israel, du Bresil, de l'Argentine et de la Corée du Sud", *Congrès International des économistes de la langue française*, May 1984.

[37] Jacques Fontanel, "Militarisation dans l'hémisphère sud", *op. cit.*

[38] Edward Kolodziej, "Whither Modernisation and Militarisation, Implications for International Security and Arms Control", *Peace, Defence and Economic Analysis*. Proceedings of a Conference held in Stockholm jointly by the International Economic Association and the Stockholm International Research Institute, Christian Schmidt and Frank Blackaby, eds. (London, Macmillan Press, 1987).

some exporting activities are a cause of impoverishment, in particular when the terms of payment become difficult or even impossible, and when the arms enterprise, which is heavily subsidized, is left to sell at a loss - to the community.[39] The present situation of a vague wish for disarmament tends above all to restrict the degree of legitimacy as national governments are called into question and to lead very slowly to a reduction in military expenditure in relation to the national wealth generated annually.

Deger and Ball consider that national armament is a cause of underdevelopment, whereas Looney[40] is of the opinion that this relationship cannot really be sustained except for countries that are not arms producers. This latter idea preoccupies Nicole Ball, who also sees some advantages in national production of arms such as the saving on scarce foreign currency, the mastery of technology and the possible introduction of a policy of industrialization gaining ground through military investment that would not otherwise have been made for civilian purposes. However, no Third World country can support such a policy unless it already has a sufficiently strong and diversified industrial sector.[41] David Whynes[42] even suggests that only large developing countries in the area investigated, in particular Brazil and perhaps Indonesia, can really derive sufficient multiplier effects from military outlay to limit the effects of eviction. José Dummond-Saraiva[43] considers scarcely plausible the hypothesis that the Brazilian economy could benefit from the impetus arising from military industrialization because the stimulation of economic activity, which is an interesting economic effect, appears to be overshadowed in the long term by the effects of substitution and eviction. Disarmament would tend to be positive for the Brazilian economy as a whole, even though Herrera-Lasso is of the opinion that the arms industry may be a powerful economic development vector for Brazil.[44] However, these thoughts have still not been

---

[39] Ron Smith, Anthony Humm and Jacques Fontanel, "The Eeconomics of Exporting Arms", *Journal of Peace Research*, Vol. 2, No. 3 (1985); François Chesnais, *Compétitivité internationale et dépenses militaires* (Paris, CPE, *Economica*, 1990); Jacques Fontanel, *French arms industry* (Grenoble, *Cahiers du CEDSI*, No. 10, Université des Sciences Sociales, 1990).

[40] Saadet Deger, *Military Expenditure in Third World Countries: the Economic Effects* (London, Boston and Henley, Routledge & Kegan Paul, 1986); Nicole Ball, *Security and Economy in the Third World* (Princeton, Princeton University Press, 1988); Robert Looney, *Third-World Military Expenditure and Arms Production* (Basingstoke and London, Macmillan Press, 1988); Jacques Fontanel, "The Economic Effects of Military Expenditure in Third-World countries", *Journal of Peace Research*, Vol.27, No.4 (November 1990).

[41] Herbert Wulf, "Developing Countries", *The Structure of the Defense Industry*, Nicole Ball and Milton Lietenberg, eds. (London, Croom Helm, 1983).

[42] David Whynes, *The Economics of Third World Military Expenditure* (London, Macmillan, 1979).

[43] José Drummond-Saraiva, "L'industrie brésilienne d'armement" (draft economics thesis, Grenoble, for publication late 1991).

[44] Luis Herrera-Lasso, "Economic Growth, Military Expenditure, the Arms Industry and Arms Transfer in Latin America", *The Economics of Military Expenditures: Military Expenditures, Economic Growth and Fluctuations*, Christian Schmidt, ed. (London, Macmillan, 1987).

supplemented by an analysis of the relationship between the rapid development of the arms industry and the indebtedness of Third World countries.   Christian Schmidt concludes with the statement that the ultimate effect of arms programmes on the indebtedness of Brazil, Argentina, South Korea and Israel is more dependent on American geostrategic considerations than on purely economic considerations, and that although United States aid does help to lighten the financial burden of national armament programmes, it also increases US debt, which has appreciable effects on the value of the dollar.[45]

In the main the staff employed in the arms industries are young and well-trained; nevertheless their productivity is low. Those who support the idea that military industries are the "key sector" of national industry believe that disarmament would be likely to lead to a serious rise in unemployment and a considerable drop in the earnings of workers. Nevertheless most present studies tend to reveal armament as a sector that generates little employment; in terms of opportunity costs, the military sector employs half the number of staff for the same expenditure in many cases. Consequently, the arms race has not been a remedy for the problems of employment - quite the opposite. Nor, however, is disarmament the panacea for this unemployment, since there is also a need to ensure redeployment of the employees of the military sector, and it is probably easier to transfer military personnel employed in offices to the civilian sector than in the case of highly specialized jobs.

The impact of military expenditure on growth is dependent on effective use of the productive capacity of national economies. In terms of opportunity costs, civilian investment is *a priori* more favourable to economic development than is military investment. However, this assessment must be qualified, on the one hand because all civilian investment (in particular investment that gives rise to demonstration effects or that arises from an error in assessment of the market) is not equally profitable and, on the other hand, because the military sector may, through its orders, maintain the level of output and of competitiveness of whole sectors of the economy (principally aeronautics, computers and shipbuilding). Through their inertial effects on economic flows, military budgets maintain the activity of entire branches of industry, providing them with a measure of security and an additional growth potential through the rapid expansion of economies of scale and effects of domination.

---

[45]   Christian Schmidt, "Industrie d'armement et endettement dans les pays en voie de développement: les exemples d'Israël, du Brésil, de l'Argentine et de la Corée du Sud". Congrès International des Economistes de Langue Française, Clermont-Ferrand, May 1984, reported in *Revue de Défense Nationale* (October 1984).

Are the Anticipated Influences of Generalized Disarmament Highly Positive for Developing Countries?

Two main types of effects are likely to emerge, other things being equal, in a context of generalized disarmament: initially a limitation on the militarization of the economy, followed by some fairly positive effects of the transfer from military activities in favour of civilian production.

1. *The progressive demilitarization of economic life and national policy*

There are great differences in the situations in Third World countries. However, since the early 1980s we have been witnessing a demilitarization of central governments that has been particularly apparent in Latin America. This demilitarization has brought about through a reduction in the power of the military in civilian society, through the absence of military political organization or through the "civilianization" of the armed forces.

The results of Looney's econometric analysis[46] show that politico-bureaucratic influences are more important in the definition of military expenditure than are international rivalries. On the other hand, effects of substitution are less important in arms-producing countries than in countries that are exclusively importers of the arms needed for their defence. Lastly, military expenditure has played only a small part in the rapid development of the indebtedness of Third World countries, particularly those in the southern hemisphere. In any case, according to Ball, they have not played the essential role that with hindsight, some individuals would have wished them to play.

A recent econometric study[47] clearly brings out the dangers of the militarization of governmental organization. The aim of the study was to demonstrate certain variables which could explain arms imports by geographic zones: national characteristics (land mass and population), the nature of the government (democracy or military dictatorship), the extent of militarization (in particular, military expenditure), economic conditions (level of wealth and signficance of international trade) and international conflicts. Generally speaking, military characteristics logically dominate the explanation of arms imports, and the effects of inertia give prominence to a real market with customers and sellers. A disarmament effort would be likely ultimately to reduce this dangerous link; even if there is always the risk in the short term of an arms enterprise seeking to re-sell surpluses, the developed countries, held back by international agreements, would be led to abstain.

Disarmament brings us into the presence of a "civilianization" of modern societies, a retreat from the ideas of militarism, the hierarchy, discipline, nationalism, patriotism and

---

[46]   Robert Looney, *Third-World Military Expenditure and Arms Production* (Basingstoke and London, Macmillan Press, 1988).
[47]   Frederic Pearson, "The Correlates of Arms Importation", *Journal of Peace Research*, Vol. 26, No. 2 (1989).

xenophobia. Militarism emerges with the State system. The social position of the military is of importance. The army is often the symbol of national unity, even if the key factor is its central place in the military-industrial complex. The military holds power in the name of its ability to defend the basic interests of the nation. That is why societies that have conscription appear less productive of militarism. Militarism arises from clashes of interest, as well as from a belief in violence and force. Nevertheless, mentalities and behaviour are not decreed.

The function of the armed forces has sometimes only been one of internal repression. Chile and Argentina are cases in point. In the opinion of many specialists military expenditure is dependent on a variety of factors: the influence of external and international conflicts, the quantity of available national resources, the inertial effects of the State budget, bureaucratic pressures, the social influence of the military (corporate interests, personal gain, coups and military regimes), the part played by world and regional powers (colonialism or neocolonialism, direct intervention, military assistance, sales of arms) and the perception of national security.[48] The army is not involved solely with its military duties, but is also directly concerned with social life and with ideals. It may frequently happen that the military is more preoccupied with internal policy than with the defence of a country that is only slightly threatened. A disarmament procedure would inevitably tend to restrict that type of behaviour.

However, the fact of an increase in the military expenditure of two hostile States often has the result of merely maintaining or even worsening international security; under these conditions a negotiated reduction of military expenditure could be envisaged, other things being equal. On the hypothesis of a lasting peace, military expenditure inevitably has an adverse effect on world economic development. It often happens that the domination engendered by military strength or by some forms of militarization of the economy has positive effects on that dominant national economy. The reduction of effects of domination may be a positive element for developing countries.

2. *Three models which the conclude that a disarmament procedure has positive effects for economic growth*

A reduction of military expenditure has been simulated by three models of the world economy.[49]

---

[48]   Jan Tinbergen, "World Peace Policy", *Peace, Defence and Economic Analysis*. Proceedings of a Conference held in Stockholm jointly by the International Economic Association and the Stockholm International Research Institute, Christian Schmidt and Frank Blackaby, eds. (London, Macmillan Press, 1987).

[49]   Jacques Fontanel, "Désarmement et pays en voie de développement", *Désarmement, développement, emploi, informations et commentaires*, No. 68 (Revue trimestrielle, Lyon, juillet-septembre 1989).

- The world model of Leontief and Duchin[50] arrives at the conclusion that the transfer of resources to poor countries promotes their economic development; in that sense, disarmament is desirable for development. A degree of disarmament would have a positive effect for all the regions of the world, the transfers of resources appreciably increasing per capita consumption and GDP both in the arid countries of Africa, and in the countries of Asia and tropical Africa with low incomes. Spectacular as these results may appear for the underdeveloped countries with low populations, they are nevertheless not very significant. Thus, a reduction of military expenditure by 1.2 per cent annually between 1980 and the year 2000 would further economic growth as follows: 1 per cent for Japan, 0 per cent for the OPEC countries, 1.5 per cent for North America, 3 per cent for Europe, 10 per cent for the countries of Asia with a planned economy, and 20 per cent for the countries of Asia with low revenues and for tropical Africa. The figures are not very significant but give an overall impression of the economic impact of disarmament. Unlike the hypothesis of a reduction in the demand for raw materials following a reduction in military expenditure, the model of Leontief and Duchin demonstrates that the new growth engendered by this disarmament does not threaten the economy of the countries that produce raw materials, which are generally Third World countries, as the Table 8.1 demonstrates
- A simulation based on the UNITAD world model[51] tests one scenario in which there is no distribution of incomes resulting from a disarmament procedure, and another that suggests a policy founded on the satisfaction of basic needs, on the hypothesis that the credits freed are used to promote small-scale and highly productive economic activities in developing countries. Two cases are analysed: (1) disarmament makes it possible to realize the objective of public assistance to development in the amount of 0.7 per cent of GNP, and (2) one-third current of world military expenditure is transferred to development programmes for developing countries (either by direct aid from developed countries corresponding to an additional expression of solidarity of the order of one-third of their savings on military expenditure, or by transfer of internal allocations of military resources to productive civilian activities). Whereas the creation of jobs seems modest for the developed countries, the outcome is different for the developing countries. In the short term, the reduction of military expenditure depresses demand and is conducive to job losses, until the point is reached at which the consequences of the

---

[50]   Leontieff and Duchin, "Worldwide Implications of Hypothetical Changes in Military Spending" (Report for the United Nations, New York, 1980); Leontieff and Duchin, *Military Spending: Facts and Figures, Worldwide Implications and Future Outlook* (Oxford University Press, 1983).

[51]   J. Royer, *Long-Term Employment Impact of Disarmament Policies* (ILO, December 1985).

Table 8.1
Evolution of the Demand for Raw Materials
Assuming either Disarmament or Continuation of the Arms Race

Resource	Continuation of arms race	Disarmament
Oil	3.9	1.0
Nickel	3.1	2.2
Copper	-0.3	2.4
Zinc	-0.3	2.7
Bauxite	-1.1	3.0
Tin	-1.8	3.2
Iron	-3.9	3.4
Coal	-5.5	4.0
Natural gas	-6.5	3.4

growth of the developing countries find expression in an increase in demand in the direction of the more developed areas. If the improvement in assistance is combined with policies focused on basic needs, the result is a considerable additional annual growth and considerable job creation. These effects are even greater if steps are taken to ease restrictions on markets and on currency. However, these gains may easily be swept away by the terms of exchange or by increases in the rate of interest and the debt payments with which the developing countries are burdened. Lastly, disarmament alone is incapable of resolving all the problems of the developing countries. In particular, even in the most satisfactory hypothesis, the real consumption per inhabitant of Africa south of the Sahara will continue to decline owing to population growth and the weakness of agricultural production. It is scarcely possible to improve the well-being of the vast majority of the population of the African continent without substantial improvements in agricultural productivity. The main efforts have to be made by the developing countries themselves;

Table 8.2
Simulations of the Effects of Disarmament

Hypotheses; annual percentage	Average growth rate (1990-2000)			
Disarmament hypotheses	Developed countries		Developing countries	
	Without redistribution of incomes	Basic needs	Without assistance	Basic needs
Disarmament with public assistance, 0.7% of GNP	3.3	3.6	7.7	8.9
Disarmament: 1/3 of military expenditure	3.5	3.7	8.6	9.4
	Job creation (millions)			
Public assistance, 0.7% of GNP	2	8	19	127
Disarmament: 1/3 of military expenditure	7	10	73	169

- According to the LINK model,[52] reductions of military expenditure of the order of 10 per cent accompanied by an increase in aid (0.7 per cent of the GNP) would lead to a growth of 1.7 per cent in the GNP of the developing countries and of 0.2 per cent in the developed countries on the maximum hypothesis that transfer would apply essentially to capital goods. Were the aid to be squandered, the growth of developing countries would remain the same, whereas the growth of the developed countries would decrease by 0.3 per cent. The developing countries have to use at least 60 per cent of their aid resources for the developed countries not to experience a reduction in their growth in relation to growth on the basic hypothesis. In another scenario of the LINK model, the United States, the USSR and Japan are the main donors of $53 billion until 1993 on the basis of their

---

[52] The model cited by Robin Luckham in "Disarmament and Development in all its Aspects with a view to Drawing Appropriate Conclusions". (Draft prepared for the United Nations Department of Disarmament Affairs, January 1986).

disarmament and in favour of the development of Third World countries. In that case, the growth path of the world economy increases from 0.9 to 1.7 per cent per year, but the developed countries experience an annual decrease of the order of 0.2 per cent relative to the normal trend, whereas the developing countries receive an additional impetus ranging from 10 per cent for the countries of Africa south of the Sahara to 2 per cent for the petroleum-exporting countries of the Middle East.[53]

However, disarmament cannot be restricted to quantitative choices on the limitation of military expenditure. In effect, it must not be forgotten that national governments always have to defend the interests of the peoples that they represent in an international environment considered to be hostile. Disarmament calls for a series of decisions on political priorities, the international economic order, the nature of development, and the rate and direction of the technological progress that can be developed in a less militarized society, on the management of the natural environment and on the reallocation and distribution of economic resources.

3. *National studies of reconversion with or without transfers*
The analyses that have been made of reconversion of the military activities of Third World countries are usually presented in accordance with the two hypotheses of the presence or absence of resource transfer from the developed countries in a disarmament situation.

- In the absence of transfers, the effects of a reduction of military expenditure, unless offset by at least an equal expenditure on the maintenance of internal order or on the purchase of imported luxury goods, are positive for countries that do not have arms industries, even in the short term, because they are conducive to the more efficient use of scarce resources. For arms-producing countries a disarmament procedure may have distorting effects in the short term, in particular for the industries and regions directly affected by the activities of the arms industry. In the long term, the effects should be positive provided that the economic regression brought about by the reduction of internal arms purchases does not lead to irreversible effects, in particular as regards the conversion of activity. It is even likely that good management of the reduction of military expenditure would have positive effects in the long term on civilian research and development, on the real productivity of national economies, and on confidence in

---

[53]   Lawrence Klein, "Disarmament and Development", *Science, War and Peace*, Jean-Jacques Salomon, ed. (Paris, Economica, 1990).

international exchange relations, which cannot be measured by econometric studies that have regard in general only to short-term developments in which the past (characterized by the arms race) recurs in the future. However, although many developing countries do devote a not insignificant proportion of their resources to military purposes, the large sums tied up in armaments should be concentrated in a small number of countries. Basically, disarmament appears to have favourable effects on the economy in Third World countries, even if the arms-producing countries are in danger of encountering some short-term difficulties in conversion that will be largely offset by the reduction of imports relating to the outlay on military industries and by the matching increase in civilian public expenditure;

- Disarmament accompanied by resource transfer in favour of Third World countries will benefit economic development only provided that it is not sequestered by a particular social group that decides to devote it to unproductive uses (for example, exports of capital and imports of luxury goods). In other words, transfer is of significance only provided that it is expressed in highly productive activity. Because of the demonstration effects that it prompts, transfer may sometimes have an adverse effect through the inflationary tensions to which it gives rise. In addition, resource transfer may be the occasion of gaining new markets for the developed countries and new dependence for the poor countries. Thus, James Lebovic[54] has been able to demonstrate the predominance of politico-military considerations in American foreign aid, both during the Carter presidency, despite its being heavily imbued with defence of the rights of man, and during the Reagan presidency, extensively influenced by the quest for the military power needed for American security. In that case transfer initially responds to politico-military considerations, thereafter to the economic interests of the donor and only ultimately to the economic development needs of Third World countries. Developing countries have, therefore, to avoid the overall effect of transfer being impoverishing. If the transfer is made in non-convertible currency, the recipient country must of necessity get its supplies in the donor country, which may take advantage of this fact to re-introduce unequal exchange flows. If the transfer is made in kind, it is not obvious that the product concerned satisfies the development needs of the recipient countries; for example, should the aid apply to a commodity that is in direct or indirect competition with the national industry of the poor country, the end result may be extremely adverse for the Third World, the more so because every product bears the stamp of the culture and the dominant values of the society in which it was created.

---

[54] James H. Lebovic, "National Interests and United States Foreign Aid", *Journal of Peace Research*, Vol. 25, No. 2 (June 1988).

Lastly, it is of interest to analyse the traditional opposition between military expenditure and expenditure on health; this opposition is not always justified because it is unusual for an increase in military expenditure to be reflected simultaneously in a reduction in the public outlay on health. While the reports of Brandt, Palme and Thorsson[55] assert that military expenditure threatens economic growth and development and, consequently, tomorrow's security, they condemn the use of public funds in the military sector to the detriment of health and education. As also found for developed countries, economic studies on the negative relationship between health and military expenditure yield contradictory results. Thus, while Deger and Looney confirm this hypothesis, it is questioned by Kennedy, by Ames and Goff, by Hayes and by Verner.[56] Basically, one may entertain doubts concerning the durability of a relationship that may in effect change in response to the actual economic setting in which choices are made by governments. Most analyses made in developing countries conclude that those with low military expenditure are also restrained consumers when it comes to education and health (and vice versa), that military expenditure is at least as vulnerable as other forms of public expenditure to a reduction of the State budget, and that an increase in military expenditure has scarcely any consequences on outlay for health and education. In the most recent study by Harris, Kelly and Pronowo,[57] the hypothesis that the larger the porportion of public expenditure devoted to military expenditure, the lower the proportion of expenditure on health and education is borne out in only 40 per cent of the instances listed in an examination of 50 countries. Furthermore, it is necessary to consider the vulnerability of

---

[55] W. Brandt, "La folie orchestrée. La course aux armements et la famine dans le monde" (Paris, Economica, 1988 - French edition); Willy Brandt *et al.* (Independent Commission on International Development Issues), *North-South, a Programme for Survival* (New York, Pan, 1980); *The Relationship between Disarmament and Development* (United Nations publication produced under the direction of Inga Thorsson, Sales No. A 36 356; New York, 3 September 1981); Olof Palme, *Common Security: a Programme for Disarmament* (London, Pan, 1982 - the report of the Independent Commission on Disarmament and Security Issues, under the chairmanship of Olof Palme).

[56] Saadet Deger, "Human Resources, Government, Education, Expenditure and the Military Burden in Less Developed Countries", *Journal of Developing Areas*, Vol. 20, No. 3 (1985); Robert Looney, "Austerity and Military Expenditures in Developing Countries: The Case of Venezuela", *Socio-Economic Planning Sciences*, Vol. 20, No. 3 (1986); Gavin Kennedy, *The Military of the Third World* (London, Duckworth, 1974); Barry Ames and Ed Goff, "Education and Defense Expenditure in Latin America 1948-1968", Liske, Loehr and McCament, eds., *Comparative Public Policy: Issues, Theories and Methods* (New York, John Wiley, 1975); Margaret Hayes, "Policy Consequences of Military Participation in Politics: An Analysis of Trade-Offs in Brazilian Federal Expenditures", Liske, Loehr and McCament, eds., *Comparative Public Policy: Issues, Theories and Methods* (New York, John Wiley, 1975); Joel Verner, "Budgetary Trade-Offs between Education and Defense Expenditure in Latin America: A Research Note", *Journal of Developing Areas*, Vol. 18, No. 3 (1983).

[57] Geoffrey Harris, Mark Kelly and Pronowo, "Trade-Offs Between defence and Education Health Expenditures in Developing Countries", *Journal of Peace Research*, Vol. 25, No. 2 (1988).

military expenditure to a reduction of public expenditure possibly hoped, despite the considerable inertial effects that exist in this type of activity considering the large allocation to personnel costs. The analysis of Hicks and Kubisch[58] emphasizes that social expenditure is less vulnerable to a reduction of public expenditure in the developing countries than is expenditure on defence and administration, and markedly less vulnerable than expenditure on the productive sectors and the infrastructure. This study was continued in a more detailed form by Harris, Kelly and Pronowo, whose main conclusion draws attention to the faster reduction of the military budget by comparison with public expenditure on health and education on the hypothesis of a reduction of public expenditure. However, this analysis leads its authors to conclude that no real effects of substitution exist between social expenditure and military expenditure.

This conclusion by Harris, Kelly and Pronowo is nevertheless somewhat too hasty, because it fails to take into account the redistribution of the social security expenditure borne by the various social categories. Social security expenditure actually turns out to be quite vulnerable to a reduction of State expenditure, which obviously tends to detract appreciably from the aim of the well-being of the population to the advantage of national defence. Basically, if health expenditure remains steady, the reimbursement of treatment is not guaranteed for all social categories; under these conditions, with equivalent expenditure, the availability of health services is heavily modified by virtue of the considerable contraction of the public health insurance system. There is at least an indirect relationship between military expenditure and social expenditure, if we include in the latter the allocation of treatment and the overall availability of medical equipment to the social strata of a country. A country-by-country study yields divergent results, which provides general confirmation of the absence of direct links between military expenditure, expenditure on health and expenditure on education.

As regards development, the facts should be treated with caution. Whereas it is undoubtedly the case at the global level that developing countries bear the burden of their armaments, suppression of the latter may have irreversible military, strategic and economic effects that undoubtedly worsen their poverty. It is therefore incorrect to state that disarmament invariably leads to an improvement in well-being; it may be the occasion of decline if it is accompanied by the maintenance of inequalities or by political, economic and military domination by another country.

It is still difficult to say whether the as yet quite weak process of disarmament entered into by the Great Powers will have positive effects for the countries of the Third World. What can be asserted, on the other hand, is that in the absence of any real willingness on

---

[58]   Norman Hicks and Ann Kubisch, *The Effects of Expenditure Reductions in Developing Countries* (Washington, World Bank, 1983); Hicks and Kubisch, "Cutting Government Expenditure in LDCs", *Finance and Development*, Vol. 21, No. 3 (1984).

the part of the industrialized States to assist Third World countries to find a way out of their economic stagnation, the conditions for a lasting peace will never be assembled and the disarmament process will rapidly be doomed to failure.

References

Aben, J., "Désarmement, activité et emploi". *Défense Nationale*, May 1981.

Ames, Barry and Goff, E., "Education and defense expenditure in Latin America, 1948-1968". *In* Liske, Loehr and McCament (eds.), *Comparative Public Policy: Issues, Theories and Methods*. New York, John Wiley, 1975.

Baldwin, D.A., *Economic Statescraft*, Princeton University, 1985.

Ball, N., "Defence and development: a critique of the Benoît study". *Economic Development and Structural Change*, Vol.31, pp.507-524, April 1983.

Benoît, E., *Defence and Economic Growth in Developing Countries*. Boston, Heath, Lexington Books, D.C., 1973. "Growth and defence in developing countries". *Economic Development and Cultural Change*, Vol. 26, pp.271-280, January 1978.

-- "Growth and defence in developing countries". *Economic Development and Cultural Change*, No.2, January 1978.

Brandt, W. *et al.*, *North-South, a Programme for Survival*, New York, Pan, 1980. (Independent Commission on International Development Issues).

Brito, D. and Intriligator, M., "Arms races and the outbreak of war: application of principal-agent relationships and asymmetric information". *In* Schmidt, C. and Blackaby, F., (eds.) *Peace Defence and Economic Analysis*. Proceedings of á conference held in Stockholm jointly by the International Economic Association and the Stockholm International Research Institute, London, Macmillan Press, 1987.

Cars, H. C. and Fontanel, J., "Military expenditure comparisons". *In* Schmidt, Christian and Blackaby, Frank (eds.) *Peace, Defence and Economic Analysis*. Proceedings of a conference held in Stockholm jointly by the International Economic Association and the Stockholm International Research Institute, London, Macmillan Press, 1987.

Chesnais, F., *Compétitivité internationale et dépenses militaires*, Paris, CPE, Economica, 1990.

Colard, G. and Fontanel, J., *Le désarmement pour le développement, un pari difficile*, Paris, Les Sept Epées, 1981. (Fondation pour les études de défense nationale).

Cooper, J., *The Scales of Output of Civilian Products by Enterprises of the Soviet Defence Industry*, CREES, University of Birmingham, 1988. (SITS Paper No. 3).

Decornoy, J., "Sortir du bourbier militaire, rebâtir une économie civile", *Le Monde Diplomatique*, July 1990.

Deger, S., and Smith, R., "Military expenditure and growth in less developed countries", *Journal of Conflict Resolution*, 1983.

-- "Human resources, government education expenditure and the military burden in less developed countries", *Journal of Developing Areas*, Vol. 20, No. 3, 1985.

-- *Military Expenditure in Third World Countries: The Economic Effects*, London, Boston and Henley, Routledge & Kegan Paul, 1986. (International Library of Economics).

Drummond-Saraiva, J., "L'industrie brésilienne d'armement". Premiers documents d'une Thèse d'economie à Grenoble (to be published late 1991).

Fontanel, J., *Military Expenditures and Economic Growth (France, Morocco)*, Grenoble, 1980. (Report for the United Nations Group of Experts on Disarmanent for Development).

-- "Aspects économiques de la militarisation et de la démilitarisation dans l'hémisphère sud", Symposium Géostratégie dans l'hémisphère sud, Ile de la Réunion, June 1990 (forthcoming).

-- "Désarmement et pays en voie de développement", *Informations et commentaires*, No. 68, "Désarmement, développement, emploi", Lyon, July-September 1989.

-- "Economie du désarmement", *Stratégique* (No. spécial désarmement).

-- "French arms industry", *Cahiers du CEDSI*, No. 10, 1990. (Université des Sciences Sociales, Grenoble).

-- *L'économie des armes*, Paris, La Découverte, 1984.

-- "Les comparaisons des dépenses militaires dans les pays de l'OCDE", *ARES, Défense et Sécurité*, Vol. XI, No. 1, 1989. (Collection Course aux armements et désarmement. Guilhaudis and Fontanel éditeurs).

-- "The economic effects of military expenditure in Third World countries", *Journal of Peace Research*, Vol. 27, No. 4 (November 1990).

Fontanel, J. and Saraiva, J., *Les industries d'armement comme vecteur du développement économique des pays du tiers-monde*, Paris, Institut français de polémologie, 1986 (Etudes polémologiques No. 430).

Fontanel, J. and Smith, R., "Analyse économique des dépenses militaires", *Stratégique*, Paris, troisième trimestre 1985. (Fondation pour les études de défense nationale).

Gyimah-Brempong, K., "Defense spending and economic growth in sub-Saharan Africa: an econometric investigation", *Journal of Peace Research*, No. 1, 1989.

Harris, G., Kelly, M., and Pronowo, "Trade-offs between defence and education health expenditures in developing countries", *Journal of Peace Research*, Vol. 25, No. 2, 1988.

Hartley, K., "Reducing defence expenditure: a public choice analysis and a case study of the UK". *In* Schmidt, C. and Blackaby, F. (eds.), *Peace, Defence and Economic Analysis*. Proceedings of a conference held in Stockholm jointly by the International Economic Association and the Stockholm International Research Institute, London, Macmillan Press, 1987.

Hayes, M., "Policy consequences of military participation in politics: an analysis of trade-offs in Brazilian federal expenditures". *In* Liske, Loehr and McCament (eds.), *Comparative Public Policy: Issues, Theories and Methods*, New York, John Wiley, 1975.

Herrera-Lasso, L., "Economic growth, military expenditure, the arms industry and arms transfer in Latin America". *In* Schmidt, Christian (ed.) *The Economics of Military Expenditures, Economic Growth and Fluctuations*. Proceedings of a Conference held by the International Economic Association in Paris, London, Macmillan, 1987.

Hicks, N. and Kubisch, A., *The Effects of Expenditure Reductions in Developing Countries*, Washington, World Bank, 1983.

-- "Cutting government expenditure in LDCs", *Finance and Development*, Vol. 21, No. 3, 1984.

Kennedy, G., *The Military of the Third World*, London, Duckworth, 1974.

Klein, L. R., "The economics of turning swords into plowshares", *Challenge*, March-April 1990.

Kolodziej, Edward. "Whither modernisation and militarisation. Implications for international security and arms control". *In* Schmidt, C. and Blackaby, F. (eds.), *Peace, Defence and Economic Analysis*. Proceedings of a conference held in Stockholm jointly by the International Economic Association and the Stockholm International Research Institute, London, Macmillan Press, 1987.

Lachaux, Lacorne, Lamoureux and Labbe, *De L'arme économique*, Paris, Les Sept Epées, 1987. (Fondation pour les études de défense nationale).

Lambelet, J. C. and Luterbacher, U., "Conflict, arms races and war: a synthetic approach". *In* Schmidt, C. and Blackaby, F. (eds.), *Peace, Defence and Economic Analysis.* Proceedings of a conference held in Stockholm jointly by the International Economic Association and the Stockholm International Research Institute, London, Macmillan Press, 1987.

Lebovic, J. H., "National interests and United States foreign aid", *Journal of Peace Research*, Vol. 25, No. 2, June 1988.

Leontieff, W. and Duchin, F., "Worldwide implications of hypothetical changes in military spending", New York, 1980. (Report for the United Nations Group of Experts on Disarmament for Development).

-- "Worldwide implications of a limitation on military spending", New York, 1980. (Report for the United Nations Group of Experts on Disarmament for Development)

-- *Military Spending. Facts and Figures. Worldwide Implications and Future Outlook*, Oxford and New York, Oxford University Press, 1983.

Looney, R. E., *Third World Military Expenditure and Arms Production*, London, Macmillan Press, 1988. (Foreword by Robert L. West).

-- "Austerity and military expenditures in developing countries: the case of Venezuela", *Socio-Economic Planning Sciences*, Vol. 20, No. 3, 1986.

Maynes, C. W., "America without the cold war", *Foreign Policy*, Spring 1990.

Melman, S., *The Permanent War Economy*, New York, Simon & Schuster, 1974.

Nishihawa, J., "Note on the impact of military expenditure on the Japanese economy". *In* Schmidt, C. (ed.), *The Economics of Military Expenditures, Economic Growth and Fluctuations.* Proceedings of a conference held by the International Economic Association in Paris, London, Macmillan, 1987.

Palme, O. *et al.*, *Common Security*, New York, Simon & Schuster, 1982. (Independent Commission on Disarmament and Security).

Pearson, F., "The correlates of arms importation", *Journal of Peace Research*, Vol. 26, No. 2, 1989.

Pilandon, L., "Quantitative and causal analysis of military expenditures". *In* Schmidt, Christian (ed.) *The Economics of Military Expenditures, Economic Growth and Fluctuations.* Proceedings of a conference held by the International Economic Association in Paris, London, Macmillan, 1987.

Royer J., *Long-Term Employment Impact of Disarmament Policies*, ILO, December 1985.

Russett, B., "Economic change as a cause of international conflict". *In* Schmidt, C., and Blackaby, F., (eds.) *Peace, Defence and Economic Analysis.* Proceedings of a conference held in Stockholm jointly by the International Economic Association and the Stockholm International Research Institute, London, Macmillan Press, 1987.

Sandler, T., "NATO burden-sharing: rules or reality?" *In* Schmidt, Christian and Frank Blackaby (eds.) *Peace, Defence and Economic Analysis.* Proceedings of a conference held in Stockholm jointly by the International Economic Association and the Stockholm International Research Institute, London, Macmillan Press, 1987.

Sapir, J., "URSS. La conversion de l'industrie militaire vers le secteur civil", *Informations et commentaires*, No. 68, July-September 1989.

Schultze, C., "Use the peace dividend to increase saving", *Challenge*, March-April 1990.

Sen, A., "Public action and the quality of life in developing countries", *Oxford Bulletin of Economics and Statistics*, November 1981; "Development - which way now?" *Economic Journal*, Vol. 93, pp. 745-762, December 1983.

Smith, R., and Smith, D., *The Economics of Militarism*, London, Pluto Press, 1983.

Smith, R., Humm, A. and Fontanel, J., "The economics of exporting arms", *Journal of Peace Research*, Vol. 2, No. 3, 1985.

Struys, W., *Défense et économie: mythes et réalités*, Centre d'Etudes de Défense, Bruxelles, No. 26, May 1989.

Thorsson, I., *In Pursuit of Disarmament. Conversion from Military to Civil Production in Sweden*, Stockholm, 1984. (Report by the special expert Inga Thorsson).

Tinbergen, J., "World peace policy". *In* Schmidt, C. and Blackaby, F., (eds.) *Peace, Defence and Economic Analysis.* Proceedings of a conference held in Stockholm jointly by the International Economic Association and the Stockholm International Research Institute, London, Macmillan Press, 1987.

United Nations, *Study on the Relationship Between Disarmanent and Development*, New York, 3 September 1981. (Prepared under the direction of Inga Thorsson) (A 36 356).

Varas, A., "Military spending and the development process", *Disarmament*, Vol. IX, No. 3, New York, Autumn 1986. (Review by the United Nations).

Verner, J., "Budgetary trade-offs between education and defense in Latin America: a research note", *Journal of Developing Areas*, Vol. 18, No. 3, 1983.

Whynes, D., *The Economics of Third World Military Expenditure*, London, Macmillan, 1979.

Wulf, H., "Developing countries". *In* Ball, N. and Leitenberg, M., (eds.) *The Structure of the Defense Industry*, London, Croom Helm, 1983.

Chapter 9

Global Changes and the Disarmament Process: Some Political and Economic Consequences on the Western Hemisphere

Luis Herrera-Lasso
Javier Diaz de Leon

Soviet perestroika and rapid changes in Eastern Europe have modified European and worldwide scenarios to a significant extent. For some analysts in the United States this can be interpreted as the victory of the Cold War. For others, the foreseeable future is far from clear and any interpretation implying victory can be considered simplistic and even dangerous. So far, facts tend to show that any changes in American global strategy are going to be slow and cautious.

More obvious and quick have been the consequences of those changes in US policy towards the hemisphere. In light of the changes in Eastern Europe, analysts in this part of the world pointed out two possible options for the United States towards the hemisphere: on one side, the obvious consequences of the willingness of the Soviet government to move into a new era of co-operation with a rapid withdrawal from regional conflicts could encourage the United States to diminish its presence in conflicts with an ostensible communist threat, specially in Central America, and give way to a scheme of coexistence. The second interpretation asserted that the United States now had a clearer horizon to consolidate its hegemonic position in the area, with very low risk of external interference. The second interpretation seems to be more accurate, at least for the time being.

For almost four decades, since the containment of communism became the main strategic priority of the United States, its main concern in the area was to involve Latin American governments in this crusade. During the 1960s, the Alliance for Progress, a programme of economic co-operation and aid oriented to the most needy sectors in these countries, also aimed to prevent communist advances in the area. Results were rather poor - as were the resources devoted to the programme - and in less than ten years, the main Latin American countries had military governments, specially in the South Cone; counter-insurgence became the main instrument to prevent and control any socialist or even leftist project.

After the failure of the United States to roll back the Cuban revolution, some drastic adjustments were made in several countries: Dominican Republic in 1965, Chile in 1973 and Grenada in 1983, while authoritarian governments in most other countries did their part in the containment scheme. In the 1970s, US policy was concentrated on other scenarios and very low attention was given to Latin America.

By the end of the decade, warning signals were visible in several countries, while a general perception of weakness and loss of power invaded political elites and eventually public opinion in the United States. Since then, a "roll back" strategy has been initiated in the continent, concentrated in the Caribbean Basin, with a new strategic approach called "low-intensity war". The worldwide economic crisis had an enormous impact on the region, augmented by the burden of an external debt without parallel. While most countries hardly managed to survive the crisis - in a sense the economic crisis helped the return of democracy in several countries - US policy was concentrated on strategic priorities, highly ideologized, with an East-West conflict perspective.

Disarmament processes between the Super Powers (related to strategic arms or chemical weapons as well as negotiations in Europe between countries of the two alliances on security matters) have not directly affected the economies of Latin America, since these countries are not part of any strategic alliance of global dimension. Nevertheless, changes in the global political scenario have already had significant political effects for the hemisphere. We must also say that the economic impact of the recent East-West evolutionary process on Latin America is intimately related to the US policy towards the region and for that reason we devote much of this chapter to that aspect.

In the first part we present an overview of US policy towards the Caribbean Basin, the results and current scenarios. In the following section, we devote our attention to Latin American countries southwards, in recent years not very much involved in the global dimension of the East-West conflict. The old and new challenges and general terms and perceptions of forthcoming relations with the United States are also discussed. In this part, we decided to include a description of the recent "Enterprise for the Americas" (27 June, 1990), since we consider this proposal the first wide response to the question: what should happen in this hemisphere *vis-à-vis* the great changes that are taking place all around the world?

In the next section, we attempt to identify on one hand, the US hemispheric agenda for the new era, its priorities and guidelines and on the other side, Latin American priorities and main challenges. Preliminary final remarks are devoted to the future of this relationship.

We conclude this chapter by trying to identify some of the main trends concerning the "peace dividends" of disarmament for the countries of the region, and some of their foreseeable consequences.

US Policy Towards the Caribbean Basin

In 1979, the last year of his term in office, President Carter showed special concern for the Caribbean. During the 1970s, Cuba had been rather successful in gaining friends and allies in the region - Jamaica, Guyana, Surinam, Grenada; meantime, the United States lost influence both in the Caribbean and Central America. In Nicaragua, a leftist revolution took power in 1979. Several Presidential directives in that year mapped out a comprehensive strategy in the Caribbean which in the long term was quite successful. During the first Reagan administration this strategy was consolidated and integrated in a more general strategy that included the Caribbean and Central America. In 1982, an effort was made to involve in this strategy other regional actors - Canada, Mexico and Venezuela - but the strategic and political conditions of the initiative posed by the United States prompted a withdrawal by these potential partners. In July of 1983, the "Initiative for the Caribbean Basin" was approved by Congress with the sole participation of the United States. In October of 1983, Grenada was invaded; the roll back strategic approach rapidly gained momentum, and with very good results.

In Central America, changes tended to be slower and US policy faced many difficulties. The strategy of low-intensity war, implemented towards Nicaragua and El Salvador, had a high political cost, specially for the executive branch. Quick results were not achieved and illegal actions, such as the "Iran-Contras" affair, did significant damage to that policy. Absence of apparent results in El Salvador also gave rise to severe criticism of the efficiency of the counter-insurgence strategy.

In the same years, US policy had to face, as never before, diplomatic resistance from Latin American countries with a clear activism: first, the Contadora Group, followed by the Group of Eight. Those efforts, oriented to reach a negotiated solution of conflicts, permanently denounced all military solutions led or supported by the United States.

Despite all such setbacks, in the first year of the current Republican administration some main objectives were reached. The Sandinistas lost general elections in Nicaragua (February 1990), an outcome that can be considered a sound victory for low-intensity war. Two months before (20 December 1989) the US military troops invaded Panama in order to protect American citizens, to capture the Chief of the Panamanian Defence Forces (accused of drug trafficking by the courts in Miami) and to re-establish democracy. This meant the self-designation of the candidate supported by the United States in the elections of May 1989. As in most recent elections in Central America, the winner was the candidate who openly received economic support from the United States during the campaign. This stratagem includes Violeta Chamorro in Nicaragua, Rafael Leonardo Callejas in Honduras and Rafael Calderon Fournier in Costa Rica. In the case of Panama, having a friendly government in power seems to be a priority if renegotiation of the Canal Treaty was the undeclared objective of the invasion.

The US intervention in Panama was of major significance in that for the first time in the past four decades, the political justification for intervention was not the containment of communism. In the absence of a communist threat, drug trafficking appeared a perfectly good cause for intervention which gained wide support inside the United States and abroad.

If we look at the consequences of these policies for the subregion, it is a fact that the risk of a military conflict in Central America is lower now than five or even one year ago. There is an on-going process of demilitarization in Nicaragua that includes a substantial reduction of troops and military expenditure. The major threats that were faced in the past years, the "Contras" and a feasible military intervention by the United States have been lifted. This means, at least theoretically, that Nicaragua is now on the path of economic recovery.

Since war and its preparation are not the main concern of Nicaragua's new government, military expenditure should decrease, perhaps significantly. A troop reduction announcement from 60,000 to 40,000 by the end of July was made by Violeta Chamorro, which could represent a saving of 10 per cent of government expenditure. Mrs Chamorro announced a future goal of troop reduction to merely 20,000 and a civilian security force such as Costa Rica's, pending negotiations with Honduras.

The cost of Nicaragua for the United States will be lower and no longer a controversial issue as it was during the low-intensity war years. If we consider that from December 1981 to February 1988 (when last disbursement of "Contra aid" was approved by the Congress) the US devoted $195 million to support the "Contras" (57 million in humanitarian aid), resources widely oriented to war-making and destruction, the same funds could now have a geometric effect on economic recovery. However, it is not likely that US aid will continue with the previous sense of urgency since Nicaragua is no longer a security priority. According to available estimations, the war against the "Contras" forced the Nicaraguan government to devote 60 per cent of its national budget to defence; per capita income fell 60 per cent during the war, and total investment dropped 75 per cent. In terms of human casualties, the number of victims, in relation to the country's total population, is 179 per cent higher than those of all wars the United States has participated in during the current century. So far, $300 million has been approved for Nicaragua, but the disbursement of these funds was postponed until May. From this package, 32 million will be distributed for the re-accommodation of the "Contras".

Nevertheless, the economic challenges for the new government are enormous. In 1989, GNP fell by -3.0 per cent for the decade. External debt was 1.8 billion in 1980, while in 1990 it amounted to 11 billion. For the same period, economic growth suffered an accumulated variation of -9.6 per cent for the decade. In addition, one of the achievements of the revolution - the increase of social expenditure - will have to be maintained if the new government wants to avoid destabilization. In this context, in order to have a lasting victory, the United States will have to make an additional economic effort to consolidate the new democracy. Otherwise, social and political problems could rise again, specially if we consider that the Sandinistas were defeated in the electoral process as a consequence of the economic situation, but they are still there and enjoy significant support from a large part of the population.

The Sandinistas' defeat was also "good news" for neighbouring governments. Honduras and Costa Rica finally had the chance to get rid of the "Contras" operating in their territories. Specially to Honduras, the defeat of the Sandinistas meant a decreasing need for a US military presence on its territory. In this new context, a process of negotiated demilitarization between Nicaragua and Honduras could take place over a period of time.

Although Honduras was not directly involved in armed conflict during these years, its economic situation is also worse now than ten years ago. The rate of growth between 1981 and 1989 was 19.8 per cent. Nevertheless, per capita GNP had an accumulated variation of -12.0 per cent between 1980 and 1989, which shows that the economy did not have the capacity to absorb the enormous immigrant flows that the country endured during the war. External debt is now US $3,260 million, US $1,872 million more than in 1979. In other words, even though Honduras was not involved in the war and did not have to pay the economic cost of militarization and war on her own territory, her economy is no better off now than ten years ago. Moreover, exchanging a US military presence for economic aid has been less than significant. Between 1980 and 1987, economic and military aid from the United States amounted to US $1,260 million.

To Costa Rica, the Sandinistas' defeat and the invasion of Panama prompted a return to its proclaimed neutral status. Although Costa Rica has not had a formal army since 1948, the national guard and police forces grew from 4,000 men to 14,000 - its highest point during the decade. This represented an increase of military expenditure in real terms that should not be underrated. Some of these expenses were covered by military and economic assistance from the United States.

In the case of Panama, the invasion caused a great shock. Different estimations after the intensive bombing over urban areas, suggest as many as 4,000 casualties. The cost of destruction was not less than $3 billion, not taking into account the impact of the economic blockade which began 26 months earlier. Since the invasion and the virtual disappearance of the defence forces, which had 14,000 regulars there is now only a 2,000-man police force, still under US command. In this scenario, the military budget has fallen drastically. Nevertheless, economic aid coming from the US has been much lower than expected. So far, a package of only US $243 million has been arranged, a figure even lower than the US $500 million retained from the US executive, as Panama's share from the Canal operation income.

In El Salvador, things have not changed very much yet. The Sandinistas' defeat and the invasion of Panama were welcomed by the government because those changes tended to isolate, at least politically, the FMLN which will probably now have more difficulty in acquiring military equipment from abroad. Nevertheless, the FMLN still has sufficient resources not to give up the armed fight. Since November's offensive, they have shown more willingness to negotiate, but this can be hardly attributed to a perceived military weakness that they could be defeated easily now or in the future.

The cost of war in El Salvador during the past years has represented more than 70,000 civilian deaths, nearly 25,000 on the military side. The country's GNP growth rate has passed from -1.7 per cent in 1979 to -1.0 per cent in 1989, with a cumulative variation between 1980 and 1989 of -6.3 per cent. The GNP per capita variation has also fallen from 1980 to 1989 by -17.4 per cent. El Salvador's external debt has increased from US $1,176 million in 1980 to US $1,825 million in 1989. Between 1980 and 1987, the United States provided US $2,793.7 million in aid to El Salvador, 27.7 per cent of which consisted of military aid, but much of the economic aid was also indirectly absorbed by the war effort.

In 1990 the war in El Salvador was still in stalemate. The FMLN's offensive of November 1989 proved that neither side had the capacity to win the war on the field. The events in Nicaragua and Panama could facilitate approval by the US Congress of more military aid to this country, in the hope of ending the war. Nevertheless, recent events have shown the existence of a different attitude: there is a strong movement inside Congress to reduce military aid to El Salvador by as much as 50 per cent, from US $85 million to US $42.5 million. The lack of control over the radical right groups and the death squadrons (which were blamed for the assassination of the Jesuit priests in the Central American University of San Salvador), as well as strong suspicions of deep corruption in the ranks of the military, have fostered this position.

What we have in Central America at the beginning of the 1990s is a subregion devastated by war - more than 300,000 deaths and almost two million refugees from a total population of 22 million. Basic needs are too great to be compensated for only by savings in military expenditure. However, nowadays the population of those countries seems to prefer personal security and survival rather than revolutionary or socialist regimes that will nver prevail over all the pressures and hostility coming from the North. Nevertheless, without real economic recovery with a reasonable distribution of income, social movements and political discontent could again provoke instability, social disruption and a new cycle of confrontation and war. In other words, in order to have a stable Central America, a new model of development and political participation (beyond "democratic elections" with all manner of foreign interference) seems to be required.

In this context the question is not so much the economic consequences of disarmament but the need for economic adjustments in order to strengthen stability and democracy and to avoid new conflicts. There is a trend for decreasing military expenditure (Nicaragua, Panama, Honduras and Costa Rica), but also a trend to maintain it at high levels and even to increase it (El Salvador and Cuba).

In Washington, we notice some signs of concern. Politicians seem to be aware of the precarious equilibrium in the area, due to the fragility of the new democracies. They are searching for collaboration in Western Europe and Japan in order to consolidate the new democracies with international economic support in a joint effort led by the United States. That may or may not work, depending on European preferences to have their own presence in the area, as has been the case since 1984.

A normalization of relations between Cuba and the United States should be easier to achieve now, since the Caribbean island is rapidly loosing strategic weight in the global dimension of the East-West conflict. Cuba is no longer a strategic threat to the United States. However, if we consider the adjustments of US policies to Central America, we can also appreciate that for the first time the United States has a chance to intensify pressure on Cuba without the risk of a serious confrontation with the Soviet Union or even with the rest of the hemisphere. Military invasion still appears as a high-cost option. Low-intensity war, which in the end proved to be successful in Nicaragua, seems to be the most likely course of action.

Global political changes favouring democracy and modernization can also lead US policy-makers to launch diplomatic initiatives with other countries of the hemisphere with the goal of exerting more pressure on Cuba. The almost immediate withdrawal of Eastern European support and the anticipated lowering of Soviet aid, although at a slow pace, could leave Cuba in a very difficult economic situation in the near future. This scenario could aggravate the internal situation while more resources were being allocated for defence. After its victories in Nicaragua and Panama, the US executive could concentrate on a low-intensity war in this one country with a better likelihood of getting the necessary funds. Political isolation, combined with a deeper economic crisis, could lead Cuba very rapidly into a most vulnerable position.

Low Intensity Conflict, Stability and Economic Recovery

A return to democracy and economic crisis were the two main features of major Latin American countries during the 1980s. With the exception of Mexico, which is unusual in its stability, the return to democracy in South America still faces great challenges. The military left power in varying circumstances and new democratic governments, without exception, have had to face one of the worst economic scenarios of their current history.

Military expenditure has decreased in most countries where the military left power, and economic crisis has limited unnecessary arms purchases. Military industries remain viable and are even growing, especially in those countries with the capacity to maintain a share in the international arms market. Inter-state conflicts tend to receive low attention and there is no government prone to reactivate old disputes when simple economic recovery seems to surpass their capacities. Moreover, relations between Latin American powers, especially between Brazil and Argentina, have reached a high point of co-operation, apparently irreversible, that includes the freezing of the development of nuclear energy projects oriented to the building up of nuclear weapons. Foreign military intervention is almost out of question and great efforts of co-operation are being made to face the great economic challenges.

It must be said that since World War II, US military assistance to Latin America has been oriented basically to counter-insurgence efforts, since Washington concluded that the communist threat was inside and not outside national boundaries. Most governments acquired sophisticated weaponry - aircraft, vessels and submarines - and developed military industries under European agreements. In Washington the prevailing approach was that Latin American countries did not need sophisticated armaments to fight internal enemies. In the last ten years, US military assistance has been concentrated in Central America and in those countries more directly involved in drug production and trafficking.

Military budgets in most countries of the area are not likely to grow in the forthcoming years, but neither will they suffer severe cuts, since national defence systems are designed to maintain subregional balances, and no foreign military attack is expected. Moreover, there is an optimistic view in some circles that changes in the global economy and correlated domestic programmes will presage a much better outlook for social and political stability. In this context, military conflicts are not very likely.

Nevertheless, there is one phenomenon creating all sorts of problems and distortion, mainly involving the Andean countries and to a lesser extent most Caribbean Basin nations: illicit drug production and trafficking. This phenomenon has created a new hemispheric agenda in terms of security. For the United States it has become the main security threat in the hemisphere. For the Andean countries, drug production and trafficking have had all sorts of consequences: serious distortions in their economies, an unprecedented climate of violence and a great threat to the stability of the State. In the case of Mexico and other countries of the region, the increasing importance of this problem for the United States has complicated its internal and external behaviour.

Although this phenomenon can hardly be inserted in the East-West conflict, it has significant implications for the re-accommodation of US strategic priorities and planning in this hemisphere. The drug crusade requires great quantities of all kinds of resources. Additionally, it can be said that the United States government - with a strong internal support for this new crusade - will make increasing co-operation in this area a condition for co-operation in other areas, especially trade and finance. This process will inevitably touch any effort to develop a hemispheric economic bloc - as envisaged in the new US initiative.

Global changes already have economic implications for most countries in Latin America, which go beyond traditional security issues. The "victory" of the United States over the Soviet Union in the East-West conflict has led to a consensus among current Latin American governments that any "non-capitalist model for growth and development" is nowadays hopeless.

After a decade of debt crisis, we notice a clear trend in the US to favour of regimes with sound economic programmes, neoliberal models and very ambitious programmes of stabilization: large reductions of the fiscal deficit, much less intervention in the economy, substantial reductions in state apparatus and export-oriented models. Nevertheless, economic instability is a real threat to social and political stability and an obstacle for consolidating democracies. Prevailing economic models tend to sacrifice employment, better distribution of income and social expenditure, while giving priority to the equilibrium of macro-economic variables, open markets for trade and investment and special support to the most dynamic sectors of the economy.

Within this context, we also find the idea that the current difficulties of the US economy leave very little space for real co-operation with Latin America, and history tells Latin Americans that US concerns towards the region are exclusively in terms of security and strategic priorities (containment of communism in the Cold War years or drug trafficking in the new era). Economic crisis in Latin America during the 1980s was never a main concern of the US government, with the exception of Mexico, an interest very much related to the foreseeable consequences of a deeper economic crisis in a neighbouring country. Additionally, there is a widespread idea that Eastern European countries are poised to absorb all the available resources in the international financing system.

The "Enterprise for the Americas" seems to be a general answer to these questions. President Bush announced (27 June) a new scheme for hemispheric relations, with the central idea of achieving, for the first time, a hemisphere of freedom and democracy. The solution for economic recovery is not aid, but trade and foreign investment. Support should be given to those countries whose economies are oriented to liberalizing trade and giving every facility to foreign investment. Reductions of US official debt - amounting US $12 billion - are to be offered to those countries working towards these goals. Preference will be given to debt-equity and nature-for-debt swaps.

The initiative includes a worldwide fund-raising effort. The first reaction of the G-7 in Houston (10-11 July 1990) was not very enthusiastic. It has yet to be seen if, after almost two centuries of the Monroe Doctrine in this hemisphere, Western European countries and Japan, will be willing to participate in the initiative or would prefer to keep their own independent areas of influence in this part of the world.

The initiative contemplates some financial resources through the IDB to support programmes of economic reform - so far US $100 million - but, as with the Caribbean Initiative, most of the results are expected to come from the inner nature of the economic programmes: free trade, foreign investment, open economies, less regulation and much lower state interference in the economy. Results in the Caribbean Basin have been far from outstanding.

After four decades of successful capitalism in the major countries of the region, at the beginning of the 1980s it was obvious that the benefits of growth and development had not reached major sectors of population.

To most Latin American countries, the situation after the "lost decade" in terms of economic growth and development is rather critical. Debt restructuring processes have been on-going with the international financial community, but still the debt service burden is rather significant, even for most successful cases such as Mexico. On the other side, the competitiveness of most countries to operate in free markets is, with very few exceptions, still very low. If foreign investment is to replace state participation in the economy, how can the enormous challenges of income distribution be tackled?

The most developed countries, Mexico and Brazil, also share the worst income distribution. In both countries, nearly 40 per cent of the population are below the minimum diet requirements for normal development. In other countries, like Colombia and Chile, it is not unusual to find one third of the population in extreme poverty. With such problems and anachronisms in most countries, public investment, and specially social expenditure, attempted to soften this situation - those were the "good days" of capitalism in Latin America. In other words, we are far from having the answers to the question: How should the new model work to attain development and well-being for the majority? In the first paragraph of the last G-7 communiqué, there is an interesting phrase: "when people are free to choose, they choose freedom. However, for large sectors of the population, at least in Latin America, this "freedom" means "freedom to starve". Grand-sounding answers to these questions would seem inappropriate.

Hemispheric Agenda for the New Era

After several decades of very low priority to Latin America, the United States is now giving major attention to the region. The main guidelines of current US policy can be summarized as follows:

1. Democracy should be the prevailing political model for all countries of the hemisphere. Moreover, democracy is a value that should prevail even above sovereignty. Democracy means free elections of civil governments. Democracy is intimately related to human rights, also a universal value;

2. Free-market economies are the logical corollary of freedom and democracy. Besides, globalization of the economy makes this option in the only possible means to survive and to achieve growth and development. State interference should be kept as low as possible;

3. In a new world of democracy and freedom with a globalized free-market-oriented economy, the main threat to hemispheric security is drug production and trafficking. This is a major common concern that deserves increasing joint effort and co-operation;

4. Environmental deterioration is also a common challenge, a supranational threat that should be tackled with a hemispheric strategy;

5. All efforts at the hemispheric level should concentrate on working towards these objectives.

From the Latin American perspective this new agenda poses several problems that can be summarized as follows:

1. Democracy as a universal value can give way to foreign intervention in internal affairs. In this scheme, at least, there is no room for a socialist Cuba. Foreign observers and external funding for electoral campaigns can serve to influence internal political processes in one or another direction, as has been the case of military assistance. Hemispheric organizations - as noticeable in the OAS's record - can also be used to intervene in internal affairs. This applies to human rights as well;

2. The drug trafficking crusade also poses delicate problems for several countries. Particularly in the Andean countries, this is not a health problem but a national security issue. States are permanently threatened by the drug lords and by the resulting violence of this business. Besides, drug trafficking delivers a significant income of hard currency not easy to replace in the current economic situation. In this context, US pressures to fight this phenomenon deeply and openly create additional problems. Giving legal authorization to US agencies to operate abroad diminishes sovereignty and has a negative effect on co-operation schemes, not to mention the possibility of US military forces in this crusade escalating to the extreme of military intervention;

3. That can also be the case for environmental concerns with special reference to the Amazonian Forest and the creation of natural reserves that can be accommodated within the scheme of debt-for-nature swaps. This area may be a priority for the United States but not necessarily for the communities that can survive only by exploiting such resources;

4. In the economic realm things are not less complicated. "Economic structural adjustment" is nowadays the current catch phrase in Latin America. In most countries levels of consumption are lower today than ten years ago. Adjustment must continue in most cases according to the "text book". However, real benefits are still far out of reach. To this lack of synchronization, the Enterprise for the Americas gives more recipes than solutions. Overcoming the economic crisis will depend once again on internal efforts, but now in a more competitive world and with an accumulated lag;

5. The lack of synchronization between current expectations and concrete results could lead to very difficult scenarios. Democracies in most countries are precarious. Political and social instability exist and can easily be aggravated if growth and distribution of wealth proceed too slowly. In those scenarios we cannot dismiss a *coup d'état* and return of the military to power. If scenarios created by drug trafficking are not corrected soon, Andean countries could enter a new decade of national crisis with deep consequences for their economies;

6. Central America is still far from reaching a stage of stability. For some analysts, recent events have given way to rapid economic recovery, since open military conflict is now very unlikely and conditions are rather suitable for strong co-operation among all governments in the subregion, with good chances of taking advantage of external economic aid. The other interpretation, not as

optimistic, stems from the fact that economic co-operation, especially from the United States, is very much below what was expected and too low in relation to what is needed for the recovery of a region that has suffered the worst economic and social crisis of its modern history. Moreover, the structural internal causes of the conflicts are still there, aggravated by almost a decade of war and economic crisis. In the Caribbean, the future of socialist Cuba is at stake.

To conciliate the US agenda for the hemisphere and Latin American priorities and concerns is not going to be an easy task. The United States is now in a better condition to conduct hemispheric policy according to its own priorities. On the other side, space for manoeuvre for Latin American countries seems rather limited. Thus no major changes are to be expected in US policy towards the region.

"Peace Dividends" of Disarmament

The United States is one of the two main actors involved in global changes and disarmament processes. In consequence, disarmament should have direct effects on the US economy. However, several facts tend to neutralize most "peace dividends". On one side, disarmament schemes do not seem to result in significant savings, at least not in the short term. Destruction of chemical weapons, for example, demands fresh money in considerable amounts to reach this aim. Reconversion of military industries into civil industries seems to face many different sorts of problems. Reconversion, where possible, takes time and also requires new investment. Additionally, military expenditure cuts are not very significant yet and, according to governmental programmes, it will take years before substantial reductions are reached.

On the other side, the United States is entering this process when its economy faces historical deficits, fiscal and commercial, with the Gulf War probably neutralizing any benefits already gained. Besides, a rapid decrease of military production means unemployment and contributes to a recession, at least in the short term.

In this context, to talk about "peace dividends" from disarmament in this hemisphere can be no more than an illusion. In Central America, for example, co-operation and economic aid are essential preconditions to strengthen the new democracies. However, US officials have already stated that there are no resources for these purposes. In other words, new funds for co-operation with Latin America are at this moment out of the question. In the most recent US initiative, the Enterprise for the Americas, it is explicitly stated that the era of aid has passed; trade and open markets will bring new solutions. If economic recession comes in the short term in the United States, Latin American exports will again be in trouble and debt service will increase in proportion to the increase in interest rates. A major military solution to the crisis in the Persian Gulf is likely to cause serious damage to the US economy with unforeseeable effects in Latin America.

If disarmament is a sustainable trend there will be a period of transition when all arms producers will try to allocate their production in Third World countries, with lower prices and better conditions of payment. This is already a current fact and Latin America is not the exception. "Peace dividends" of disarmament for Third World countries can mean a cheaper market for new acquisitions. Again, the Middle East can become the new opportunity for arms dealers. Additionally, we have to consider the absence of any agreement to ban the conventional arms trade - except in the case of political decisions of governments, for governmental sales - leaving considerable space for "free traders", in many cases with non-official governmental backing.

The future of the economies of Latin America is very much related to the evolution of the US economy. In its current state, despite the real achievements in disarmament already reached, no "peace dividends" are to be expected for the Latin American region.[1]

---

1   Most figures come from CLEE's data bank which includes economic reports from CEPAL, the World Bank and other economic and financial sources.

Chapter 10

Responses

First Response

Ednan Agaev

As disarmament turns into a fact of life and as both the reduction and elimination of armaments take effect, a question arises about the economic consequences of this process. It goes without saying that the funds released in the future as a result of disarmament may stimulate economic development and be used for helping developing countries. But at present practical disarmament itself requires additional funds. This concerns the very processes of weapons elimination, ensuring verification over the implementation of obligations and also the need for conversion and redirection of branches of industry participating in the production of weapons to be reduced or eliminated. As a result the so-called "peace dividend" in essence becomes rather meagre, thus making it necessary to introduce certain realistic adjustments to the formula "disarmament for development".

Evidently, it will be necessary to find additional financial resources even before their part is released as a result of disarmament for the solution of a whole number of rather serious issues confronting the countries on the road to disarmament. In other words, we are not speaking about reducing expenditures to date, but rather about their growth. Naturally, expenditures, inevitable in the process of weapons elimination and verification, considerable as they are, cannot be compared with military costs. It is also evident that they will not be constant since they are limited in time. Nevertheless, it would be naive to expect that immediately after disarmament there would come "an epoch of prosperity" which can bring "a golden shower" of investment for the purposes of development.

The reality also is that until now only the so-called developed countries have been involved in the processes of disarmament. At the same time the arms race in the Third World countries is not decelerating but on the contrary becoming more intensive. A whole number of countries, while paying lip-service to disarmament and persistently pushing for the formula "disarmament for development", are not even considering the practical implementation of a comprehensive development strategy. They spend enormous amounts of money on purchasing weapons and on their production, as well as on nuclear energy development programmes, the scales of which often surpass the limits of reasonable sufficiency in the field of peaceful uses of nuclear energy. Perhaps it would be wiser for this category of states not to wait for the developed countries to solve their problems related to arms reduction and thus release the means for providing aid, but rather to start now attacking the tasks of socio-economic development while simultaneously cutting their own military expenditures. The necessity of such measures is also dictated by enormous social problems in Third World countries, including those which are actively investing funds to enhance their military potentials.

There is yet another problem relating to arms reduction prospects in East-West relations on the one hand, and to the simultaneous continuation of the arms race the Third World countries on the other. Thus, forthcoming agreements on conventional armaments in Europe create the problem for European states of eliminating a significant quantity of armaments. It cannot be ruled out that attempts will be made to address this problem in the most "economically simple" way - that is, to export armaments that are subject to reduction to Third World countries. Already the world armaments market is getting "overheated", with exporting nations fiercely competing and offering their customers sophisticated types of armaments, even supplies of the most dangerous and destructive types of weaponry. This trend may become stronger in the future unless a solution is found to the question of economic compensation for arms producers.

One may predict that in future, even in the foreseeable future, military production will enter a period of crisis resulting from an inevitable decline in arms procurements by governments. Such a crisis is comparable to that of the so-called traditional industries such as the steel industry, for example, which laid its grip on industrialized nations in the 1970s. Many industries disappeared and many were converted. In the process, difficult social problems were concurrently addressed. From the experience of conversion in the 1970s we remember that governments provided considerable support to industries that had been struck by the crisis. Now governments will be required to make similar efforts especially because, for many years, they were the ones to stimulate active defence production. It can be foreseen that conversion of a large number of enterprises and concerns will require a considerable amount of investment over a long period of time.

To summarize the above-mentioned problems, the conclusion is that "peace dividends" should only be regarded as viable in the long term. At present, however, there is a need to have realistic perceptions of the situation and to face the fact that the initial stage the disarmament process will require additional funds and intensive effort to address the socio-economic problems caused by conversion. In addition, it is also essential gradually to eradicate demagogical contentions related to disarmament and development problems, which are being used by certain countries as a cover-up for their own unattractive positions on both disarmament and development.

Second Response

Chin Kin Wah

The assumptions behind the East-West disarmament process are not wholly applicable to the Southeast Asian security environment where the arms build-up, especially after the American withdrawal from continental Southeast Asia in 1975, has been influenced more by East-East (i.e. conflict within the Communist bloc) rather than East-West conflict. Many unresolved East-East cold war issues in Northeast and Southeast Asia have also meant that the post-cold war confidence-building processes and mechanism in Europe have yet to find parallels in the wider Asia-Pacific region.

The so-called "peace dividend" generated by East-West détente is also less apparent in Southeast Asia. Nor is the economic challenge of the "conversion issue" posed by the East-West disarmament process necessarily felt in the same way in Southeast Asia, where arms procurement and defence industrialization are being pursued in varying degrees by the regional states.

The less developed states of the region do not necessarily reap the peace dividend of Super Power détente. If the peace process has meant a lessening of US strategic interest in the Philippine bases (of course, conflict elsewhere may once again underline the importance to America of these bases), then the prospect of a thinning out of the American presence has actually exerted new economic pressures on the Philippines whose capacity for national defence (without American protection) is woefully inadequate given its low level of armaments, extensive coastline, large exclusive economic zone and its myriad security problems. On top of all that, it has a government which, having survived six coup attempts since coming to power in 1987, is understandably suspicious of sections of the military.

In continental Southeast Asia, we find that a combination of internal Soviet economic problems and the East-West peace process itself have led to an attenuation of Soviet interest in having a military presence in Vietnam. This however creates an added economic challenge to Vietnam which continues to have a security problem in Cambodia (posed by the Khmer Rouge) that in turn poses complications in the Sino-Vietnamese relationship. But even a thawing out of the Sino-Vietnamese relationship may not necessarily suggest a quick solution to the security problem posed by the Khmer Rouge - which, among other factors, is a major obstacle to the Cambodian peace process. Indeed, China's arms transfers to the Khmer Rouge may ironically lead to an increasing inability on China's part to influence its regional ally - producing in effect a situation in which "the tail wags the dog".

For the newly industrializing countries of the region which are looking *inter alia* towards defence industrialization, the East-West disarmament process offers economic opportunities of a different order. It has been observed for example, that some ASEAN countries have acquired the technology (through compensatory trade agreements) during the early phase of their defence industrialization by taking advantage of adverse market conditions encountered by major arms exporters. Today the economic challenge is posed by the need to find new market opportunities for their products, the need for industrial complementation to reduce competition, and diversification (as in the case of Singapore's aerospace industry) into civilian sectors.

These brief observations point to the need for a closer look at developments and trends within regions even as we reflect on broad changes affecting the international system as a whole.

Third Response

Michael D. Intriligator

There has been a *change in the arms race* in recent years, which will probably accelerate in the future. The "old" arms race, involving competition between the East and West, especially between the Soviet Union and the United States, has been replaced by a new set of arms races in the Third World, among medium and smaller powers in Asia, the Middle East, Africa, and Central and South America. The East-West arms race has been characterized by the use of high technology, and it has resulted in a stabilizing regime of mutual deterrence. By contrast, the new arms races in the Third World are characterized by the use of medium and low technology, and they result in severe instabilities that could lead to regional conflicts or wars.[1] The new arms races and the resulting instabilities are aggravated by three factors. First is the presence in the Third World of on-going international and civil wars, subnational liberation fronts and conflicts of ideology. Second is the fact of disarmament in the East and West, both because each side is, as a result, less able to control client states in the Third World and because the attempts to keep military production lines going, to recoup investments made in weapons plants and to earn foreign exchange will lead to massive arms sales by both East and West to the Third World. Third is the example set by the East and West which have, for decades, sought security through military expenditures. As a result, the Third World sees weapons acquisition as a means to security, including the acquisition of conventional capabilities, chemical weapons and even nuclear weapons.

It is also important to note the *flaws in the UN view on this issue.* The UN view on disarmament and development makes three assumptions, all of which are questionable. First, it assumes that there will be disarmament in both East and West but, while there have been some reductions, armaments have been continuing to grow. Second, it assumes that disarmament will release resources for use elsewhere (the "peace dividend"), but disarmament will lead to severe problems of conversion,

---

[1]   For a further discussion of the new arms races see Michael D. Intriligator and Dagobert L. Brito, "A Possible Future for the Arms Race" *in* N.P. Gleditsch and O. Njolstad (eds.), *Arms Races: Technological and Political Dynamics*, London, Sage Publishers.

including unemployment of factors specialized in the production of military goods. It will require resources in order to retrain workers, build new capital and, in general, to train or build factors which can produce non-defence goods and services. Third, it assumes that the resources released by disarmament could be used to support economic development in the Third World. But the resources are few, if any, and it is not clear that they will be channelled into the Third World, as opposed to national development or investments in the East or West. Furthermore, the Third World is itself engaged in various arms races that will themselves absorb resources.

Fourth Response

Jun Nishikawa

The East-West rivalry which has characterized the post-war world seems to be approaching an end, with the adoption of a "perestroika" policy by the Gorbachev administration in USSR and with the successive US-USSR summit meetings between 1985-90. Recent political changes in East Europe seem to testify to the acceleration of the formation of a more interdependent and more horizontal world order. The disarmament process between the East and West is now fully under way.

What will be the consequences of this East-West disarmament process on third parties, in particular developing countries? Before reflecting on this question, we have to think about the reasons which have led the Super Powers, in spite of the existence of a "military-industry complex" on both sides, to control their "equilibrium of fear" and even disarm their strategic and intermediate nuclear arsenals. One is the rise of public opinion in the world, particularly in Europe, against the deployment of nuclear forces in this region, and the more rationalistic judgement of Super Power leaders to accept world opinion which has been expressed in UN and other forums. However, the major reason seems to be the decline of the Super Powers' economic positions. Large US fiscal and trade deficits and the USSR's economic stagnation in the 1980s were crucial to forcing both leaders to decide to suspend an endless arms race, whose costs have become more and more detrimental to their respective economies.

The decline of both economies was accelerated by the rise of Japan, the NICs and other industrializing economies on the world scene. It is understandable in a sense that this industrialization in developing countries has been accompanied by the growth of armament industries. Today, China, Brazil, Argentina, Israel, Egypt and North Korea are emerging as major producers and exporters of arms and munitions in the Third World. It is true that, with growing debt problems, these developing countries have made efforts to export arms in order to earn foreign exchange. From 1976 to 1986 (both five-year averages), the exports of major weapons from developing countries to the world market rose from US \$278 million to \$2,634 million (in constant 1985 US \$). Except for China, the major Third World producers and exporters produce sophisticated modern arms under licence from developed countries and transnational corporations (or other developing countries).

Argentina, Brazil, Egypt and South Korea produce helicopters and submarines; Brazil and South Korea, towed howitzers; Nigeria, Chile, Thailand and Pakistan, trainers; Egypt, mobile SAM systems, anti-tank missiles and MBTs; India, helicopters, anti-tank missiles, submarines, fighters, MBTs and air-to-air SSMs; North Korea, MICVs, MBTs and SSMs; Taiwan missile launchers, MBTs and frigates (SIPRI Yearbook 1989).

We see that trainers, fighters, helicopters, submarines, frigates, tanks, missiles and missile-launchers are more and more produced locally and exported to other parts of the world, including developed countries (France has bought trainers from Brazil; Spain has bought trainers from Chile; Turkey has bought fighters from Egypt, etc.).

However, with the atmosphere of détente in the world, as well as the end of several major wars in the Third World (the Iran-Iraq war, and the Soviet withdrawal from Afghanistan, in particular), we observe a depression in the armament industry in the world, not excluding the Third World.

Actually, we may envisage several scenarios for the future of the growing arms industry in the Third World.

First, in combination with government, the arms industry may try to create and develop a market for conventional arms. However, since Third World governments, unlike those of the Super Powers, still have little ability to create regional tensions and conflicts for the sake of the military-industrial complex, and since the weight of the arms industry in developing countries has not been very great, it is unlikely that regional conflicts will be created and intensified for the cynical purpose of promoting the interests of arms production and exports.

Second, if world opinion in favour of lasting peace becomes stronger, the arms industry in the developing countries will face the problem of conversion to civil industries. This is the destiny that the East European arms industries are actually facing. However, since these arms industries produce weapons mostly under licences from developed countries and TNCs, and since they lack their own R&D and technological base, they will face difficult problems with conversion.

Is there any scenario which can integrate these arms industries for the peaceful, overall benefit of the developing countries? Several factors would be necessary to realize this scenario.

First, it would be necessary, following the partial nuclear disarmament of the Super Powers, to promote overall nuclear disarmament, as well as reductions in conventional arms on a worldwide scale.

Second, if savings on military expenditures, which were reduced by disarmament, were directed towards the overall development process in the developing countries, they might reduce the possibility of both regional and internal conflicts.

Third, technical co-operation from international organizations and the developed countries could be vital in achieving the conversion from arms to civilian industries in developing countries. UNIDIR could take the initiative to study the possibility of this conversion in each country, and create forums for information exchanges to promote civilian conversion. Some defence industries will continue to operate; however, the possibility of arms exports might be greatly reduced in the context of the peaceful atmosphere promoted by two worldwide efforts mentioned above.

In conclusion, the East-West disarmament process, together with an atmosphere of détente on a worldwide scale, have caused a depression in the rising arms industry in the Third World. It is necessary, however, to promote further disarmament in the area of conventional weapons and to transfer the resources thus liberated to productive fields. This will also accelerate peaceful development, which is crucial to the welfare of the majority of people, as war can destroy in one night all past development efforts. The conversion of arms industries both in the developed and the developing world should be on the agenda of the international community. Concerned governments, industries and scientists must co-operate in order to bring about this conversion.

Part 4

Economic Implications of a Chemical Weapons Convention

Chapter 11

Economic Incidences of a Convention on the Elimination of Chemical Weapons

Herbert Beck[1]

Since 1968-69 the United Nations Conference on Disarmament has been engaged in negotiations for a comprehensive disarmament agreement in the field of chemical weapons. After more than 20 years an agreement built upon the three principles of comprehensiveness, universality and verifiability has received general consensus.

As this general political consensus nears agreement, no less important questions need to be raised. For example, how much will it cost and who will pay for it?

The purpose of this paper is to examine certain economic consequences which can be identified at this stage through a detailed cost analysis will not be possible for some time. The aim of this article should rather be to contribute to an introductory debate.[2]

In my view two main economic effects can be recognized with respect to the projected Chemical Weapons Convention:

- Firstly, direct consequences of the treaty in terms of setting up appropriate organizations and operating costs for a verification regime; and
- Secondly, indirect effects that have to do with the actual working of such a regime.

The Direct Costs of the CW Regime

Before turning to questions concerning the cost aspects of the projected convention, it seems necessary to ask which areas will be regulated by the CW Convention.

The Scope of the Projected CW Convention

In contrast to the 1925 Geneva Protocol, which was essentially a "no-first-use" treaty, the CW convention aims at prohibiting production and possession of any toxic substance which was not specifically intended for some non-CW purpose. The aim of

---

[1] Please note that this article represents only the opinion of the author.

[2] Economic aspects of the CW Convention have attracted surprisingly little attention. However many facts necessary for a reliable estimation are still subject to debate. Most attempts to evaluate these factors were made in the context of the CD negotiations themselves. For a first attempt of a model calculation, see Beck, H., "Verifying the Projected Chemical Weapons Convention: A Cost Analysis", *AFES-Report*, No.13, 1988.

creating a universal and comprehensive treaty made it necessary to prohibit production and to verify this prohibition reliably. One of the most interesting - but also most difficult - features of the CW convention is the fact that many chemicals used for entirely civilian purposes share precursors which are also pre-products of chemical warfare agents. Therefore the striking characteristic of the CW convention is - in contrast to almost any other industrial field - the verification of non-production of chemical weapons by the civilian chemical industry.

The best way to understand this is to look into the draft treaty that is the text of the convention on which consensus has more or less been reached in the Geneva CD negotiations. Article I of the projected convention states that each State Party undertakes not to develop, produce, otherwise acquire, stockpile or retain chemical weapons, or transfer, directly or indirectly, to anyone (para 1) or assist, encourage or induce, in any way, anyone to engage in activities prohibited to parties under the convention (para 2).[3] Further, each State Party undertakes not to use chemical weapons (para 3), nor to prepare the use of CW (para 4). Para 5 provides that all chemical weapons should be destroyed and all chemical weapons production facilities should be destroyed (or dismantled) (para 6). The term chemical weapons applies to chemical substances which hold a certain toxicity and are intended for purposes prohibited by the convention (Article II, para 1). Purposes not prohibited by the convention are industrial, agricultural, research, medical or other peaceful purposes, domestic law enforcement purposes and military purposes not connected with the use of chemical weapons, i.e. protective measures (para 3). This "general purpose criterion", although complicated in its wording, is necessary in order to include all substances which possess a dual capability, i.e. chemical weapons or their precursors on the one hand and important compounds for civilian production on the other. The transformation of this general statement into practice is achieved by so-called schedules of compounds. All chemicals (or group of chemicals) relevant to chemical warfare are listed in these schedules according to their military importance and economic significance. Schedule 1 comprises "supertoxic lethal chemicals", i.e. in the first place the present chemical warfare agents. Schedule 2 contains precursors of Schedule 1 agents. Schedule 3 includes those compounds which might be used or were used as chemical warfare agents but play such an important role in the commercial field (in terms of function and production size) that they can neither be prohibited nor strictly verified.

With regards to control this means firstly that all chemical weapons shall be destroyed within 10 years (Articles IV, para 5 and 6); secondly that all chemical weapons production facilities shall be closed and destroyed/dismantled (Article V, para 8); thirdly, that all facilities that produce a limited amount of chemical agents for protective purposes (up to one ton/annum) shall be verified (Article II, para 3b); and fourthly, that enterprises of the civilian chemical industry which produce or process

---

[3]   Conference on Disarmament, Document CD/961, 11 February 1990.

toxic chemicals and their precursors for purposes not prohibited by the convention shall be subject to controls under the verification regime (Article II, para 3b).

In order to fulfil these tasks an International Agency is to be established. Within this agency, a Consultative Committee shall be responsible for the functioning of the convention. However, it shall delegate the actual implementation of duties to an Executive Council. This Executive Council shall supervise the Inspectorate and shall serve as the point of reference for all State Parties. Finally, a technical secretariat is charged with the task of carrying out the inspections (Article VIII).

Additionally, each State Party is obliged to adopt any measures to implement the convention, particularly to establish or designate a National Authority (Article VII).

One of those measures to be adopted by the State Parties will be legislation which obliges chemical enterprises falling under the provisions of the treaty to accept inspections and to submit production data.

Cost Structure

Looking at the structure of the projected convention from an economic perspective, one has to distinguish various factors deriving from the obligations laid down in the treaty.

Firstly, institutional arrangements have to be found to fulfil the tasks required for by the treaty. An International Agency has to be set up, buildings found, laboratory facilities provided, etc. National agencies have to be established according to the rules.

Secondly, all those countries possessing CW are obliged to destroy their stocks. Besides the political and technical problems,[4] this poses a heavy economic burden on CW possessing countries. Several hundred millions US dollars are and will be spent by the two Super-powers in order to fulfil this obligation.[5]

Thirdly, genuine costs in connection with *verification* will be incurred on three different levels:

1. The *International Agency* carrying out the actual verification, employing inspectors, applying control instruments etc.
2. *National Agencies* serving as linkages between the national chemical industry and the international agency.
3. The national *chemical industry* as far as it falls under the provisions of the convention.

However these costs, which might be termed *actual verification costs*, are only those which incur directly from the verification process. On the level of the chemical

---

[4]   Public protest (as the example of Chapayevsk shows) and technical considerations, such as the decision by the US Government to build destruction facilities near the location where CW are stockpiled, are also consequences which have to be recognized in economic terms.

[5]   The US Government spends between US $100 and 400 million per year for its demilitarization programme. See in this context also the article of Ron Sutherland in this volume.

industry, additional (indirect) costs might be caused by the fact that a free market situation will be changed into a case of state or international regulation, so-called *regulation costs*.

But before going more profoundly into the area of regulation costs, it is useful to distinguish parameters which shape the actual level of costs of the convention.

On the one hand the time factor plays an important role. A relatively short *preparatory phase* - in which the verification regime shall be brought to the point of full-scale functioning - is followed by the *destruction phase* (lasting approximately 10 years) in which all warfare agents, production and stockpile facilities will be destroyed. This period of time will be the most intense in terms of workload and consequently the most expensive.[6] After that the (in its temporal dimension) unlimited *control phase* has to deal primarily with the verification of non-production of chemical weapons.

A second factor shaping the verification costs is the *control intensity* of the verification regime. In this context it is important to determine on which concept the verification process is based. One can define verification as the establishment of the truth or correctness (of something) by examination or demonstration. The political question of compliance with the treaty is translated into technical questions which then are tried to be answered by technical methods ("Do the data actually found coincide with what was expected?"). Whether the technical evaluation re-translated into the political sphere is considered as satisfactory is again a political assessment based on existing security standards. However, the need on the inspecting party's side to know as much as possible is limited by the need for confidentiality when the inspecting party becomes the inspected one. Therefore several mechanisms - particularly in the case of the chemical industry - were proposed in order to protect the legitimate rights of companies competing on the world chemical markets. In practical terms the most important is to classify chemicals according to their commercial importance. As has been said before, those chemical companies producing e.g. Schedule 3 chemicals are normally only obliged to submit certain production figures to the national and/or international agency. Besides this routine inspection approach, challenge inspection poses a permanent threat to the commercial secrecy interests of an enterprise. In this case the principle of "negative proof" is of utmost importance. Negative proof means that an inspection of a chemical company should generally not lead to a "positive" identification of the produced compounds, but only to the information that no chemicals prohibited by the treaty or those which were not notified to the international agency are present. If doubts occur further measures might lead in the last instance to the actual analysis of the chemical compound.

---

[6]   In this context one has to take into account bilateral agreements concerning unilateral destruction of CW before the actual coming into force of the convention. The understanding of the USSR and the United States to reduce their current CW stocks independent of the Geneva negotiations does not curtail the actual destruction costs but might significantly lower the verification costs, depending on how many stocks had been destroyed by the time the convention comes into force.

Besides the number of facilities and companies which have to be controlled, the frequency of visits is one of the decisive cost factors. Sites where warfare agents are destroyed will probably be monitored permanently, whereas closed former production facilities will be visited only three or four times a year in order to verify that they have not been re-opened. A complementary measure to control declared sites (those which have been reported to the international agency as falling under the provisions of the treaty) are on-challenge inspections. Theoretically speaking every location where chemical agents *could* be produced might be subject to on-challenge inspections. To secure personal rights the principle of negative proof becomes even more important. The difficult task of the negotiators in Geneva consists in balancing the deterrence function of intensive verification against reasonable, cost-effective assurance. Closely related to questions of frequency and control intensity are technical decisions such as how many inspectors should form an inspection team, how extensive their inspection schedule should be, how fast the information gathered during the inspection should be available at the international verification headquarters, and so on. Although several ideas have been brought forward it is not yet certain how intense the control will be. Some sort of synergetic effects from other arms control negotiations could occur.

At the moment it seems that the verification regime will depend heavily on inspectors carrying out on-site inspections and being assisted by instrumentation whenever possible. Therefore labour costs should be the most important cost factor on all three levels (international agency, national agencies, chemical industry). The workload itself lies very much on the shoulders of the international agency, whereas the national counterparts have more co-ordinating functions. In the matter of direct costs, the chemical industry is hardly affected.

The Indirect Costs of the CW Regimes

The effects of the projected CW Convention are not limited to the actual economic costs described above. The chemical industry in particular is affected by consequences that derive from legislation itself. I will call these *regulation* or *indirect costs*.

What is meant by the notion of indirect costs? What are the ideas underlying this concept?

The initial idea is that market forces are best suited to shape the economic relations between individuals. However, political aims and considerations (in form of legislation) are constantly intervening into the market sphere for (generally) honourable reasons. This is also the case with the CW Convention. In order to reach a status where all chemical weapons are banned from the entire world, measures have to be taken to ensure this - knowing that short supply might cause increased demand and higher profitability. Because of the fact that chemical weapons and commercially-used compounds can often only be distinguished by (legal) definition, the chemical industry plays an important role in shaping a convention which is constantly in tension between political aims and economic interests.

Theoretical Foundations of the Cost Analysis of Legal Regulations

Since, as Dicke and Hartung stress,[7] a number of different notions exist as to what costs are in economic terms, it seems indispensable to differentiate between internal and external costs. The notion of transaction costs also plays a central role in the relationship between the economy and legislation.

Internal and External Costs

> In terms of allocation theory external costs are all costs of an economic activity (consumption or production of a good) which are not borne by the consumer, but by a third party.[8]

Thus, for example, costs of environmental pollution are not normally incurred by the polluter, but by many others who are not involved and who have to pay in the form of a prejudiced quality of life.

In the case of legislation, the notion of external costs is totally different. The producer, in this case the law giver, generally externalizes all his costs, because at the end of the day the citizen has to pay the costs of governmental activities. Internal costs in this sense are only those incurred through executing the laws, thus in administration. Internal costs differ from all others incurred outside the state sector and which can therefore be called the external costs of the legislation.

Legal Order and Transaction Costs

The basis of all management is the exchange of rare goods:

> Each transaction is connected with economic costs, consequently with the consumption of scarce resources: the party to a contract (search costs), alternative options must be reconsidered *vis-à-vis* profitability, information about the qualities of the subject matter of the contract as well as the reliability of the contracting party must be gathered (information costs) and the precise conditions have to be negotiated (negotiating costs) ... . If feasible transactions from which all parties would benefit do not come about, it might be due to such transaction costs.[9]

Legal intervention in the freedom of contract (at least in market economies) is justified by the argument that the state lowers transaction costs. It ensures, for example, that negotiations between a producer of external effects and parties having suffered damage come to an optimal solution. In the case of the Chemical Weapons convention the opportunity to produce chemical warfare agents would be an external

---

[7]   Dicke, H. & Hartung, H.: Externe Kosten von Rechtsvorschriften - Möglichkeiten und Grenzen der ökonomischen Gesetzesanalyse. Tübingen, 1986, p.9.

[8]   Ibid. p.9.

[9]   Ibid. p.11.

effect of the production of industrial chemicals. State intervention is based upon the assumption that it can assess the reaction correctly and that the State behaves as a maximizer of welfare. This statement is frequently questionable, often because a legal regulation cannot differentiate very closely. With respect to the long duration of the negotiations for a Chemical Weapons convention, this aspect is reflected by the question as to what chemical weapons precisely are and to what extent the freedom of action of economic subjects should be limited by the treaty. To date - apart from the actual warfare agents - it is not totally certain which compounds will be attached to which schedule.[10] The chemical industry tries - quite understandably from its point of view - to discourage regulation as much as possible. But if regulation is unavoidable, it should be extremely precise in order to avoid uncertainty. Increased transaction costs also incur if, for example, legal or illegal detours are taken in order to avoid laws or if a black market is being built up, in which case information procurement is much more expensive. On the level of nation states, one speaks in this context of false regulatory policies, of "state failure". Less, more precise or no regulation at all might often be more efficient and certainly cheaper. This attempt to assess external costs shall be exemplified by the Chemical Weapons Convention.

Methodology of Cost Analysis

Mechanisms of Cost Causation

For the analysis of cost causation one can as a matter of principle distinguish between two levels: the effects on the individual enterprise concerned and the effects on the national economy as a whole.

On the level of enterprise this means that - in terms of business - costs can be defined as *consumption of real resources*. They are performances which an enterprise has to make without the realizable performances arising on the market. They include the existing costs caused by a new law.

On the national economy level the effects of laws can be understood in terms of "welfare losses", i.e. *non-optimal allocation of existing resources* (for interference in the market mechanisms), whereby only additional costs which exceed the transfer sum are of any relevance.

---

[10]   Another feature of this aspect is whether the chemicals subject to systematic verification measures had to be identified specifically and individually, or whether whole families of chemicals should instead be specified - in the interest of closing loopholes. The West European chemical industry federation (CEFIC) favoured the first option, following a strategy which Brickman, Jasanoff & Illgen called an "arms length relationship" between industrialists and bureaucracy. (See Brickman, R., Jasanoff, S. & Illgen, Th.: *Controlling Chemicals. The Politics of Regulation in Europe and the United States.* Ithaca and London, 1985, 218 pp.

Finally, a macro-economic analysis has to answer the question whether *chances for economic growth* have been impaired. If an enterprise abstains from activities because of a law, costs incur.

Registration on the Business Level

Particularly relevant are those cases where laws have little or no effect on factor deployment which consequently cannot flow into the cost centre accounting. Dicke/Hartung suggest disclosing those costs by comparative calculation of net returns, collating the real incurring costs with those of a hypothetical enterprise which does not fall under the new legislation.

> The difference, i.e. the lost profits due to higher capital costs, is a measure of the legal costs for an enterprise.[11]

In the case of the Chemical Weapons Convention the costs for the chemical industry can be estimated to be rather low. The labour costs in an enterprise as large as BASF will not exceed two fully employed clerks plus staff. The effects on the profitability, as mentioned above, should be small if at all traceable. The cost factor should be inversely proportional with the size of the company, i.e. smaller factories will be charged relatively more than larger ones. On the other hand it seems plausible that in general a smaller-sized factory will have a smaller variety of products and will therefore be controlled less. The possibility of specialized enterprises should not be neglected either. At the Government-Industry Conference Against Chemical Weapons (GICCW) held in Canberra in 1989, industry representatives of industrialized countries stated that their existing accountancy and record-keeping practices would easily satisfy the data-requirements of the CW regime. "The chemical industry in industrialized countries has for a long time learned to account for every kilo of its production", said a French spokesman.[12] However this might not be true for developing countries, so that in several cases international assistance might be needed.[13]

The limitations of pure business analysis are based primarily on two facts: firstly, business accounting collates only primary and not secondary costs, such as costs incurred outside the enterprise. Secondly, one cannot assume that costs caused by legislation remain entirely within the enterprise. On the contrary, it is probable that at least a share of the costs will be shifted onto prices and therefore affect the whole national economy.

---

[11] Dicke & Hartung, p.24.
[12] Michel Peslin (UIC), statement in the Industry Forum, 20 September 89, GICCW/INFO/27.
[13] Ambassador N. Elaraby (Egypt), GICCW/WSI/7, para 4 and Ter Haar (NL), GICCW/WSI/3, para 26. Sweden emphasized in this context that such assistance might bring additional benefits for environmental and labour protection in the countries with a weaker national legislative framework.

Registration on the National Economy Level

An interesting approach for evaluating macro-economic effects is provided by investigating tax legislation. From the entrepreneurial standpoint taxes do not differ from other costs; they merely represent a transfer of resources from the private sector to the state.

Those costs which increase the loss of purchasing power in the private sector are important.

Recktenwald distinguishes the following additional burdens:[14]

1. An *evasion burden* is incurred when economic activities are shifted legally or illegally from the regulated into a non- or less-regulated area, for instance abroad, in future consumption or the shadow economy. In the case of the Chemical Weapons Convention this point only becomes relevant if the production of a compound is prohibited - if it is assigned to Schedule 1. In all other cases its production is controlled but no "evasion" is necessary.
2. The *excess burden* represents the loss of welfare due to a deteriorated supply of goods, i.e. the amount of money a regulated enterprise would be ready to pay in order to avoid falling under the regulation. Looking at the schedules being discussed at the Conference on Disarmament, it is not easy to imagine what sort of a regulation measure would necessarily lead to a deteriorated supply of goods. What was mentioned above in (1) also applies here: to create excess burden, chemicals must be prohibited.
3. *Bureaucracy costs* in the true sense of the word, i.e. consequential costs due to controls and molestation. These costs are recordable on the business level.
4. *Levying costs* are costs which accrue by registration and enforcement of legislation. Included are also court fees in the case of legal disputes. The more often review conferences in which a redistribution of Schedule 1 and 2 chemicals take place, the higher the levying costs will be. This is because it makes a difference whether a company's products fall into Schedule 2 or 3.
5. *Efficiency losses* occur if, by means of legislation, deficient regulatory policy has been pursued, whose goals would have been better achieved by different means.

The bureaucracy costs, as mentioned above, have already been submerged into the business accounting process. The levying costs are part of the "internal costs" and the efficiency losses will be discussed later within the aspect of dynamic analysis. Thus we can concentrate for the moment on the excess burden. A welfare theoretical

---

[14] Recktenwald, Horst C.: "Neue Analytik der Steuerwirkungen - Ein Konzept für vernachlässigte Forschung". *Wirtschaftswissenschaftliches Studium*, 1984, Vol.13. pp.393-400.

approach can be valid for all laws which lead to welfare losses, due to the change of relative prices.

> The essential problem of a welfare theoretical registration of legal costs is to distinguish that part of the costs of the actual excess burden, representing a welfare loss not only for individual economic actors but for the economy as a whole, from that part which represents only a transfer".[15]

The beneficiary must be identified and the value of the implicit transfers which he receives must be subtracted from the charge in order to discover the excess burden. The question of the amount of money an enterprise would be willing to spend to evade certain services it otherwise would have to render depends primarily on its elasticity of supply. At this point business and welfare theoretical considerations meet: the collective charge of enterprises results from the sum of bureaucratic costs, collected in the business, and the excess burden. The overall economic charge is of interest only for the excess burden. Dicke/Hartung stress in this context that by discussing these questions no statement is made concerning the quality of the services claimed. In other words, it is not certain whether the services are necessary nor whether the state might have reached its goals in a cheaper way.

> Thus it is supposed implicitly that the services claimed would have a positive welfare effect which corresponds justly with the operating costs, respectively the paid taxes.[16]

One difficulty is that laws which constitute obligations *vis-à-vis* third parties (for example labour or social legislation) cannot generally be exactly quantified. Another point to be mentioned is the question of cost shifting: if an enterprise is at any time able to forward its excess burden then no excess charge incurs to the company itself. However, Dicke/Hartung stress:

> With cost shifting the overall economic welfare loss does not disappear at all; it will be shifted likewise ... . So, for example, after a shift of legal costs onto the employees by means of wage reduction, the elasticity of supply of the primary charged enterprise is no longer relevant for calculating the excess burden, but the wage elasticity of labour supply. For a theoretically complete registration of the excess burden, it would be necessary to know the elasticities of all directly involved markets as well as the amount of all shifting processes.[17]

In case this is impossible, one has to be reminded that the inclusion of only those enterprises directly concerned can merely represent a first approximation. Applying these considerations to the Chemical Weapons Convention, one first has to ask what is the motive for buying oneself exemption from the regulations. As mentioned above

---

[15]   Dicke & Hartung, op.cit., p.35.
[16]   Dicke & Hartung, op.cit., p.36.
[17]   Ibid. p.37.

these concern the classification of the chemical compounds whether their production is *prohibited* by the convention or not. A further point connected with this question is whether and to what extent competing companies are affected and, thirdly, how good the chances are of shifting incurred costs. If one examines Schedule 1 of the rolling text, only pinacolyl alchohol possesses a limited relevance as a lubricant.[18] All other compounds either have no use (the genuine gases) or can easily be substituted by (harmless) compounds in their civilian field of application. A good example is the substitution of alkylphosphonyldifluoride by dichloride. The more limited the economic relevance of a compound the smaller the excess burden or, to put it differently, the smaller the sum an enterprise is willing to spend on avoiding the prohibition. As the excess burden concerning pinacolyl alcohol is minimal, any welfare effects are not detectable.

With regard to the shift of costs one can assume that they are shifted totally to the consumers. This is especially true if the goal of the Convention, to become a universal treaty, is to be accomplished. One result will be non-discrimination with respect to cost effects. Theoretically some states could conceivably offer themselves as "production resorts" of otherwise prohibited chemicals by not acceding to the Convention. Article XI of the draft treaty dealing with economic and technological development can be seen as a carrot to induce states to join the treaty or as a stick to penalize those that do not. In fact Article XI seems to be a direct interface between political and economic interests and can be used as a means to encourage states to adhere to the treaty, accept controls and benefit from the free exchange of goods and transfer of know-how. All others should recognize the price for their standing aside. One precondition for the effective working of this approach is of course that all important chemical nations seek accession to the treaty.

A further methodological aspect to be considered is the dynamic macro-economic analysis. In contrast to the static or static-comparative approaches hitherto, the dynamic analysis tries to provide criteria for the transformation of laws into entrepreneurial decision-making processes. Finally, the dynamic analysis deals with the adaptive behaviour of enterprises. The core question is to find out whether undesired consequences of legislation can be traced back to an under-exposure of such adaption processes.

The following points are important:

1. *Increase of entrepreneurial risk.* Obscurely worded laws, strong dissent about the final shape of a law and/or frequent modification are factors which provoke

---

[18]   If pinacolyl alcohol is listed as a key precursor in Schedule 1, its production on an industrial scale will be prohibited. In the other case, if listed in Schedule 2 (which is much more probable at the moment), it will be verified as other compounds such as arsenic trichloride etc. Its industrial use is secured. Nevertheless, pinacolyl alcohol demonstrates the tension between comprehensive preventive measures against the circumvention of the Convention and the interests of industry to be hampered as little as possible in its research and development efforts.

uncertainty towards the framework conditions of entrepreneurial decision-making. It is still too early to say anything about the clearness of the CW convention. With regard to other international agreements it can be noted, however, that once a treaty has been concluded the contents are unlikely to be altered. Review conferences are always prepared very carefully and are therefore rare. How far obscure wording might lead to insecurities on the entrepreneurial side with respect to the agreement's implementation is not clear yet. One might hope to draw on the experience of national bureaucracies.

2. *Reactions vis-à-vis mobility restraints.* In this case one has to consider first of all costs which may result from a delayed or even hampered introduction of products. Mobility restraints in terms of the labour factor and (under certain conditions) of the land factor are important. Furthermore, attention has to be paid to adaption problems which may occur with interventions in the internal organization and decision-making structure of an enterprise.

   Internal organization and decision-making structures are not touched by the Convention itself, but delays or even hindrances of the introduction of products are at least theoretically possible. For example, a compound of great commercial promise might be prohibited on grounds of its utility as a chemical warfare agent. Observing the actual negotiations in Geneva, however, the impression is gained that the notion of "economic relevance" has a quasi veto function. Thus, with proper timing it should be possible to avoid any mobility restraints.

3. As a final point in this context, the question of the *innovation behaviour of an enterprise* has to be posed. If innovation speed is dampened generally, the costs consist of the missed chances for growth, the loss or reduction of competitiveness and the restriction of occupational opportunities. Besides cost effects which may occur concerning patent regulations, one may refer in this context to too-narrowly defined norms or safety requirements. In particular, cases where not only goals but also the means for achieving those goals are prescribed can result in more costs.

   At present, it is difficult to imagine that the prohibition of pinacolyl alcohol (and that is the only compound with any economic potential) could significantly influence the investment ability of an enterprise. So one could argue from a pragmatic standpoint that the inclusion of pinacolyl alcohol in Schedule 1 can be justified. This does not mean that a careful evaluation process is unnecessary for every single case.

The Non-Proliferation Aspect

The picture painted so far supposes that the civilian chemical industry - that has the technical potential to produce CW agents - is not interested in circumventing the convention's goals. In most cases this might be so, but there are always exceptions. Simple economic logic asserts that shortages in goods result in higher prices (assuming that demand remains constant). The chemical industry as such was determined to support the international community in its endeavours to ban chemical weapons.

However, two basic approaches were possible. One was a global ban on chemical weapons with all the provisions and obligations necessary as described above. On the other hand a mere non-proliferation regime was conceivable that would concentrate on measures to limit effectively the spread of chemical weapons without impeding trade between economically important regions (such as EEC, EEC-US, etc.). Efforts to harmonize and expand national chemical export controls in the Western (OECD-) Group go back to 1984, when the "Australian Group" founded. Similar attempts were made in the East by the "Leipzig Group".

The problem behind this attempt was of course whether this non-proliferation regime would be recognized as a first step towards a global treaty or whether it seen as a last resort in curbing chemical weapons proliferation. Even if the latter solution had been the most sensible from an economic point of view (from the industrialized countries' perspective), its disadvantages quickly became obvious: no real incentive would have existed for developing countries to support a chemical weapons ban, and all the political reservations and difficulties which accompanied nuclear non-proliferation would have been repeated. The question finally resolved in favour of a global agreement when at the Government-Industry Conference against Chemical Weapons in Canberra 1989, the world's chemical industry committed itself to practical support for the Chemical Weapons Convention.

Nevertheless the problem of the spread of chemical weapons still exists. Some countries feel that chemical weapons are indispensable for their national security as the war between Iraq and Iran has shown. Originally those countries tried to acquire precursors on the open market, willing to pay high prices for specialized compounds. With the growing effectiveness of export controls - co-ordinated by the Australia (and Leipzig?) Group - and increased consensus between the Super-powers about non-proliferation policies, a trend became visible of the respective states trying to become self-sufficient. The strategy chosen by countries interested in establishing their own production capacities was to acquire the appropriate technology in order to produce chemical warfare agents under their own direction. The best known example for such an attempt might be the case of Imhausen Chemie which planned a CW production facility in Rabta (Libya). The Imhausen case in particular shows the soft spots of present national legislation and the lack of international control mechanisms in cases of circumvention of export laws. In this respect the Chemical Weapons Convention can serve as a switch-key between those who accept international regulations (and enjoy transfers of technical know-how) and those who do not want to be controlled (and might lose touch with international developments in the chemical field).

Conclusion

The following points can be noted:

1. The projected Chemical Weapons Convention can be seen as a highly successful example of how various interest groups influence a negotiating process in order to achieve a cost-effective treaty.
2. The tension between political aim and economic interests results from the fact that:

   - The chemical industry produces compounds that can be used to produce chemical weapons and that therefore an effective control regime had to be installed.
   - Legitimate commercial secrecy interests exist.
   - Equal production environments should be secured so that no competitor could profit from standing outside the control regime.

3. With regards to what is called the "peace dividend", it seems that the CW Convention will be a rather poor example. It seems doubtful whether there will be any dividend payment in the short or medium term.[19]
4. Finally one should not forget what weight costs should have in comparison with political considerations. The German Federal President, Richard von Weizsäcker, noted in this context: "Anybody, who doesn't take the financial aspects of political decisions seriously acts irresponsibly. But, whoever fixes his political principles only on cost considerations hasn't got any principles.

---

[19]   See in this connection Ron Sutherland's article.

Chapter 12

The Economic Consequences
of Chemical Weapons Disarmament

Ronald G. Sutherland

Introduction

The economic consequences of chemical weapons disarmament will be significant.
The heart of a chemical weapon is a toxic chemical whose effect is quite simply the
death or incapacitation of humans and animals alike. Since the effect is physiological,
it follows that the destruction of such weapons will have to be carried out with great
care so that the employees, nearby residents and the environment of the chemical
facility are not harmed in the process.

The actual costs of the destruction of chemical weapons will be high, further
exacerbated by the public's fear of the environmental consequences of accidents
occurring when such weapons are moved from storage to destruction sites. This means
that possibly many more destruction plants will have to be built than absolutely
necessary on the basis of agent tonnage.

There are many factors that will contribute to destruction costs. Among them are:

- the number of agents;
- the different types of munitions;
- the number of production facilities;
- the number of stockpiles; and
- the movement of chemical weapons.

As well as the costs of destruction that may be ascribed to disarmament, there will
be costs associated with arms control - the process which prevents the possible
production of additional chemical weapons anywhere in the global chemical industry.

The global total of chemical weapon agents is of the order of 100,000 tons at
present. The USSR has stated that its stockpile is not larger than 50,000 agent tons,
and analysis of data from the US suggests a stockpile of about 32,000 tons. Apart
from Iraq, there are no other admitted possessors or manufacturers of chemical
weapons but the discussions on proliferation which are based on information not
verifiable by any multilateral process, have suggested between 15 and 20 nations in
that category. It is unlikely that any such possessor will have large stockpiles; 12
stockpiles of 1,500 tons would seem to be a reasonable basis for discussion purposes.

Despite massive research efforts dating back to the First World War, the actual number of agents currently weaponized is small, as shown in Table 12.1.

Table 12.1
Chemical Warfare Agents

Agent	US	USSR
Mustard (H, HD, HT)	Yes	Yes
Lewisite (L)	Obsolete	Yes
Tabun (GA)	Obsolete	No
Sarin (GB)	Yes	Yes
Soman (GD)	No	Yes
VX	Yes	Yes
Mustard/Lewisite	No	Yes

The United States has residual stocks of tabun and lewisite although these are no longer considered to be militarily useful. The agent BZ is currently being destroyed and is not listed as a weapon. Table 12.2 lists the weapon systems described by the USSR at Shikhany, as reported in CD/789. See Table 12.2.

Table 12.3 gives a summary of published US disposal plans, with the locations of eight stockpiles and their current percentages of the overall stockpile. The stockpile in the FRG will be moved to Johnston Atoll in the summer of 1990. On present indications, the Johnston Atoll destruction plant will be closed after the elimination of the Pacific and German stockpiles, probably before a Chemical Weapons Convention (CWC) enters into force. Storage sites in the continental United States are referred to as Oconus, while the others are known as Oconus stockpiles. The Rocky Mountain Arsenal site is no longer utilized. See Table 12.3

The data given in CD/789 is the only information available on Russian chemical weapons, together with the statement that the total stockpile is 50,000 agent tons. This figure has been the subject of intense debate and is not yet accepted by all. There is no published information on CW stockpiles, Chemical Weapons Production Facilities (CWPF) nor their locations in the USSR. Speculation suggests that there are ten production sites and nine stockpile locations.[1] The USSR has also stated that all CW

---

[1]   "Soviet Chemical Weapons Threat", 1985, Defence Intelligence Agency, USA.

are kept within its borders and that none of its Allies has CW or CW production facilities.

Table 12.2
Soviet Army CW Agents

Agents Types	Delivery System
Blister Agent Mustard/Lewisite	Chemical Bomb Spray Tank
Lewisite	Artillery Shells
Nerve Agent Sarin	Artillery Shells Rockets Chemical Bombs
VX	Artillery Shells Rockets Tactical Missiles
Viscous VX	Tactical Missiles
Thickened Soman	Spray Tanks
Irritant CS	Hand Grenades

Source: CD/789.

In July 1988 the United States in CD/844 submitted data to the Conference on Disarmament (CD) on its production facilities. The status of these CWPF is given in Table 12.4. See Table 12.4.

Many observers were surprised when President Mitterand stated that France did not possess chemical weapons nor production facilities. The statement caused public confusion because of previous speculation in the literature[2] and because of the negotiating position of the French delegation at Geneva in 1988, especially with respect to the concept of "security stocks".

---

[2]   G. Stashevsky, "Chemical Weapons: The View from Moscow", *Novosti Press Agency*, Moscow, 1988.

Table 12.3
Summary of Disposal Plan

Depot (%)	Agent	Form	Disposal	Time (Years)
Tooele (42.3)	H HD HT GB VX	Projectiles, TC[1] Cartridges, Projectiles, TC Cartridges, Projectiles, Cartridges, Projectiles, Rockets, Bombs, TC Projectiles, Rockets, Mines, Spray T, TC TC	MMF[2] BF[3]	4 4
Pine Bluff (12)	HD HT GB VX	Cartridges, TC TC Rockets, TC Rockets, Mines	MBZ[4]	?
Umatillo (11.6)	HD GB VX	TC Projectiles, Rockets, Bombs TC TC	MMF	3
Pueblo (9.9)	HD/HT HD	Cartridges Projectiles	MMF	1
Anniston (7.1)	HD/HT GB VX	Cartridges Projectiles, TC Cartridges, Projectiles, Rockets, TC Cartridges, Projectiles, Rockets, Mines, TC	MMF	3

Table 12.3 continued

Depot (%)	Agent	Form	Disposal	Time (Years)
Aberdeen (5.0)	HD	TC	BF	2
Newport (3.9)	VX	TC	BF	2
Lexington (1.6)	H GB VX	Projectiles, TC Projectiles, Rockets, TC Projectiles, Rockets, TC	MMF	1

[1] TC = One ton container
[2] MMF = Munitions (mixed) Facility
[3] BF = Bulk Facility
[4] MBZ = Modified BZ Facility
Compiled from various sources

Table 12.4
Chemical Weapons Production Facilities

Location	Agent	Status
Rocky Mountain Arsenal	Sarin (GB)	Standby 1957
Newport	VX	Standby 1969
Pine Bluff	Difluoro (DF) QL	Operational Binary Operational Binary
Muscle Shoals	Dichloro	--
Aberdeen	Pilot Plants	--

There is considerable speculation that a number of nations in the Middle East have acquired chemical weapons and production facilities. Discussions on proliferation have mostly focused on that region. There is no doubt that Iraq acquired capability during the Iran-Iraq war and it is believed to have the capacity to produce mustard gas, Sarin and Tabun. Syria has been reported to have a production facility, and the most recent controversy involves Libya. The complex at Rabta is believed by some to be a CWPF. There are statements that Iran has acquired chemical weapons and that Egypt has attempted to improve its CW capability. Claims have also been made that Israel has a production capacity for mustard gas and nerve agents.

Table 12.5 lists those countries which have been the subject of most discussion in the literature concerning their possession or production of chemical weapons.

Table 12.5 lists those countries which have been the subject of most discussion in the literature concerning their possession or production of chemical weapons.

Table 12.5
Known and Suggested Chemical Weapons Possessors

Known	Suggested	
US	Angola	Laos
USSR	Burma	Libya*
Iraq	China	North Korea
Iran	Cuba	Pakistan
	Egypt	South Africa
	Ethiopia	South Korea
	France*	Syria*
	India	Taiwan
	Israel	Thailand
		Vietnam*

* The asterisks indicate those countries which have been the subject of most speculation.

In addition to current possessors of CW and CWPF, there are also a number of nations that were possessors at one time; these will likely have responsibilities in the destruction of chemical weapons or former facilities. Table 12.6 lists countries that possessed such weapons at one time.

Table 12.6
Former Possessors of Chemical Weapons and Facilities

Australia	Italy
Canada	Japan
China	Kenya
Czechoslovakia	Nigeria
Egypt	Poland
France	Singapore
Germany (FRG and GDR)	South Africa
Hungary	USSR
India	UK
Indonesia (Netherlands)	US

Source: Based on a table from SIPRI Yearbook 1988 (p.103).

The Chemical Weapons Convention

The Chemical Weapons Convention (CWC) has been under negotiation by the Conference on Disarmament (CD) at Geneva for many years. The results of each year's negotiations are presented as a "rolling text" which is updated at least annually to reflect the state of the negotiating process. The current text is included in CD/961 of February 1990. The outline is given in Table 12.7.

The preliminary structure in Table 12.7 details the compliance activities of the States Parties and the verification activities of the International Inspectorate which will act for the Technical Secretariat of the International Organization to monitor compliance with the provisions of the CWC. Article 1 presents the general provisions on scope. Each State Party undertakes not to develop, produce, otherwise acquire, stockpile or retain chemical weapons or transfer, directly or indirectly, chemical weapons to anyone. In addition to undertaking not to use chemical weapons, States Parties would agree not to induce anyone else to engage in activities prohibited by the CWC. States that possess CW and CWPF are required to destroy them within a ten year period. The thrust of Articles IV and V and their annexes is chemical disarmament. No weapons should remain after ten years. There are substantial costs associated with the destruction of CW and CWPF at the national level, as well as international costs associated with the multilateral verification of national compliance. Article VI is an arms control measure whereby the chemical industry will be monitored to ensure that new chemical weapons are not produced. Article VII is concerned with the provision of National Authorities for all States Parties. These organizations will provide the information required by the International Organization described in Article VIII. The interaction of the Articles which represent compliance and verification activities is shown in Table 12.8.

Table 12.7
Preliminary Structure of the Chemical Weapons Convention

Preamble	
Article I	General Provisions on Scope
Article II	Definitions and Criteria
Article III	Declarations
Article IV	Chemical Weapons
Article V	Chemical Weapons Production Facilities
Article VI	Activities not Prohibited by the Convention

Table 12.7 continued

Article VII	National Implementation Measures
Article VIII	The Organization
Article IX	Consultations, Co-operation and Fact-finding
Article X	Assistance and Protection against Chemical Weapons
Article XI	Economic and Technological Development
Article XII	Relation to other International Agreements
Article XIII	Amendments
Article XIV	Duration and Withdrawal
Article XV	Signature
Article XVI	Ratification
Article XVII	Accession
Article XVIII	Depository
Article XIX	Entry into Force
Article XX	Languages and Authentic Text
Annex on Chemicals	
Annex on the Protection of Confidential Information	
Annex to Article III	
Annex to Article IV	
Annex to Article V	
Annex 1 to Article VI	
Annex 2 to Article VI	
Annex 3 to Article VI	
Preparatory Commission. Addendum to appendix 1: Protocol on Inspection Procedures	

The Destruction of Chemical Weapons and their Production Facilities

The cost both of CW destruction and of the eventual dismantling of the military facilities that produced them is considerable. The initial estimate of the cost of destroying unitary weapons in the United States was placed at $2.3 billion. By the time the Stroessel Commission[3] reported, it was $2.7 billion; it is now about $5 billion with a ceiling of about $6 billion. There has been no discussion of the USSR, but its

Table 12.8
Compliance and Verification Activities

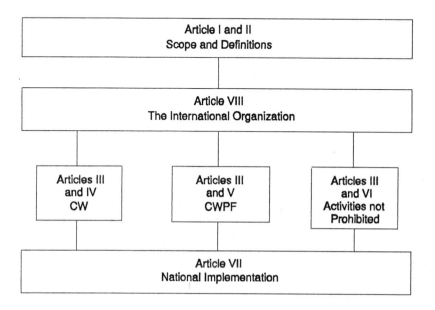

stockpile is about 50 per cent larger. Moreover it is unlikely to benefit from any economies of scale if the technology employed is similar to that used by the US.

Until 1969 the accepted methodologies of destruction included ocean dumping, land burial and open-pit burning. As such methods are now environmentally unacceptable, the United States has put considerable effort into alternative technology, in the process destroying several million kilograms of agents. In early programmes, the mustard was incinerated and the nerve agents chemically neutralized. The experimental programme at Tooele in Utah (CAMDS) is based on incineration of all agents; Tooele was used as a model for the first full-scale plant at Johnston Atoll (JACADS). This plant is undergoing testing and should become fully operational in late 1990. It will be the prototype for all other destruction facilities in the US. It will be used to destroy the stockpile at that location and also to destroy the US stocks transferred from the Federal Republic of Germany after which it will be

---

3   Report of the Chemical Warfare Review Commission, Chairman, W.J. Stroessel, 1985.

decommissioned. The Environmental Impact Study (EIS) carried out by the US military came to the conclusion that all CW agents should be destroyed at their stockpile locations in the United States. Table 12.9 gives the location and the estimated agent tonnages for the United States, together with the presumed number of locations and agent tonnages for the USSR.

Table 12.9
Unitary Chemical Stockpiles of US and USSR

Country	Agent Tons*	Agents
US 8 [conus] 1 [FRG] 1 [Johnston Atoll] USSR (9)	(32,000) (500) (1,600) 50,000	VX, GB, GA, H, HD, HT, L VX, GB, H/L, L, GD

* ( ) estimates appearing in unofficial sources

It has been reported that the construction of the incineration plant at Johnston Atoll cost $305 million and that the projected cost for Tooele is about $138 million at present. The completion date for the Tooele plant is December 1992, with destruction of CW taking place between January 1993 and April 1997. Construction of the planned facility at Aberdeen should begin in June 1992 and be completed in spring 1994. Destruction of HD at that location should begin in spring 1995 and take 18 months to complete. The United States is committed to the construction of nine demilitarization plants to destroy its CW stockpile of unitary weapons. It is assumed that the first two plants will cost about $966 million if the cost of Tooele is representative. Thus the construction costs are likely to total about $2 billion. The Tooele facility will have about 400 employees and the planned programme will last for four years. Hence the wage bill will be for approximately 1,600 person years. The cost of moving CW is also very high. The US stockpile in FRG consists of about 10,000 artillery shells loaded with Sarin or VX. This stockpile will be moved by September 1990 by the Clausen - Miesau - Nordenham - Johnston Atoll route at at a cost of $50 million to the US and DM 40 million to the FRG (excluding security costs) for about $70 million in total.

The destruction of a CWPF will cost several million dollars. In CD/844, the United States suggests tens of millions as an estimate. There would have to be a planning and public review process leading to an environmental impact statement. This process could take about two to three years and the slow decontamination/destruction process another two years. This suggests that about $100 million would be required to close down the US facilities; the process would take up to five years after the decision to go forward with closure was made.

The USSR has given no information on its stockpiles except a total figure of 50,000 agent tons, although they did display a variety of munitions and agents at Shikhany in October 1987, with details being presented to the Conference on Disarmament in CD/789. Estimates in the literature suggests nine stockpiles and ten production facilities. The USSR appears to have little experience in the destruction of chemical weapons. A recent description by Evstafiev[4] of the pilot plant planned for Chapayevsh and now designated as a training facility indicated that the agents would be neutralized at 100-140 Celsius scale with one volume of CW agent producing about three volumes of waste which would then have to be removed by rail from the site for subsequent destruction (i.e. eventually 50,000 tons of CW would produce 150,000 tons of liquid waste for further processing). This seems to be much less efficient then the US incineration process where only solid and gaseous effluents have to be handled; the former will not likely be particularly hazardous and the latter can be cleaned up by an industrial scrubbing process. It is not possible to produce any effective cost estimates but the following can be suggested:

1. The USSR will require destruction sites at each stockpile location;
2. Considerable work on the process technology is still required;
3. Given the size of their stockpile it is unlikely to cost less than the corresponding US programme;
4. This would give a cost range of $5 to 6 billion.

The same will apply to the decontamination/ destruction of the USSR's CWPFs. The number is unknown but is of the order of ten. The disassembly costs will likely be tens of millions of US dollars per plant. An estimate of $100 million is not unreasonable given the current lack of information.

The literature on the proliferation of chemical weapons and their production is voluminous but its accuracy is impossible to assess. For the sake of estimating cost, 12 nations besides the US and USSR can be assumed to possess chemical weapons. Each site will require a destruction facility whose cost will depend on the technology employed. It is unlikely that any possessor could move its stockpile(s) to another country for destruction because of environmental concerns. The construction costs would be of the order of $100 million per site or in the billion dollar range globally. Similar arguments apply to production facilities.

Inspection Requirements Under a Chemical Weapons Convention

The entry into force of a chemical weapons convention will take place after ratification by a specified number of States Parties. The period between signature and entry into

---

[4]   I.B. Evstafiev in National Implementation of the Future Chemical Weapons Convention, edited by T. Stock and R.G. Sutherland, SIPRI and Oxford University Press, 1990.

force will be about two to three years and will require about 60 signatures. This will have a bearing on the number of inspectors required by the Technical Secretariat since many activities, including on-site inspection, will be required almost immediately. The Secretariat will also have to ensure that:

- Declarations are made within 30 days;
- Plans are submitted for destruction;
- Detailed plans are submitted within six months;
- Destruction can be commenced within 12 months.

In principle all States Parties must be able to demonstrate compliance with the International Organization as represented by its inspectors. In practice the range of obligations will depend on whether or not a State Party possesses CW and/or CWPF.

With regard to chemical weapons stockpiles, the International Inspectorate needs to know each location, the number and types of munitions and the chemical agents employed. It must verify that the sites are secured, that the contents are sealed and that no CW is moved without its knowledge before a destruction plant becomes available. It then has to be continuously on-site until the stockpile is destroyed. These are two different tasks and could require different personnel.

Manpower requirements will depend on the number of stockpiles worldwide. The US has eight stockpiles, assuming that Johnston Atoll has attained its objectives. The munitions and bulk stock will have to be destroyed over a nine year period. This implies that about 30,000 tons will have to be destroyed under international supervision. It is assumed that there are nine stockpiles in the USSR containing about 50,000 tons. If we also assume that there are 12 other CW possessors, then there will be 12 additional stockpiles i.e. eight US, nine USSR and 12 others i.e. (14 declarations of CW possession and 29 locations). The inspectors will have to visit all sites and ensure that no weapons leave before a destruction plant becomes available; movement to any other destruction location would have to be overseen. For simplicity it will be assumed that destruction occurs on-site; the continuous presence of inspectors might be unnecessary if the sites could be electronically secured until destruction of CW commenced, but at that stage it must be assumed that teams will be continuously present. If there are five inspectors at each US/USSR site, then the initial requirements are as shown in Table 12.10.

It is suggested that three-man teams will initially be sufficient at other stockpile locations since it is unlikely that any destruction plants will be available before entry into force. It is also assumed that stockpile inspection will be a full-time task without rotation to other duties. Stockpile destruction is mandated to commence 12 months after entry into force. All teams would then be at full strength as shown in Table 12.11.

The analysis in Table 12.11 suggests that the first-year requirement for inspectors is 201 rising to 241 for 29 sites. The actual numbers could be larger depending on the number of shifts worked at the destruction sites and could be lower if full-time manning before the beginning of destruction is not required.

Table 12.10

Inspection Requirements for Stockpiles - 1 year

	Stockpiles	Inspectors	Total Inspectors (1.66)[a]
US	8	40	66
USSR	9	45	75
Others	12	36	60
Total	29	121	201

[a]   The planning factor, 1.66, assumes that each inspector works 220 days per year and that inspection requires 365 days availability.

Article V requires the destruction of all chemical weapons production plants. The data in the table summarizes speculations made in the literature and would mean that 23 CWPF would have to be destroyed. Only the US number of five is definitive. There is also a requirement related to former CWPFs, but this is unlikely to be a costly proposition.

Table 12.11

Inspector Requirements for CW Stockpile Destruction

	Stockpiles	Inspectors	Total Inspectors (1.66)[a]
US	8	40	66
USSR	9	45	75
Others	12	60	100
Total	29	145	241

[a]   The planning factor, 1.66, assumes that each inspector works 220 days per year and that inspection requires 365 days availability.

The inspector requirement for CWPF is difficult to assess. Their presence will be required during destruction. They will then have to verify that the CWPF is closed, raw materials and stocks are sealed, and that only safety and closure activities are carried out. Each facility will have to be visited, inventories audited, seals emplaced and monitoring instruments installed. A continuous presence will be required until the instruments are functioning: if two inspectors are required then 46 active inspectors would be assigned, requiring 75 to be available in total.

Table 12.12
Chemical Weapons Production Facilities (CWPF)*

Country	Number
US	5
USSR	(10)
France	(1)
Iraq	(2)
Iran	(1)
Syria	(1)
Libya	(1)
Egypt	(1)
Israel	(1)
Total	23

* Number in brackets unconfirmed.

The actual cost of inspection is difficult to assess. Using the safeguards division of IAEA as a model, it would appear that US $200,000 will be required to keep an inspector in the field, with projected total costs as follows.

Table 12.13
Estimate of Inspection Costs

Activity	Inspectors	Cost (US $ million)
CW Stockpile	201	40.2
increasing to	241	48.2
CWPF	75	15.

This leads to an estimate that the inspectorate for the verification of the destruction of all chemical weapons and production facilities will range in size from 276 to 316 at a cost of US $55 to $63 million. The cost of electronically securing all sites is of the order of US $20 million but this sum could change depending, for instance, on the level of inspectors permanently assigned to sites. These then are estimates of the annual costs required for the implementation of Articles IV and V of the CWC.

Article VI:
Activities not Prohibited by the Convention

This Article controls toxic chemicals seen to be a risk to the Convention, the aim being to prevent further production of chemical weapons. The chemicals of concern are assigned to schedules on the basis of risk; allowed production of schedule 1 chemicals will be carried out at a single facility under government control. This is the Single Small-Scale Facility (SSSF). The monitoring of these will involve the International Inspectorate in on-site visits and possibly the emplacement of instruments to monitor activities between inspections. An assessment of the possible number of such SSSFs leads to an estimate of 43 including NATO, WTO and other nations. Each facility would have to be visited extensively in the first year of CWC; such inspections would last a week and involve about five inspectors; instruments, if required, would have to be installed at a second visit during that year. Electronic monitoring could be expensive. The actual annual inspections could be carried out by six inspectors if the visit required only two days. This would cost about US $1.2 million.

The verification of non-production in the chemical industry is complex since it involves a combination of on-site inspection, data collection and analysis. The complications and potential costs are difficult to assess. This estimate uses papers on the Netherlands and Federal Republic of Germany as starting points in the discussion.[5,6]

The cost analysis must take into account the following:

- an Inspector Year;
- number of Inspectors per Inspection;
- the Duration of an Inspection;
- the Number of Facilities; and
- inspection Frequency.

This paper assumes that an Inspector Year consists of 40 days out of the approximate 220 day working year. It appears that, initially, an inspection team will consist of five inspectors from an analysis of National Trial Inspection (NTI) data. For planning purposes it is assumed that an inspection could last for five days. The assessment of the number of facilities that will require inspection under the rolling text of the CWC and under other tentative inspection modalities is extremely difficult, as is the inspection frequency that will eventually be decided upon.

For industry, those plants that manufacture Schedule 2 chemicals will require closest inspection since they are most likely to be misused or generate suspicion. Examination of the literature suggests that 200 is a reasonable starting point for

---

5   "The size and structure of a Chemical Inspectorate: the Netherlands", CD/445, March 1984.

6   H. Beck, "Verifying the Projected Chemical Weapons Convention. A Cost Analysis", AFES Press No.13, Mosbach, 1988.

calculations. Each facility attachment for subsequent inspections and random but routine inspections thereafter. It is assumed that each site could be inspected annually.

There is speculation that many chemical plants are CW-capable and would require inspection, although this is not yet part of the rolling text. It is suggested in this paper that there could be above 1,000 such plants which should be visited once every three years.

Schedule 3 facilities are not currently subject to inspection under the draft text. There may well be fewer such plants because of the tendency of industry to centralize facilities that produce large tonnage chemicals. It is assumed that their number is of the order of 100 and that they could be examined by teams of three in a three-day period.

In terms of inspection needs there are three situations (i) monitoring Schedule 2 facilities, (ii) monitoring CW capable facilities, and (iii) monitoring Schedule 3 production. Only (i) is agreed in the present status of the negotiations although the others are the subject of debate. The results of this analysis are shown in Table 12.14.

It should be noted how sensitive the numbers in Table 12.14 are to the parameters listed and that the addition of a CW-capable category doubles the costs. The required inspection of Schedule 2 costs $25 million; this increases only slightly with the inclusion of the type of inspection of Schedule 3 facilities suggested.

Challenge Inspection

The actual demand for challenge inspection is difficult to quantify and the estimates of inspectors required presently vary from 0 to 80. As the negotiators currently agree that each State Party has the right to request such an inspection, the potential number will be a function of:

- the number of States Parties;
- the efficiency of routine verification;
- the confidence of all States Parties in the verification procedures; and
- the number of undeclared sites.

If we examine the prior estimates in this paper, there are approximately 1,400 sites; of these, about 1,100 are not subject to routine inspection under the draft text. The following assumptions would project a need for 138 inspectors:

- 1,100 locations;
- one challenge per location per five years;
- five inspectors per inspection;
- five days duration.

If we use the same frequency as suggested for CW-capable, this increases to 230, that is, there is a trade-off between costs incurred under Articles VI and IX.

Allegations of use would also require challenge inspections. These would be difficult to cost but the Interntional Organization should have the capacity to mount two per year if required. The team would likely require assistance from outside experts.

Table 12.14
Estimates of Inspectors Required for Various Inspection Types and Costs

A. *Inspectors for Schedule 2*

Schedule 2 Plant	200
Inspection Frequency	1 per year
Inspectors/Inspection	5
Duration	5 days
Inspectors	125
Cost	$ 25 000 000

B. *Inspectors for CW-Capable Plants*

CW-Capable Plants	1 000
Inspection Frequency	1 every 3 years
Inspectors/Inspection	5
Duration	5 days
Inspectors	208
Cost	$ 41 600 000

C. *Inspectors for Schedule 3*

Schedule 3 Plants	100
Inspection Frequency	1 per year
Inspectors/Inspection	3
Duration	3 days
Inspectors	23
Cost	$ 4 600 000

Other Inspection Modalities

There are a number of proposals under discussion by the CD in Geneva as to the comprehensiveness of the verification procedures laid down in the rolling text and as to whether this problem can be ameliorated by *ad hoc* inspection modalities. The basic problem is that the declaration procedures only target facilities that have actually produced scheduled chemicals. There is a fear that CW-capable facilities might become production centres unknown to the International Organization, whether producing chemicals for legal or illegal purposes under the CWC. The Australians proposed "Spot Checks" in CD/791 and 869 and the UK "*Ad Hoc* Inspections" in CD/909.

The problem with the approach is its sheer size. There could be anywhere between 50,000 and 100,000 facilities worldwide. What frequency of inspection would be needed to effectively check on misuse? How would one organize the detailed negative inspection required? Would it be worth the effort?

The Australian approach was basically directed to Schedule 3 problems. The FRG based its approach on a "National Register" of potential facilities. The UK used active and passive quotas to dampen the costs of such an inspection modality. Tables 12.15 and 12.16 illustrate the potential costs. It should be noted that the final number of States Parties will be in the region of 150 thus raising the costs of *Ad Hoc* Inspections under this formulation since 338 inspectors would be required rather than 135.

Table 12.15
Ad Hoc Checks

Number of facilities	50 000 - 100 000
Inspection frequency	1 every 5 years
Inspectors/inspection	2
Inspection duration	2 days
Inspectors	1 000 - 2 000

Table 12.16
Ad Hoc Inspections

Maximum Number of Inspections/State Party	6 per year
State Parties	60
Number of Inspectors/Inspection	5
Inspection duration	3 days
Inspectors	135

The Size and Cost of the International Inspectorate

By considering all the estimates provided earlier in this review, we can assess the likely total cost of the Inspectorate. The tasks assigned by the CWC with respect to verification of CW stockpiles, CWPF and the SSSF would appear to require about 340 inspectors or $68 million exclusive of capital costs to secure these sites and perhaps specialized equipment for the inspectors.

The only other routine monitoring currently required is in the Schedule 2 area; the estimate here is 125 inspectors or $25 million.

Challenge inspection could possibly be managed by 138 inspectors, assuming 220 such inspections a year at a cost of about $27 million.

This leads to an estimate of approximately 600 inspectors at a cost of $120 million. It should be noted that this cost is a global figure and encompasses support staff etc., raising the total staff of the Technical Secretariat to about 1,000.

Other inspection modalities will necessitate substantial additional resources. The question is whether the increased confidence thus gained will be worth the additional fiscal costs. There will be other costs associated with the headquarters of such an inspectorate, but no attempt has been made to assess its cost at this stage.

The States Parties and the Chemical Industry

So far we have discussed the costs associated with destroying of chemical weapons and production facilities, the costs of supervising such activities by an International Organization, as well as the international costs associated with verifying compliance with non-production in industrial facilities. There are two other areas that require study. These are the costs of the National Authorities set up to demonstrate compliance with a CWC, and the costs that will have to be absorbed by industry both in preparing the data required by National and International Organizations and in their involvement in the inspection process.

National implementation regimes will differ for host States Parties. They all have the same instrinsic obligations but their requirements will depend on: (i) possession or non-possession of chemical weapons; (ii) possession or non possession of production facilities; (iii) former possession of (i) or (ii); (iv) potential to produce chemical weapons; and (v) the nature of a States Party's chemical industry. Those States Parties that have obligations under (i) and/or (ii) may well require an independent agency, while others will be able to assign the task to an existing agency. It is almost impossible to develop accurate estimates for either situation. For the former, the costs will be trivial relative to the expense associated with destruction. For the latter the situation is obscured by the lack of finality about the range of inspection processes required by the Convention. For example the lack of current Schedule 2 production would substantially minimize inspections for many States Parties but CW-capable or *Ad Hoc* inspections will lead to inspection efforts in all States Parties, within the CWC. Disregarding possessor nations, it is possible to divide States Parties into those with a substantial and those with a developing chemical industry: OECD members account for the bulk of chemical trade at present, but Beck has noted that some 33 countries have produced key precursors or compounds likely subject to control. One could thus conclude that two countries will have large National Authorities, about 30 of intermediate size and the remainder (say 120) of modest size, suggesting the following:

Table 12.17
Costs of National Authorities for States Parties

Size	Number	Cost	Total Cost
1. Large	2	2 500 000	5 000 000
2. Intermediate	30	500 000	15 000 000
3. Small	120	100 000	12 000 000

This would lead to an annual cost for national authorities of approximately $32 million.

Given the uncertainties, it is not possible to assess the costs which will accrue to industry in supplying data and in involvement in inspection processes with the new National Authority and International Organization. But every dollar spent in regulation will probably have to be matched by industry.

Conclusion

Any country interested in acquiring chemical weapons should be dissuaded by the briefest examination of the costs associated with the destruction of such weapons. Over the next decade the major possessors will expend about $12 billion in demilitarizing their stockpiles and production facilities. Over the same period the International Agency will spend about $1.2 billion verifying compliance, with a continuing cost of about $60 million to the International Authority after the destruction phase is over. The National Authorities could spend about $300 million over that destruction period; again one would anticipate reductions in costs after that period for possessor nations, but for no one else. It is safe to assume that industry's costs will parallel those of the regulatory agencies for the monitoring of non-production.

Acknowledgements

This paper was prepared while on leave of absence from the University of Saskatchewan at the Verification Research Unit of the Arms Control and Disarmament Division of External Affairs and International Trade Canada. I wish to thank Mr. F.R. Cleminson and Mr. G.K. Vachon for many helpful discussions.

References

Soviet Chemical Weapons Threat, 1985, Defence Intelligence Agency, US.

Stashevskey, G., *Chemical Weapons: The View from Moscow*, Novosti Press Agency, Moscow, 1988.

Thatcher, G., "Poison on the Winds", the *Christian Science Monitor* Special Report, December, 1988.

"Information on the Presentation at the Shikhany Military facility of standard chemical munitions and of technology for the destruction of chemical weapons at a mobile facility", CD/789, December 1987.

Information Presented to the Visiting, Soviet Declaration at the Tock Army Depot, 18-21 November 1987, CD/830, April 1988.

"Chemical Stockpile Disposal Program CD/711", July 1986.

Stringer, H., *Deterring Chemical Warfare: US Policy Options for the 1990s*, Institute for Foreign Policy Analysis Inc., Cambridge, Mass., 1986.

Beck, H., "Verifying the Projected Chemical Weapons Convention. A Cost Analysis", AFES Press No. 13, Mosbach, 1988.

Chemical and Biological Weapons, Vol. 4, Stockholm, SIPRI, 1986.

Chemical Weapons Convention Bulletin, Nos. 1 to 4, Federation of American Scientists, Washington, US, 1988 and 1989.

"Systems Study of an International Verification Organization on Chemical Weapons", Canada, October 1987.

"Chemical Stockpile Disposal Program: Final Programmatic Environmental Impact Statement", Vol.1-3, Aberdeen Providing Ground, Maryland, US, January 1988.

Canada Handbook for the Investigation of Allegations of the Use of Chemical or Biological Weapons, November 1985.

National Trial Inspections, Australia CD/910, Belgium CD/917, Brazil CD/895, Czechoslovakia CD/900, Finland CD/CW/WP.233, F.R. Germany CD/912, France CD/913, FRG CD/899, Hungary CD/890/Add.1, Italy CD/893, Japan CD/CW/WP.228, Netherlands CD/924, Sweden CD/CW/PW.216, Switzerland CD/CW/WP.247, US CD/922, USSR CD/984, Chairman's Papers CD/CW/PW.213, 236, 217, 237, and 248.

Methodology and Instrumentation for Sampling and Analysis in the Verification of Chemical Disarmament Vols. A1, A2, B1, B2, B3, B4, B5, C1, C2, C3, C4, D1, and E1, The Ministry for Foreign Affairs of Finland, Helsinki, 1977 to 1988.

Hensley, John, *The Soviet Biochemical Threat to NATO*, New York, St. Martin's Press, 1987.

Seagrave, Sterling, *Yellow Rain*, New York, M. Evans and Company, 1981.

The Arms Control Reporter, 1984 to present, Institute for Defence and Disarmament Studies, Brookline, US.

"Destruction and disposal of Canadian stocks of World War II Mustard Agents", CCD/434, July 1974.

"Disposal of Chemical Agents", CD/173, April 1981.

"Size and Structure of a Chemical Inspectorate", CD/445, March 1984.

"Application of (Nuclear) Safeguards Remote Verification Technology to Verification of a Chemical Weapons Convention", CD/79, January 1988.

"Verification of Non-Production of Chemical Weapons and their Precursions by the Civilian Chemical Industry. Trial Inspection of an Australian Chemical Facility", CD/698, June 1986.

"Making the Chemical Weapons Ban Effective", CD/769, July 1987.

"Verification of Non-Production. The case for Ad Hoc Checks", 791 CD/79, January 1988.

"Factors Involved in Determining Verification Inspectorate Personnel and Resource Requirements", CD/823, March 1988.

"Past Production of Chemical Warfare Agents in the United Kingdom", CD/856, August 1988.

"Verification of Non-Production of Chemical Weapons Ad Hoc Checks", CD/869, September 1988.

"Report of the Ad Hoc Committee on Chemical Weapons to the Conference on Disarmament", CD/961, February 1990.

"Verification of the Chemical Weapons Convention: Practice challenge inspections of military facilities", CD/921, June 1989.

"Verification Laboratory, General Features and Instrumentations", CD/CW/WP.253, June 1989.

"Report of the Technical Group on Instrumentation", CD/CW/WP.272, January 1990.

SIPRI Yearbook 1988, Oxford University Press, 1988.

"Report of the Chemical Warfare Review Commission", Chairman W.J. Stroessel, 1985.

Barnaby, F., Tauris, *The Invisible Bomb*, London, 1989.

National Implementation of the Future Chemical Weapons Convention, Stock, T. and Sutherland, R.G. (eds.), SIPRI, Oxford University Press, 1990.

Lundin, S.J., *Estimation of tasks for, size of, and necessary resources for a Technical Secretariat under a Chemical Weapons Convention*, SIPRI, 1989.

The Chemical Weapons Convention and the International Inspectorate: A Quantitative Study, Canada, August 1990.

Chapter 13

Responses

First Response

Salah Bassiouny

This paper will deal with the perception of the Third World regarding the topic under discussion.

With the ongoing world changes, with what looks like the final phases of the end of the Cold War and with the emergence of a new world order, we have witnessed the speedy steps undertaken by the US and the USSR in the direction of an agreement on chemical weapons.

This is a plausible achievement. Within developed societies which have maximized their defences within the capabilities and socio-economic structures of their states, the road to arms control, in general, can be seen as relatively easy and smooth. On the other hand, such a hopeful outcome has not prevailed in other regions, where persistent and longstanding conflicts are still dominant in shaping the policies of states and their economies of warfare. Of course, I cite here the Middle East as an example.

As demonstrated by the policies of many States, those who have relatively limited resources will assess the economic benefits of a weapon according to its cost-effectiveness and the range or degree of national security it offers. Certainly, chemical weapons fall within the category of mass destruction weapons which are low-cost in production but relatively highly effective as a defensive or offensive weapon.

The cost of arms in the Middle East is extremely high; military expenditure has reached US $70 billion annually. This represents 16 per cent of the region's gross national product. Such figures also indicate the serious imbalance between military expenditure and development. If such a situation continues, the economic burden will increase and more allocations for military production and procurement will persist.

Coming back to the topic under discussion, and after listening to the comprehensive analysis presented by Mr. Beck and Mr. Sutherland, I wish to emphasize that the paper dealt mainly with cost analysis within the context of highly industrialized countries. With both the capital and the latest technology, they can either directly produce certain substances or replace them, or can stop the production of some chemical substances for use in chemical weapons without too much economic loss. The same applies to the destruction of stocks of chemical weapons.

In fact, I find such prospects very encouraging so long as the economic cost can be absorbed and certain basic rules forming a code of conduct can also be established to avoid indirect competition. Also, the great chemical corporations, which control the know-how, have committed themselves in principle to this code of conduct.

If we try to apply the same rules of analysis and perception to the developing countries, we face a completely different picture. In principle, all developing countries accept the aims of this convention. However, we can sense some hesitancy or reluctance on their part when dealing with the different obligations imposed on them and the economic burden they will have to shoulder:

1. In the first place, chemical industries in some countries of the Third World were established at a high cost and with what I may term old technology. In most of these industries, substances produced are of a low quality, leaving behind toxic wastes which prove to be detrimental to man and environment. To change and acquire new techniques is very costly, whether in machinery, substances or know-how. In addition, these industries are still, in most cases, labour intensive;

2. If we deal with the operation of destroying whatever stocks of Cold War, then we are facing yet another economic cost, which governments might not be able to afford;

3. Any country which has produced chemical weapons has invested additional money for necessary protective measures: masks, special shelters, special civil defence, special hospitals, etc. which will have been wasted.

   True, whatever precautions are undertaken there will always be serious harm to the population in wartime. Moreover countries who possess the weapon might feel reluctant to lose it, especially when they are facing a kind of guessing game towards their adversary in a conflict situation.

There are other elements too which we must consider.

There is the political consideration which demands serious initiatives to achieve a situation of peace in regions like the Middle East, as well as the imperative necessity to link together all mass destruction weapons - nuclear, chemical and biological. In the final analysis the notion of security cannot be divided. In this respect, if we are looking at a period of ten years for the gradual elimination of chemical weapons, I hope that within this period of time peace could be achieved and the target of elimination of mass destruction weapons be attained.

On the other hand, and bearing in mind the expected expenditure for implementing the convention, I propose that a special fund of $1 billion be established to assist developing countries to accede to the provisions of the convention. This fund should be financed by the industrialized countries, whether by governments or the chemical industries. The fund should have as part of its objective the proper modernization of chemical factories in the Third World and their required transformation to produce purely civil chemical substances.

Then, and most important, the fund should cover the high cost of the destruction of stockpiles of chemical weapons which are in the possession of some developing countries.

Second Response

Thomas Bernauer

Other contributions to this publication have tried to assess the economic consequences of the planned chemical weapons convention. They have based their judgements on the projected verification mechanisms of the treaty under negotiation. I would like to look at the cost-problem from a different perspective and examine the influence that anticipated costs of the projected treaty may have on the scope of and adherence to a chemical weapons convention. In this context, I argue that cost-benefit calculations are to some extent responsible for the willingness of states to co-operate in particular forms of the chemical disarmament effort. I would like to point to three problems in this regard:

1. As far as the question of costs is concerned, the following three factors are likely to influence a State's willingness to co-operate in a chemical disarmament regime as set forth in the present version of the rolling text: the possession or non-possession of chemical weapons; the extent to which a chemical weapons threat is perceived; and the size of a country's chemical industry. Switzerland, for example, has no chemical weapons and does not perceive a great threat, partly because it has well-developed protection measures. However, it has a large chemical industry which means that it would have to bear considerable direct and indirect costs of verifying a CW convention. Apart from motivations such as international solidarity, domestic political dynamics, etc., such States may have little incentive to join the projected treaty. In any event, it is likely that "side-payments" to less interested or less concerned states will have to be made in the negotiations in order to ensure wide adherence to the treaty. Side-payments under discussion are to link chemical and nuclear disarmament (something I do not support at all); treaty obligations concerning economic co-operation and development, including free trade of chemicals and related equipment among the parties; trade barriers against non-parties; assistance and protection against chemical weapons, etc;

2. The verification measures now envisaged for the convention may be too costly. In general terms, a balance between acceptable residual security risks due to incomplete verification, and costs of verification has to be found. This balance, i.e. the resulting extent and intrusiveness of verification, is largely a normative problem. It is influenced by the state of relations between countries, trust in the others' future behaviour, the perceived military value of chemical weapons, etc. A chemical weapons convention has not yet been concluded, partly perhaps as a result of too costly verification procedures. One should therefore think of lowering verification requirements. However, less verification may not be possible for two (political) reasons. Firstly, Western countries have long

insisted on very extensive and intrusive verification as a *conditio sine qua non* for a chemical disarmament treaty, and it may be difficult to explain to national audiences why less verification is now required. Secondly, the present structure of the rolling text, which is the result of many years of cumbersome multilateral negotiations, may be difficult to change. The historical record of other negotiations proves this point. The inability to lower verification requirements may drive certain states out of the multilateral process and seek "cheaper" solutions. This leads to the third point;

3. The bilateral US-Soviet chemical weapons agreement, signed on 1 June 1990, is a "cheap" agreement for the two countries concerned, but may be bad news for the multilateral process. It is cheap in the sense that it does not provide for the verification of non-production of chemical weapons in the civil chemical industry. Chemical weapons production and storage facilities will not be destroyed. Chemical weapons will not be completely eliminated. And the agreement does not provide for a ban on the use of chemical weapons under all circumstances (withdrawal of reservations to the 1925 Geneva Protocol). The agreement is also cheap because it may help in economizing the destruction of chemical weapons to some extent; help may be provided to the Soviet Union which, at present, does not have any destruction capacity. The bilateral accord may be bad news for the multilateral process for several reasons; the fact that the two States have not committed themselves to the unconditional destruction of chemical weapons under the projected convention constitutes a serious drawback from their previous positions. They intend to keep the production infrastructure, a limited stockpile, and the right to use these weapons until late into the 10-year destruction period envisaged for the multilateral convention. This may discourage other states from joining the convention because they may be reluctant to foreswear the CW option at the very outset of the convention if they are uncertain whether other States will completely destroy their stocks and production capacity. Moreover, the fact that the US and the Soviet Union are evidently clinging to chemical weapons for their national defence may, together with erroneous views on the impact of chemical weapons in the Iran-Iraq war, send the wrong message to governments that plan to acquire chemical weapons. The costs in security terms of this development may therefore exceed the benefits of the bilateral accord.

Third Response

Keith Hartley

Three issues need to be addressed:

1. *Is the current form of the Chemical Weapons (CW) Convention worthwhile?*
   The cost estimates suggest that destruction, inspection and verification will be a costly undertaking. The discussion has suggested little about the magnitude of the likely benefits. Indeed, the benefits have to be valued very highly to justify the costs to be incurred: if they don't, why bother? Could it be that it is the inspectors who will be the real beneficiaries from an agreement?
2. *Substitution and linkage*
   With a CW convention, biological and other weapons might be substituted for chemical weapons.
3. *Who checks the inspectors?*
   It seems to be assumed that inspectors operate impartially, pursuing the "will of the people". But the economics of regulation suggests the possibility that regulatory agencies might be captured by producers. Regulators might be influenced in their behaviour and decisions by producers (cheating) offering lavish meals, entertainment, travel gifts, bribes and future employment prospects.

Fourth Response

Michael D. Intriligator

The papers in this session suggest the need for an objective *benefit-cost analysis of the chemical weapons convention*. The direct costs of destruction of existing stockpiles are enormous, and to them must be added the cost of preventing new chemical weapons production, the cost to industry of coping with the requirements of the convention, the cost of monitoring and verification, and even the cost of procuring alternative weapons to replace the lost chemical weapons stockpiles. The resulting total costs are stupendous. What are the benefits? The convention will not prevent war, even a war involving chemical weapons. The benefits are, in fact, largely symbolic. The convention may actually not be worthwhile in terms of projected benefits and costs and, in any case, it deserves a careful and objective benefit-cost analysis. Perhaps an alternative approach to chemical weapons should be seriously considered. One such alternative might be to allow chemical weapons production and stockpiles, but to impose strong sanctions against the *use* of such weapons.

Fifth Response

Sten Lundbo

In considering the economic implications of the implementation of a Chemical Weapons Convention, we must bear in mind that the scope of this Convention will be more comprehensive than that of any other existing multilateral disarmament or arms control treaty. It will also contain more extensive verification mechanisms than any such treaty, including the INF Treaty. The cost of implementation of this Convention will therefore be considerable.

On the other hand, the know-how and intellectual resources presently devoted to developing chemical weapons in a number of countries will be released for more productive purposes. Furthermore, the implementation of an effectively verifiable, global and comprehensive ban on chemical weapons could set a precedent for implementing other global arms control treaties, for example in the area of outer space. In particular, the future negotiators will be able to draw on the experience gained when executing both the routine and the challenge verification mechanisms of a global chemical weapons ban. Thus a Chemical Weapons Convention will in many ways serve as a guideline for future global disarmament treaties, which underlines its importance both for disarmament negotiators and for government officials involved in the administration of arms control and disarmament treaties.

In the Conference on Disarmament only the United States and the Soviet Union have so far declared themselves to be possessors of chemical weapons, but there may be as many as 15-20 countries possessing or seeking to acquire such weapons. The Soviet Union has stated that its stockpiles do not exceed 50,000 tons of poisonous chemicals.[1] The United States has indicated it has less than the Soviet Union. The destruction of these stocks will be an expensive undertaking, in particular because sophisticated technology will have to be utilized. In addition, environmental protection measures have to be carefully planned. There could be spin-offs in civilian areas from the development of technology for the destruction of chemical weapons. Given the increased attention to environmental considerations, this could prove to be of importance.

The operation of a modern destruction plant was demonstrated to delegates from the Conference on Disarmament in October 1984 at the Tooele Army Depot in Utah, US, which makes use of incineration processes. At that time, it was stated that it costs about ten times more to destroy chemical weapons than to produce them. So far the United States has only one complete destruction plant - on Johnston Island in the Pacific Ocean. The Johnston Island plant will destroy the overseas American stocks, about 6 per cent of total US stockpiles. The US Government is also planning to build eight more plants in the United States to destroy chemical weapons stocks. It is

---

[1]   Document CD/CW/WP.264 of 21 November 1989.

calculated that the cost of eliminating US stocks could amount to US $4 billion in current prices.

The Soviet Union has built a destruction plant near Chapayevsk. However, the government had to cancel plans to make it operational due to the protests of the local population. An alternative national programme for destruction, which contains several options for building destruction facilities at other places, is under consideration in the Soviet Parliament. I should add that a mobile destruction unit was demonstrated to delegates from the Conference on Disarmament at the Shikhany military facility in October 1987.

At the recent Washington summit, the United States and the Soviet Union signed an agreement on the destruction and non-production of chemical weapons and on measures to facilitate the multilateral convention on a ban on chemical weapons. According to this agreement, which is considered a real milestone, the two Parties undertake to co-operate as regards methods and technologies for the safe and efficient destruction of chemical weapons. Each Party will assign the highest priority to ensuring the safety of people and to protecting the environment during its destruction of chemical weapons. The treaty further stipulates that the Parties shall negotiate a specific programme of co-operation related *inter alia* to methods and specific technologies for the destruction of chemical weapons and measures to ensure the safety and protection of the human population and the environment. In addition, they shall, where appropriate, co-operate with other States that request information or assistance regarding the destruction of chemical weapons. They may even respond jointly to such requests.

The agreement is important from a cost-effective and environmental point of view, because the two States will co-operate and share experiences between themselves and with other chemical-weapons States, thus reducing the total costs of destruction. I further draw your attention to the fact that each Party shall cease to produce chemical weapons upon the entry into force of the agreement and begin to destroy its chemical weapons by no later than 31 December 1992.

In the multilateral negotiations in the Conference on Disarmament there is agreement that each State Party of a Chemical Weapons Convention shall destroy all chemical weapons production facilities and related facilities and equipment, beginning not later than 12 months and finishing not later than 10 years after the Convention enters into force. While the production plants may be temporarily converted into destruction plants, neither the production plants nor the equipment can be converted to civilian use. This may be regrettable from an economic point of view, but the negotiators believe that this has to be done in order to secure an effective and verifiable treaty.

One of the biggest challenges facing a Chemical Weapons Convention is that important sectors of the chemical industry in each State Party will have to be monitored on a routine basis in perpetuity. The Convention will accordingly involve industry to an unprecedented degree. Due to the fact that the chemical industry to a large extent produces dual-purpose chemicals, thousands of installations around the world may have to be monitored to ensure compliance with the global ban on chemical weapons. No other disarmament treaty involves the control of a whole industry. Special precautionary measures must be agreed upon and taken in order to protect confidential business information. In addition, the inspection and control of the chemical industry have to be carried out in such a way as not to impede the normal development of the industry. The industry must provide government authorities with annual declarations as regards chemicals specified in the three schedules dealt with in the Rolling Text. Furthermore, the industry will have to abide by certain import and export regulations in order to ensure that super-toxic lethal chemicals are not misused. These obligations have, of course, direct and indirect economic implications for the chemical industry.

The question of providing humanitarian assistance and/or protective equipment to States Parties subject to or threatened by a chemical weapons attack certainly has economic aspects. However, this question has not been solved in the ongoing negotiations in the Conference on Disarmament. This also applies to the Convention's article on economic and technological development. However, there seems to be general agreement that the Convention should be implemented in a manner designed, as far as possible, to avoid hampering the economic or technological development of States parties and international co-operation in the field of peaceful chemical activities.

The extensive verification tasks will result in the establishment of a fairly large international organization. In fact, the envisaged Technical Secretariat will probably be larger than the present International Atomic Energy Agency (IAEA) in Vienna. It has been estimated that the cost of the International Inspectorate, which will employ several hundred inspectors, will amount to about US $120 million a year. The recruiting and training of the inspectors will in itself certainly be a difficult and resource-intensive task.

The States Parties themselves will need to appoint a National Authority to serve as the focal point for effective liaison with the International Inspectorate and other States Parties, and for co-operation among the relevant national ministries and industry. The need to establish such a National Authority and the appropriate supporting infrastructure underlines the extensive responsibilities of the States Parties in implementing a Chemical Weapons Convention.

Sixth Response

Johan Molander

Before discussing some economic aspects of chemical disarmament I would like to comment shortly on one assertion and two proposals that have been made in the previous discussions.

Utility of Chemical Weapons

It has been stated by two different speakers that chemical weapons are highly effective at low cost. In fact the actual military utility of chemical weapons is doubtful. Chemical weapons are effective as a weapon of terror against unprotected civilians and certainly also against unprotected enemy forces. Their use by Iraq against Kurdish civilians and untrained Iranian troops during the recent Gulf war bore out this effectiveness.

However, any military advantage is dramatically reduced when enemy forces have protection and it is nullified if they have retaliatory capacity. The unqualified assertion that chemical weapons are effective is therefore incorrect and dangerous.

Technical Assistance

Two proposals have been made in our discussion of chemical weapons. One regarding an international fund to assist smaller chemical-weapons States to destroy their stockpiles under a future Convention, and one regarding a development fund to promote the chemical industry for peaceful purposes.

The first proposal would seem perfectly valid and useful. In fact a first step in this direction has been taken by the two major chemical-weapons States which have offered to assist other States with technology for CW destruction programmes.

The second proposal for a development fund under the Chemical Weapons Convention seems much less valid. The CWC is a Convention under which *all* States shall forego the CW option and *all* possessors destroy their CW. It is therefore a totally non-discriminatory regime. What is needed is a provision for non-discriminatory trade practices inside the Convention as already foreseen by draft Article XI.

The bargain under the NPT was very different whereby the NWS, keeping their monopoly on nuclear weapons, undertook to co-operate in peaceful nuclear technology under safeguards with those States that had renounced the nuclear weapons option. No such bargain is conceivable under the CWC.

Cost of a Chemical Weapons Convention

As has been discussed in detail by the two excellent papers submitted by Mr. Sutherland and Mr. Beck, the CWC would entail substantial costs under the following items:

1. The Organization;
2. The National Authority;
3. Verification
   • on the national level, including indirect costs,

- on the international level for carrying out routine and challenge inspections;
4. Destruction.

I do not intend to discuss any of these items in detail. By and large I find Mr. Sutherland's estimates for the cost of an international Organization to the tune of some US $100-150 million a year a fair and reasonable approximation, even if I doubt whether it will be possible to employ and use some 600 inspectors within that price-tag. On the other hand I also doubt whether that many will really be needed.

Let me just add a few comments regarding the cost of destruction and challenge inspection and the "indirect costs" to industry of routine inspections.

It is necessary to face the fact - as the US and the USSR are currently doing - that the *destruction of CW* is enormously costly. The figures presented here seem to be on the low side. As far as I understand some US $5 billion are now budgeted in the US for destruction until 1997. The final bill might very well be double that. The USSR, having a bigger stockpile with a composition that presents different and partly new technological challenges for destruction, faces a formidable task not least in view of the ecological sensibility of local populations. The Soviet destruction programme will therefore be no cheaper than the American one, and this in a situation of very scarce resource.

As pointed out by Mr. Sutherland, the cost of *challenge inspections* is difficult to estimate. It seems that in order to "secure" a not very big inspection site, some 50 persons would be needed. No estimate has been made regarding equipment, transport, cost of disassembling suspect munitions, etc. Experiences from the INF point towards substantial costs for these kinds of inspections.

In his paper Mr. Beck discusses the *indirect cost to industry* of routine inspections. I think these have been vastly exaggerated. Industry runs a very substantial risk of disclosure of sensitive process and commercial information. These concerns are being met by negotiators in Geneva. If the Convention is properly elaborated and implemented, such costs should normally not occur. The experience of the IAEA shows that the actual costs for industry receiving international inspectors are indeed low. Besides, inspection is nothing new to the chemical and pharmaceutical industries, already burdened by national and sometimes foreign inspectors for compliance with various health, environment, safety and quality regulations. It is my view that inspections under a CWC would add a very marginal burden.

Economic Benefits from Chemical Disarmament

Unfortunately it is difficult to point out any direct economic advantage of chemical disarmament. The benefits are to be found in the political and security fields.

Some indirect economic benefits may however be possible to discern. The first is to avoid the inevitable and sky-high future cost of destroying chemical weapons that one has once produced. Secondly, an international regime, where every State has confidence in the implementation of the Convention, will in the long run promote trade and technology co-operation. Thirdly, a country like the Soviet Union might gain experience in applying strict norms of environmental protection.

By implementing the Convention, developing countries will be better able to control multinational and national chemical industries operating on their territory which can benefit the implementation of health and environmental regulations as well as tax collection.

Incidences of other Agreements on Negotiation on a CWC

One speaker has mentioned the incidences of former agreements on the negotiation of new disarmament agreements. This is illustrated also by the CWC negotiations. However it seems to me personally that we do not always draw the correct conclusions from former treaties. Experiences from the INF and the IAEA safeguards system have mainly been used.

The INF can certainly give guidance regarding inspections of military installations. However there is a risk that the strict and sometimes confrontational procedures of such verification become counter-productive when applied to civilian industry. In this respect I think that the Geneva negotiators should have looked more to the IAEA which emphasizes safeguards as a service designed to help the State Party (the facility) to demonstrate compliance.

In another aspect, however, I feel that the CW negotiations have made too much use of IAEA safeguards approach. The safeguards apply to nuclear material which is easily identifiable and which, because of its properties, has to be subject to containment and exact accountancy by the facility operator. Verification based on containment, surveillance and accountancy control is therefore easily applicable. This is not the case in the chemical industry, where thousands of compounds may be produced in flexible, easily modified production processes and where precise accountancy may not always be required. However, it seems that verification of Schedule 2 chemicals in the CWC is based mainly on the IAEA model. I doubt whether this is useful, and whether it would not be feasible to introduce a more qualitative verification system based on declarations, confidence-building and random or selected inspections.

Lately proposals have been made to introduce so-called *Ad Hoc* Inspections. Many delegations, especially among the non-aligned, are unwilling even to discuss these proposals. In part this is because *ad hoc* inspections have been presented as an additional measure of verification. The time is perhaps ripe to promote the qualitative *ad hoc* concept by making it a substitute for routine inspection in the chemical industry.

Under such a scheme systematic routine inspections would be limited to military CW installations (until all chemical weapons were completely destroyed) of and to the very few Schedule 1 facilities. The whole chemical industry would be subject to one qualitative *ad hoc* system which would be cheaper and more streamlined. Finally, challenge inspections or inspections on request anywhere without the right of refusal would be kept as an ultimate safety net.

It might be worth investigating whether such an approach could make the verification of a CWC cheaper but still effective, thereby enhancing the possibilities for a viable chemical weapons ban.

Conclusion

Prospects for Economic Research in the Field of Disarmament

Christian Schmidt

From the variety of opinions formulated by participants about the role and limits of the economic approach to disarmament studies related to the new political context, three main features emerged which characterized the dominant spirit of the meeting, namely: (1) *criticism* of common fallacies; (2) *scepticism* about oversimplified evaluations and solutions; and (3) the need for *future-oriented thinking* rather than that confined by historical precedents. Their contents can be summarized as follows:

1. Criticism

A lot of so-called "clichés" have been examined in order to analyse the economic dimension of current disarmament processes. Firstly, the topic of peace dividends was carefully considered. Such a formula confused different levels, which should be distinct from an analytical point of view. The first level concerns a relevant evaluation of the net benefit to be gained from the economic consequences of disarmament talks, which differs very much from one case to another. A second level corresponds to tentative benefit-sharing:

- For countries which participate directly in the negotiation process;
- For countries which are only indirectly affected by the processes (such as developing countries). There is no symmetry between countries simultaneously involved in internal economic restructuring and those not so involved.

A third level is provided by the allocative budget processes of each nation. The shift of possibilities from a military to a civil budget (health, education or anything related to social welfare) is the point in question. Even if, in spite of the economic costs of disarmament, a profit must be conjectured according to the first level, it does not mean that this would necessarily be fairly distributed among the disarmers and, especially, that a spin-off would be observed in peace activities according to the third level. Beyond such a warning, the economists have drawn up a possible research programme gathering relevant data at each level and exploring actual relationships.

Another well-known topic linking disarmament and development was also discussed at length and with caution. On the one hand, many participants underlined the fact that East/West disarmament talks do not necessarily preclude the end of the arms race. First of all because in many cases, especially for advanced industrial countries, the arms race is first and foremost a process dominated by internal factors,

221

and secondly, because there is no evidence of the impact of these negotiations on the reduction of regional arms races. Even the most pessimistic have noticed the real risk of an increase in arms dynamics in certain areas, partially due to arms exports exacerbated by arms limitations. On the other hand, a possible reduction of defence expenditures in some developed countries has till now been linked to major military budgets; thus the existence of an opportunity for economic development in Third World countries seems uncertain at least. Such an assumption postulates an international transfer which does not operate automatically. On the contrary, there is a good chance that any gains from disarmament would be used by each disarming country for its own purposes.

The knowledge of the part that illusion plays in these common views has provided a first contribution from the academic economists' point of view. The next step will be to elaborate more relevant and realistic alternative schemes in order to understand the effectiveness of the economic consequences of the disarmament process.

2. *Scepticism*

A flavour of scepticism dominated the discussion. Many participants underlined the risk of overestimating the final impact of disarmament on economics at a macro level. Indeed, all the computations which were rapidly provided by various economists (including a Nobel Prize winner) via traditional econometric models are purely mechanical. If such simulations offer a stylized picture of the chains of reaction which could be introduced by alternative hypotheses of reductions in military budgets, the results should be considered cautiously. Most often, these hypotheses are placed in macro-economic models without any additional transformation; thus, the output is interpreted under the general assumption "*sic stantibus rebus*". Some specialists suspected the existence of time-process adjustments induced by the decision of military budget cuts which are not taken into account in the models. Such an adjustment process would then tend to minimize their final impact. Therefore, the majority of participants claimed that more specific and detailed studies were needed based on a less integrated point of view.

Another, far more radical, reason to be sceptical appeared. Doubts were expressed about the ability of economic tools alone to provide a relevant interpretation of the listed phenomena. At present, the economic facet of disarmament appears dominated by political will at every stage. The initial decision process is obviously a political one. However, the linkage between, for instance, conventional weapons negotiations in Vienna and cuts in military budgets also belongs to a political process, as does the conversion from military to civil activities, where the role of the government is determinant in most cases. Finally, the economic impact of disarmament combined with a decrease in internal debt and a diminution of fiscal pressure will not have the same consequences as if it were directly coupled with a reallocation of public expenditure in favour of social activities or of industrial investment. Thus a large consensus emerged among the experts to integrate the political dimension into the studies, and to ask political scientists to join economists in mixed research teams.

The last reason why there is some doubt about economic expertise nowadays is relative to data gathering. It was mentioned many times that a large number of the studies belong to the general field of industrial economics. This is especially true of the convention negotiated on chemical weapons and also, at least partially, of the CFE negotiation. Statistical material used came not only from governmental sources but also from industrial ones. Among various other reasons, commercial considerations play a central role, and companies and professional organizations proved reluctant to release information, more particularly in academic circles. It was noticed that no representative from industry participated in the Leningrad meeting. The way to associate relevant industrial sectors in such research was then introduced as a specific open question.

3. *Future-Oriented Thinking*

Economic knowledge about defence expenditure, arms dynamics and the military industrial sector is to some extent provided by the statistical treatment and analyses of past series of data gathered from historical sources starting after the Second World War. Therefore, the regularity which has been observed, as well as the concepts elaborated to explain these phenomena, are closely related to this sample. Indeed, the United States has experimented at least twice on large-scale conversions - after the Korean and the Vietnam wars. Such experiences were carefully studied by such brilliant economists as K. Boulding. Likewise, the East-West debate during the arms control negotiation process (SALT I and II) induced a form of stabilization of the American military budget during this short period. However, except for these events, the dominant trend has been the arms race, especially among many developing countries after the 1960s. So the material gathered from the observation of past data and the economic studies, many of them under the sponsorship of the United Nations, has mainly been oriented towards an evaluation of the impact of the growth of military expenditure on macro-economic dynamics. The majority of participants could see no evidence of symmetry between economic situations generated by arms increases and arms reductions. Thus the historical background used by defence economists must be considered as a relatively poor reference in foreseeing future situations. Such an established fact is linked to a more general discontinuity between war and peace economics.

Two principal lines for future research were proposed. The first follows the idea that disarmament economics as such does not exist. On the contrary, the economic dimensions of disarmament are manifold and it is arbitrary to postulate a unified body of doctrine in order to explore them. For instance, the economic problems set by nuclear agreements are quite different from the CFE, and questions raised by a convention on chemical weapons are also different. The Leningrad meeting underlined this and warned against the temptation of transposing too rapidly certain results extracted from one set or the other. For example, the cost evaluation for the INF Treaty does not provide a correct base to estimate the economic cost of CFEI, even as a methodological guide. Another consequence of such general views is a careful account of the specificity of each kind of economy *vis-à-vis* the disarmament process. It was stressed and repeated many times, for instance, that disarmament can induce unexpected deregulatory effects, due to the specificity of arms industrialization in several countries members of the Warsaw Pact. Furthermore, the disarmament process between the US and the Soviet Union, as well as between the two alliances, has indirect consequences on the arms industry in other countries, such as Japan. These unusual cases should be analysed in greater detail.

A second suggestion formulated by many participants is to link more closely economic studies and the decision-making process in the field of disarmament. On the one hand, the advantage of such an orientation is a better integration of the political factors; on the other, it also provides the opportunity to take into account the economic purpose included in the political decision processes. A systematic exploration of the alternative strategies open to the governments involved in disarmament talks, as well as for the industrial companies which anticipate their consequences, could be a fruitful starting point. Some analytical tools elaborated by economists seemed well adapted to this task, including, for example, public choice theory and game theory in its application to industrial economics. Such a direction in research obviously does not preclude the necessity of improving the computation system of the defence sector, especially in the framework of national accounting systems. In any case, improving the analysis of the decision-making process (in a domain where economic considerations are not only a constraint but also one of the targets) is fully complementary with performing the measurement of these economic dimensions.

4. *Final Remarks*

In order to test the validity of these approaches, all the participants agreed to regular future meetings regarding specific topics in line with the large number of suggestions made. Members of the IDEA proposed to examine jointly with UNIDIR a research programme which is relevant to both the scientific canvas previously designated and to the people involved in disarmament processes. This type of co-ordination seemed to the majority of economic experts to be the best way to avoid past disillusion and to restate a new impulse in this area. Some crucial questions tentatively listed for future work included the following:

- The relationship between alternative strategic options and their economic price;
- From CFE to national defence budget allocation;
- The impact of cuts in military expenditure on industry: a comparative study;
- Disarmament and national accounting systems;
- Possibilities and limits of the conversion from military to civil activities in various economic environments.

List of Authors

Ednan AGAEV, Head of Disarmament Division, Department of International Organizations, Ministry of Foreign Affairs, Moscow, USSR

Anguel ANASTASSOV, Expert, United Nations and Disarmament Department, Ministry of Foreign Affairs, Sofia, Bulgaria

Ambassador Salah BASSIOUNY, Director, National Center for Middle East Studies, Cairo, Egypt

Herbert BECK, Attaché, Auswärtige Amt, Bonn, Germany (Federal Republic of)

Thomas BERNAUER, Research Associate, UNIDIR, Geneva, Switzerland

CHIN KIN WAH, Senior Lecturer, Department of Political Science, National University of Singapore, Singapore

Andrej CIMA, Counsellor, Deputy Head of Delegation at the Negotiations on Conventional Forces in Europe, Ministry of Foreign Affairs, Prague, The Czech and Slovak Federal Republic

Saadet DEGER, Senior Researcher, Head of Military Expenditure Project, Stockholm International Peace Research Institute (SIPRI), Stockholm, Sweden

Javier DÍAZ DE LEÓN, Research Associate, Centro Latinoamericano de Estudios Estratégicos, a.c., Mexico D.F., Mexico

Jacques FONTANEL, Director, Faculté des Sciences Economiques, Grenoble, France

Keith HARTLEY, Director, Institute for Research in the Social Sciences (IRISS), University of York, York, United Kingdom

Luis HERRERA-LASSO, Director, Centro Latinoamericano de Estudios Estratégicos, a.c., Mexico D.F., Mexico

Michael D. INTRILIGATOR, Director, Center for International and Strategic Affairs, University of California Los Angeles, Los Angeles, USA

Gennady KHROMOV, Council of Ministers of the USSR, Moscow, USSR

Edward A. KOLODZIEJ, Research Professor, Program in Arms Control, Disarmament and International Security, Department of Political Science, University of Illinois at Urbana-Champaign, Urbana, USA

Sten LUNDBO, Deputy Director General, Royal Ministry of Foreign Affairs, Oslo, Norway

Johan MOLANDER, Counsellor, Deputy Head of the Delegation of Sweden to the Conference on Disarmament, Geneva, Switzerland

Jun NISHIKAWA, Professor, Faculty of Political Science & Economics, Waseda University, Tokyo, Japan

Tibor PALANKAI, Head, Department of World Economy, School of Economics, Budapest, Hungary

Louis PILANDON, Professor, University of Clermont-Ferrand, Clermont-Ferrand, France

Christian SCHMIDT, President, International Defence Economics Association (IDEA), Paris, France

Wally STRUYS, Professor, Ecole Royale Militaire, Economie et Gestion, Brussels, Belgium

Serge SUR, Deputy Director, UNIDIR, Geneva, Switzerland

Ronald SUTHERLAND, Professor, Department of Chemistry, University of Saskatchewan, Saskatoon, Saskatchewan, Canada

Katarzyna ZUKROWSKA, Research Associate, Polish Institute of International Affairs (PISM), Warsaw, Poland

Recent UNIDIR Publications
(from 1987)

RESEARCH REPORTS

La guerre des satellites : enjeux pour la communauté internationale, par Pierre Lellouche, éd. (IFRI), Genève, UNIDIR, 1987, 42 p., publication des Nations Unies, numéro de vente: GV.F.87.0.1. Also available in English: *Satellite Warfare: A Challenge for the International Community*.

The International Non-Proliferation Regime 1987, by David A.V. Fischer, Geneva, UNIDIR, 1987, 81 p., United Nations publication, Sales No. GV.E.87.0.2.

La question de la vérification dans les négociations sur le désarmement aux Nations Unies, par Ellis Morris, Genève, UNIDIR, 1987, 230 p., publication des Nations Unies, numéro de vente: GV.F.87.0.4. Also available in English: *The Verification Issue in United Nations Disarmament Negotiations*.

Confidence-Building Measures in Africa, by Augustine P. Mahiga and Fidelis Nji, Geneva, UNIDIR, 1987, 16 p., United Nations publication, Sales No. GV.E.87.0.5

Disarmament: Problems Related to Outer Space, Geneva, UNIDIR, 1987, 190 p., United Nations publication, Sales No. GV.E.87.0.7. Existe aussi en français: *Désarmement: problèmes relatifs à l'espace extra-atmosphérique*.

Interrelationship of Bilateral and Multilateral Disarmament Negotiations / Les relations entre les négociations bilatérales et multilatérales sur le désarmement, Proceedings of the Baku Conference, 2-4 June 1987 / Actes de la conférence de Bakou, 2-4 juin 1987, Geneva, UNIDIR, 1988, 258 p., United Nations publication, Sales No. GV.E./F.88.0.1.

Disarmament Research: Agenda for the 1990s / La recherche sur le désarmement: Programme pour les années 90, Proceedings of the Sochi Conference, 22-24 March 1988 / Actes de la conférence de Sotchi, 22-24 mars 1988, Geneva, UNIDIR, 1988, 165 p., United Nations publication, Sales No. GV.E./F.88.0.3.

Conventional Disarmament in Europe, by André Brie (IIB), Andrzej Karkoszka (PISM), Manfred Müller (IIB), Helga Schirmeister (IIB), Geneva, UNIDIR, 1988, 66 p., United Nations publication, Sales No. GV.E.88.0.6. Existe également en français: Le désarmement classique en Europe.

Arms Transfers and Dependence, by Christian Catrina, published for UNIDIR by Taylor & Francis (New York, London), 1988, 409 p.

Les forces classiques en Europe et la maîtrise des armements, par Pierre Lellouche et Jérôme Paolini, eds. (IFRI), 1989, 88 p. Publication des Nations Unies, numéro de vente: GV.F.89.0.6. Also available in English: *Conventional Forces and Arms Limitation in Europe*.

National Security Concepts of States: New Zealand, by Kennedy Graham, published for UNIDIR by Taylor & Francis (New York, London), 1989, 180 p.

Problems and Perspectives of Conventional Disarmament in Europe, Proceedings of the Geneva Conference 23-25 January 1989, published for UNIDIR by Taylor & Francis (New York, London), 1989, 140 p. Existe aussi en français: *Désarmement classique en Europe, Problèmes et perspectives*, publié pour l'UNIDIR et l'IFRI par Masson (Paris), 1990, 226 p.

The Projected Chemical Weapons Convention: A Guide to the Negotiations in the Conference on Disarmament, by Thomas Bernauer, 1990, 328 p., United Nations publication, Sales No. GV.E.90.0.3.

Verification: The Soviet Stance, its Past, Present and Future, by Mikhail Kokeev and Andrei Androsov, 1990, 131 p., United Nations publication, Sales No. GV.E.90.0.6.

UNIDIR Repertory of Disarmament Research: 1990, by Chantal de Jonge Oudraat and Péricles Gasparini Alves (eds.), 1990, 402 p., United Nations publication, Sales No. GV.E.90.0.10.

Nonoffensive Defense: A Global Perspective, published for UNIDIR by Taylor & Francis (New York, London), 1990, 194 p.

Aerial Reconnaissance for Verification of Arms Limitation Agreements - An Introduction, by Allan V. Banner, Keith W. Hall and Andrew J. Young, D.C.L., 1990, 166 p., United Nations publication, Sales No. GV.E.90.0.11.

Africa, Disarmament and Security / Afrique, désarmement et sécurité, Proceedings of the Conference of African Research Institutes, 24-25 March 1990 / Actes de la Conférence des Instituts de recherche africains, 24-25 mars 1990, Geneva, UNIDIR, United Nations publication, Sales No. GV.E/F.91.0.1.

Peaceful and Non-Peaceful Uses of Space: Problems of Definition for the Prevention of an Arms Race, by Bhupendra Jasani (ed.), 1991, published for UNIDIR by Taylor & Francis, 179 p.

In Pursuit of a Nuclear Test Ban Treaty: A Guide to the Debate in the Conference on Disarmament, by Thomas Schmalberger, 1991, 132 p., Sales No. G.V.E.91.0.4, United Nations publication.

Confidence-building Measures and International Security: The Political and Military Aspect: A Soviet Approach, by Igor Scherbak, 1991, 179 p., United Natiosn publication, Sales No. GV.E.91.0.7.

Prevention of an Arms Race in Outer Space: A Guide to the Discussions in the Conference on Disarmament, by Péricles Gasparini Alves, United Nations publication (**forthcoming**)

RESEARCH PAPERS

No. 1 - *Une approche juridique de la vérification en matière de désarmement ou de limitation des armements*, par Serge Sur, septembre 1988, 70 p., publication des Nations Unies, numéro de vente: GV.F.88.0.5. Also available in English: *A Legal Approach to Verification in Disarmament or Arms Limitation*.

No. 2 - *Problèmes de vérification du Traité de Washington du 8 décembre 1987 sur l'élimination des missiles à portée intermédiaires*, par Serge Sur, octobre 1988, 64 p., publication des Nations Unies, numéro de vente GV.F.88.0.7. Also available in English: *Verification Problems of the Washington Treaty on the Elimination of Intermediate-Range Missiles*.

No. 3 - *Mesures de confiance de la CSCE: Documents et commentaires*, par Victor-Yves Ghébali, mars 1989, 112 p., publication des Nations Unies, numéro de vente: GV.F.89.0.5. Also available in English: *Confidence-Building Measures within the CSCE Process: Paragraph-by-Paragraph Analysis of the Helsinki and Stockholm Regimes*.

No. 4 - *The Prevention of the Geographical Proliferation of Nuclear Weapons: Nuclear-Free Zones and Zones of Peace in the Southern Hemisphere*, by Edmundo Fujita, April 1989, 52 p., United Nations publication, Sales No. GV.E. 89.0.8. Existe également en français: *La prévention de la prolifération géographique des armes nucléaires: zones exemptes d'armes nucléaires et zones de paix*.

No. 5 - *The Future Chemical Weapons Convention and its Organization: The Executive Council*, by Thomas Bernauer, May 1989, 34 p., United Nations publication, Sales No. GV.E.89.0.7. Existe également en français: *La future convention sur les armes chimiques et son organisation: le Conseil exécutif*.

No. 6 - *Bibliographical Survey of Secondary Literature on Military Expenditures*, November 1989, 39 p. United Nations publication, Sales No. GV.E.89.0.14.

No. 7 - *Science and Technology: Between Civilian and Military Research and Development - Armaments and Development at Variance*, by Marek Thee, November 1990, 23 p., United Nations publication, Sales No. GV.E.90.0.14.

No. 8 - *Esquisse pour un nouveau paysage européen*, par Eric Remacle, octobre 1990, 178 p., publication des Nations Unies, numéro de vente GV.F.91.0.2.

No. 9 - *The Third Review of the Biological Weapons Convention: Issues and Proposals*, by Jozef Goldblat and Thomas Bernauer, April 1991, 78 p., United Nations publication, Sales No. GV.E.91.0.5.

UNIDIR NEWSLETTER
(quarterly)

Vol. 1,   No. 1, March/mars 1988, *Disarmament-Development/Désarmement-Développement*, 16 p.

No. 2, June/juin 1988, *Research in Africa/La recherche en Afrique*, 28 p.

No. 3, September/septembre 1988, *Conventional Armaments Limitation and CBMs in Europe/Limitation des armements classiques et mesures de confiance en Europe*, 32 p.

No. 4, December/décembre 1988, *Research in Asia and the Pacific/La recherche en Asie et dans le Pacifique*, 40 p.

Vol. 2,   No. 1, March/mars 1989, *Chemical Weapons: Research Projects and Publications/Armes chimiques: projets de recherche et publications*, 24 p.

No. 2, June/juin 1989, *Research in Latin America and the Caribbean/La recherche en Amérique Latine et dans les Caraïbes*, 32 p.

No. 3, September/septembre 1989, *Outer Space/L'espace extra-atmosphérique*, 32 p.

No. 4, December/Décembre 1989, *Research in Eastern Europe/La recherche en Europe de l'Est*, 48 p.

Vol. 3,   No. 1, March/mars 1990, *Verification of Disarmament Agreements/La vérification des accords sur le désarmement*, 48 p.

No. 2, June/juin 1990, *Research in North America/La recherche en Amérique du Nord*, 72 p.

No. 3, September/septembre 1990, *Nuclear Non-Proliferation/La non-proliferation nucléaire*, 43 p.

No. 4, December/décembre 1990, *Research in Western and Northern Europe (I)/ La recherche en Europe de l'Ouest et en Europe du Nord (I)*, 72 p.

Vol. 4,   No. 1, March/mars 1991, *Research in Western and Northern Europe (II) / La recherche en Europe de l'Ouest et en Europe du Nord (II)*, 72 p.

No. 2, June/juin 1991, *Biological Weapons / Armes biologiques*, 42 p.